全国高等学校外语教师丛书 · 科研方法系列

Doing Action Research in English Language Teaching: A Guide for Practitioners

英语教学中的行动研究方法

Anne Burns（澳）著

外语教学与研究出版社
FOREIGN LANGUAGE TEACHING AND RESEARCH PRESS
北京 BEIJING

京权图字：01-2011-2952

Doing Action Research in English Language Teaching: A Guide for Practitioners (First Edition) / by Anne Burns / ISBN: 978-0-415-99145-2

图书在版编目（CIP）数据

英语教学中的行动研究方法 = Doing Action Research in English Language Teaching: A Guide for Practitioners ：英、汉 /（澳）伯恩斯（Burns, A.）著. -- 北京 ：外语教学与研究出版社，2011.10（2022.1 重印）
（全国高等学校外语教师丛书. 科研方法系列）
ISBN 978-7-5135-1440-8

I. ①英… II. ①伯… III. ①英语－教学研究－英、汉 IV. ①H319.3

中国版本图书馆 CIP 数据核字（2011）第 216545 号

出 版 人　王　芳
项目负责　段长城
责任编辑　毕　争
责任校对　郑丹妮
封面设计　覃一彪　韩　雪　华　艺
版式设计　吴德胜
出版发行　外语教学与研究出版社
社　　址　北京市西三环北路 19 号（100089）
网　　址　http://www.fltrp.com
印　　刷　北京九州迅驰传媒文化有限公司
开　　本　650×980　1/16
印　　张　16.5
版　　次　2011 年 10 月第 1 版　2022 年 1 月第 14 次印刷
书　　号　ISBN 978-7-5135-1440-8
定　　价　60.90 元

购书咨询：（010）88819926　电子邮箱：club@fltrp.com
外研书店：https://waiyants.tmall.com
凡印刷、装订质量问题，请联系我社印制部
联系电话：（010）61207896　电子邮箱：zhijian@fltrp.com
凡侵权、盗版书籍线索，请联系我社法律事务部
举报电话：（010）88817519　电子邮箱：banquan@fltrp.com
物料号：214400101

记载人类文明
沟通世界文化
www.fltrp.com

Contents

总序 文秋芳 iii

导读 文秋芳 vii

Preface xv

Acknowledgements xvii

Chapter 1 What Is Action Research? 1

1.1 What is action research? 2

1.2 Why should I do action research? I'm a teacher not a researcher! 7

1.3 What are the steps in action research? 9

1.4 How is AR different from other kinds of research? 12

1.5 Is action research the same as reflecting on your teaching? 17

1.6 Summary point 23

Chapter 2 Plan – Planning the Action 27

2.1 Finding your focus 28

2.2 Developing and refining your questions 36

2.3 Getting permission and covering ethical issues 40

2.4 Preparing your resources and materials 47

2.5 Summary point 58

Chapter 3 Act – Putting the Plan into Action 65

3.1 Collecting your data 65

3.2 Observing and describing: What do I need to see? 68

3.3 Asking and discussing: What do I need to know? 88

3.4 Cross-checking and strengthening the information 112

3.5 Summary point 114

Chapter 4 Observe – Observing the Results of the Plan 121

4.1 Preparing for data analysis 121
4.2 Analysing and synthesising qualitative data 125
4.3 Analysing and synthesising quantitative data 139
4.4 Validity in action research: Making sure your conclusions are trustworthy 152
4.5 Summary point 157

Chapter 5 Reflect – Reflecting and Planning for Further Action 165

5.1 Reflecting in the AR cycle 166
5.2 Planning the next steps 170
5.3 Sharing with others 174
5.4 On with the action! 193
5.5 Summary point 195
5.6 Final words 196

Postscript: Action Research in Action 199

Developing learners' self-assement skills S.K. AL-Sinani 201
Watching to learn or learning to watch A. Van Eysden 213
打破大学英语课堂中的沉默——提高课堂互动的行动研究 程熙旭 223

Further Reading and Resources 233

Index 239

总 序

“全国高等学校外语教师丛书”是外语教学与研究出版社高等英语教育出版分社近期精心策划、隆重推出的系列丛书，包含理论指导、科研方法和教学研究三个子系列。本套丛书既包括学界专家精心挑选的国外引进著作，又有特邀国内学者执笔完成的“命题作文”。作为开放系列，该丛书还将根据外语教学与科研的发展不断增加新的专题，以便教师研修与提高。

笔者有幸参与了这套系列丛书的策划工作。在策划过程中，我们分析了高校英语教师面临的困难与挑战，考察了一线教师的需求，最终确立这套丛书选题的指导思想为：想外语教师所想，急外语教师所急，顺应广大教师的发展需求；确立这套丛书的写作特色为：突出科学性、可读性和操作性，做到举重若轻，条理清晰，例证丰富，深入浅出。

第一个子系列是“理论指导”。该系列力图为教师提供某学科或某领域的研究概貌，期盼读者能用较短的时间了解某领域的核心知识点与前沿研究课题。以《二语习得重点问题研究》一书为例。该书不求面面俱到，只求抓住二语习得研究领域中的热点、要点和富有争议的问题，动态展开叙述。每一章的写作以不同意见的争辩为出发点，对取向相左的理论、实证研究结果差异进行分析、梳理和评述，最后介绍或者展望国内外的最新发展趋势。全书阐述清晰，深入浅出，易读易懂。再比如《认知语言学与二语教学》一书，全书分为理论篇、教学篇与研究篇三个部分。理论篇阐述认知语言学视角下的语言观、教学观与学习观，以及与二语教学相关的认知语言学中的主要概念与理论；教学篇选用认知语言学领域比较成熟的理论，探讨应用到中国英语教学实践的可能性；研究篇包括国内外将认知语言学理论应用到教学实践中的研究综述、研究方法介绍以及对未来研究的展望。

第二个子系列是“科研方法”。该系列介绍了多种研究方法，通常是一书介绍一种方法，例如问卷调查、个案研究、行动研究、有声思维、语料库研究、微变化研究和启动研究等。也有一书涉及多种方法，综合描述量化研究或者质化研究，例如：《应用语言学中的质性研究与分析》、《应用语言学中的量化研究与分析》和《第二语言研究中的数据收集方法》等。凡入选本系列丛书的著作人，无论是国外著者还是国内著者，均有高度的读者意识，乐于为一线教师开展教学科研服务，力求做到帮助读者“排忧解难”。例如，澳大利亚Anne Burns教授撰写的《英语教学中的行动研究方法》一书，从一线教师的视角，讨论行动研究的各个环节，每章均有“反思时刻”、“行动时刻”等新颖形式设计。同时，全书运用了丰富例证来解释理论概念，便于读者理解、思考和消化所读内容。凡是应邀撰写研究方法系列的中国作者均有博士学位，并对自己阐述的研究方法有着丰富的实践经验。他们有的运用了书中的研究方法完成了硕、博士论文，有的是采用书中的研究方法从事过重大科研项目。以秦晓晴教授撰写的《外语教学问卷调查法》一书为例，该书著者将系统性与实用性有机结合，根据实施问卷调查法的流程，系统地介绍了问卷调查研究中问题的提出、问卷项目设计、问卷试测、问卷实施、问卷整理及数据准备、问卷评价以及问卷数据汇总及统计分析方法选择等环节。书中对各个环节的描述都配有易于理解的研究实例。

第三个子系列是“教学研究”。该系列与前两个系列相比，有两点显著不同：第一，本系列侧重同步培养教师的教学能力与教学研究能力；第二，本系列所有著作的撰稿人主要为中国学者。有些著者虽然目前在海外工作和生活，但他们出国前曾在国内高校任教，期间也经常回国参与国内的教学与研究工作。本系列包括《英语教学中的学习策略培训：阅读与写作》、《听力教学与研究》、《写作教学与研究》、《阅读教学与研究》、《口语教学与研究》、《翻译教学与研究》等。以《听力教学与研究》一书为例，著者王艳博士拥有十多年的听力教学经验，同时听力教学研究又是她完成博士论文的选题领域。《听力教学与研究》一书，浓缩了她多年听力教学与听力教学研究的宝贵经验。全书分为两部分：教学篇与研究篇。教学篇中涉及了听力教学的各个重要环节以及学生在听力学习中可能碰到的困难与应对的办法，所选用的案例均来自著者课堂教学的真实活动。研究篇中既有著者的听力教学研究案例，也有著者从国内外文献中筛选出的符合中国国情的听力教学研究案例，综合在一起加以分析阐述。

教育大计，教师为本。“全国高等学校外语教师丛书”内容全面，出版及时，必将成为高校教师提升自我教学能力、研究能力与合作能力的良师益友。笔者相信本套丛书的出版对高校外语教师个人专业能力的提高，对教师队伍整体素质的提高，必将起到积极的推动作用。

文秋芳

北京外国语大学中国外语教育研究中心

2011年7月3日

导　读

《英语教学中的行动研究方法》一书是澳大利亚学者Anne Burns所著。2008年，笔者在德国当选为新一届国际应用语言学学会（AILA）执委会执行委员，与Anne Burns同在国际应用语言学学会执委会内工作。此后，我与她有机会近距离接触和交往。Anne Burns在学界长期从事二语教学，对英语教学中的行动研究有着丰富的经验。她为人谦和、善解人意，善于倾听不同意见，长于跨文化沟通。我们在会上和会下的交流平等、坦诚，让人感到很舒服。阅读她撰写的《英语教学中的行动研究方法》一书后，更感文如其人。全书贯彻了"读者友好"的原则，概念解释清楚，例证丰富，语言浅显易懂，便于一线教师掌握行动研究的方法，特别适合行动研究新手。

1．全书概述

全书分为5章。除第一章说明行动研究的定义外，其余4章分别描述作者提出的行动研究的4个环节：计划（Plan）、行动（Act）、观察（Observe）与反思（Reflect）。每一章的内容由四部分组成：

1）阅读前问题（Pre-reading questions），作者根据本章节的主要内容，列出问题，要求读者对其思考。目的是一方面激发读者的求知欲望，另一方面给读者提供本章的重点，期待他们能够紧扣这些问题阅读全章内容。

2）本章主体内容，一级标题标明本章涉及的问题。每个一级标题下，交叉出现"反思时刻"(Reflection point）或者"行动时刻"（Action point），要求读者参与思考或行动，此外，还穿插"课堂声音"(Classroom voices)，为教师提供典型案例，帮助教师进一步理解比较抽象的解释。

3）总结时刻（Summary point），作者将全章内容进行归纳提炼，帮助读者掌握全章的要点。

4）附录与参考文献，这部分内容为读者提供了行动研究需要的相关表格、量具以及其它资料。

从每一章的结构可以看出，作者主张教师的学习要有理论、有实践、有反思、有行动。相反，只看书或只听别人讲，自己不深入思考、不参与行动，就不可能学会行动研究的方法。同时在反思与行动时刻，特别强调与同事讨论与合作。笔者也完全赞成Anne Burns的理念，学、思、行同步，学习才有成效；团队合作好于孤军奋战，互动中思想火花碰撞，易于产生新知识、新方法。

2. 各章节主要内容

第一章为全书的开篇，着重阐述什么是行动研究。本章就4个问题分别加以说明：1）行动研究的定义；2）行动研究的步骤；3）行动研究与应用研究的区别；4）行动研究与反思性教学的区别。作者将英语教学中的行动研究解释为一种教师探究自己教学情境的方法。该方法具有对教师和教学过程的自我反思性、批判性与系统性的特点。作者指出，这里所说的批判性没有“负面” 和“否定”的含义，只是要求行动研究者对自己的教学采取质疑的态度，善于发现可改进之处，有意识地对其加以干预，旨在产生积极的变化。

Burns 根据 Kemmis & McTaggart（1988）的模型，指出行动研究的步骤呈现出循环往复的特征。她用图展示了行动研究的两个周期：第一个周期包括计划–行动–观察–反思，第二个周期包括修改计划–行动–观察–反思。在此基础上，她还总结了行动研究具有以下5个特征：1）行动研究需要教师对自己的教学进行评价与反思，目的在于使自己的实践产生不断的变化与进步；2）行动研究规模小、情境性强，要解决的教学问题源于特定的情境、特定的课堂、特定的学校；3）行动研究参与性强，并期望参与者形成共同体合作解决当时当地的迫切问题；4）不同于“直觉”教学，行动研究需要系统地收集数据；5）行动研究基于民主原则，赋予参与者改变课程实践的权力。

行动研究与其它应用研究有什么不同？这是从事行动研究的新手经常提出的问题。首先需要强调的是，“研究者是否是教师”不是区分两类不同研究的关键特征，因为教师既可以从事行动研究，也可从事应用研究。作者认为行动研究与应用研究既有相同、交叉之处，也有不同之处。他们的主要区别表现为四点：第一，应用研究强调“客观性”，力图控制某些变量，探究两类变量之间的关系；行动研究相对比较“主观”，探索解决教学实际问题的方法；第二，应用研究与行动研究都关心研究结果的应用，但行动研究的目的是解决研究者当时当地个人所关切的问题；第三，应用研究所选的研究方法结构性很强，中途不能更改，而行动研究的方法开放性高，研究者可根据实际情况随时对其进行调整；第四，应用研究从文献出发，形成理论假设，通过周密的设计，收集并分析数据，最终检验假设，从而形成为实践服务的理论，而行动研究关注能否寻找到理论来更好地阐释自己的教学实践。

行动研究与反思性教学相同吗？反思性教学只是行动研究的一部分，但善于进行反思性教学的老师很容易成为行动研究者，因为反思能力是行动研究的必备条件，同时也是行动研究继续的必要环节。与反思性教学不同的是，在行动研究中，“行动”是该研究的核心。它既是手段，又是最终的追求目标。教师的反思最终要落实到行动上。仅有反思没有行动，就不能称其为行动研究。

第二章描述设计行动方案。设计过程涉及多项任务：1）寻找研究焦点；2）形成研究问题；3）处理相关伦理问题；4）查阅文献；5）确定研究参与者；6）获得相关支持；7）准备设备与材料。寻找研究焦点是件伤脑筋的事，但作为研究者，这是一个绕不过的坎。有些人在行动研究初期就对研究焦点有非常清晰的认识，但更多的人是在行动研究的过程中才逐步形成的。常见的情况是，我们从教学实践中获得“灵感”，再由“灵感”逐步发展为研究计划。灵感来源的渠道很多，可以通过记日记、集体讨论、分析某个特定问题场景、阅读某篇文章等。事实上，教学的方方面都可能成为行动研究的对象。例如，提高学习者的自主性、理解学生的学习动机、推广小组活动等。在确定研究焦点后，需要形成具体的研究问题。问题越具体，越容易选择确定的方法收集与分析数据。研究问题的数量不能过多，一次研究最好解决一到两个问题。所要研究的问题可能在研究的过程中会发生变化，这是行动研究与其它研究的区别之一。Burns对研究问题的形成提出四点建议：第一，应避免超出你能力范围的问题；第二，提出的问题要能在你允许的时间内完成；第三，每次研究一个焦点，不要涉及面太广；第四，问题要和你教学情境直接相关。行动研究之前要处理相关伦理问题。这里需要回答3个问题：第一，你的研究要得到什么样的许可；第二，谁要受到你研究的影响；第三，你的研究结果要向谁报告。需要说明的是，根据国际规则，研究中的伦理问题不是泛泛而谈，而是有非常具体、明确的要求。例如研究之前必须要得到相关人员的书面许可。如果研究成果在杂志上发表，必须对书面许可加以说明。此外要避免对研究参与者产生负面影响，或带来不必要的伤害，同时要确保研究参与者的知情权。

第三章介绍行动研究方案的实施。本章侧重介绍各种收集数据的方法。选择收集数据的方法时需要回答两个问题：我需要看到什么？我需要知道什么？观察可以回答第一个问题，其它方法可以回答后一个问题。这里所说的观察比日常生活中的相似活动更具自我意识，主要原因是你要收集的数据有着很强的指向性、客观性、反思性、事实性与反复评价性。观察的方法有多种，可采用观察表，记录行为或事件；也可以记观察笔记，其中包括反思观察、分析观察、叙事观察、影子观察；也可用录像、录音设备将所要观察的活动进行全程或部分录制；也可用事先设计的平面图对活动场景进行描述，或者用相机拍照。回答“我需要知道什么”这个问题的方法也很多，有访谈、问卷、日记。根据访谈问题的自由度，访谈分为全结构式、半结构式、开放式。问卷也分封闭式与开放式两种。高质量数据的收集应该来源于多种渠道，互相之间可进行“三角验证”，避免主观性与片面性。

第四章阐述如何考察行动研究的结果。本章主要介绍了分析质性数据与量化数据的方法。与一般应用研究不同的是，行动研究数据的分析具有动态性、循环性与反复性。数据分析可以与行动研究同步，一边实施行动研究计划，一边分析，在分析的过程中逐步缩小研究范围，发现研究焦点。本章介绍了两种主要的质性数据分析工具：范畴化与课堂话语分析。质性数据的范畴来源于数据。换句话说，行动研究者在阅读数据前，头脑中不应有预设的范畴。研究者通过持续、反复阅读数据，对数据进行深度解读，最终聚焦的“范畴”从数据中“涌现”。这就是我们常说的自下而上的归纳法，而不是自上而下的演绎法。课堂话语分析的数据来源于录像或录音材料。研究者必须要对所听材料有深度理解。根据Richards的建议，具体分析可分四步完成：1）对总体特征进行勾画；2）识别带有全局性的明显特征；3）聚焦结构性成分；4）提供完整的描述。量化数据的分析处理过程，可用描述性统计的集中趋势与离散趋势来进行分析与报告。集中趋势有平均数、中数与众数；离散趋势有全距与标准差。评价行动研究的效度与实验研究的效度不相同，行动研究更多地考察研究结论的可靠性与准确性。

第五章阐述行动研究的最后一个环节“反思”。然而，我们说它是最后一个环节并不尽然。作者在本章开头就强调，“反思”会贯穿于行动研究的全过程。本章重点讨论了3个问题：1）反思的内容；2）下一步的计划；3）与其他人分享研究结果的方法。反思涉及的内容包括行动、研究过程、研究者自身的信念与价值观、情绪与经验。思考下一步计划通常始于对已开展的行动研究进行评估，例如是否达到预期目标、是否发现新问题，在此基础上决定是否继续前行。逻辑上说，行动研究“永无休止”，因为教学过程的改进永无尽头，教学要求不断变化，所教学生情况不尽相同，老问题解决了，新问题又出现。但在实际生活中，可能由于某种客观原因，行动研究不得不中止。无论你决定是否前行，你都要对已完成的行动研究进行总结，做出结论。研究结果的分享形式多种多样，有口头与书面两种，口头又可以分为讨论或辩论两种形式。

3. 本书的不足之处

人无完人，金无足赤。在笔者看来本书也有不足之处，主要有以下三点：

第一，在界定行动研究时，不够简洁、明了。本书第5页列出了墨西哥教师对行动研究的3种定义，接着又列出了6种其他学者所做的定义，但书中未给出作者自己明确的定义。本书是为那些行动研究者新手上路所写，是一种启蒙书。我们给出的定义越多越繁复，读者就越糊涂。笔者认为比较好的写作方法是，作者在消化、理解多种定义的基础上，提炼出核心内容，用一线教师能够理解的语言进行阐述。例如，可先将行动研究简单地定义为："行动研究是教师为解决教学实际问题或变革教学现状而采取某种新措施的研究"。接着再对行动研究的典型特征辅以例证进一步给予解释。行动研究的核心是"行动"。这里的行动不是一般意义上的行为，它是有目的、有理据、有监控、有反思的行为。行动研究所关注的问题与当时当地的教学实践直接相关，是影响教学效果且迫切需要解决的问题。行动研究都是由一线教师直接参与研究，充当教学的实施者和研究者的双重角色，具有广泛的参与性。行动研究开展的环境一般为教师所教授的自然班级，没有人为操纵的因素，具有较强的真实性。研究者（也就是教师）在整个研究过程中，需要不断地反思，包括反思教学发现研究问题、反思研究方案、修正研究设计、反思研究结果、确定下一步行动研究的问题等——这是行动研究反思性的具体体现。另外，行动研究的结果对提高教学效果有着直接的作用，具有很强的应用性。综上所述，行动研究具有当下性、参与性、真实性、反思性与应用性五个典型特点（文秋芳、韩少杰，2011）。

第二，对行动研究各个环节的介绍亦未跳出一般研究的框架，特别是对行动研究4个环节（计划、行动、观察与反思）的说明，体现不出行动研究的典型特征。首先，行动研究的核心部分应该是对所要解决的问题提出有理有据、且可操作的新行动方案，这是计划（Plan）环节的重要内容，然而本书的第二章几乎未涉及这个环节。本书中行动研究的行动（Act）环节，按理应该报告行动方案是如何实施的。遗憾的是，本环节未涉及这个议题，而是根据一般研究方法的介绍思路，说明收集数据的各种方法及其要注意的问题。第三个观察（observe）环节理应说明如何通过观察来分析行动研究的成效。出人意料的是，作者仅分别说明质性数据与量化数据的分析方法，其内容与常见的研究方法介绍无明显区别。

第三，行动研究的过程描述不完整，缺乏动态感（见P.10）。笔者认为借助图1能够更好地描绘行动研究的全过程（文秋芳、韩少杰，2011）。图中的内圈包含行动研究的四个环节：（1）聚焦问题；（2）提出（解决问题）方案；（3）实施方案；（4）评价成效。这四个环节形成一个循环链，每一次行动研究的结束将激发新的行动研究。如此循环往复，教学在研究中得以发展，研究在教学中得以深入。外圈包括三种活动：（1）向书学习，即阅读文献；（2）向人请教，即向周围人学习；（3）研究者自我反思。外圈的三种活动渗透在行动研究的全过程。为了使内圈的活动更科学、更有成效，研究者要不断地阅读文献，不断地向有经验的人求教，不断地根据新获得的外部资源与实际操作情况进行反思，并及时对行动研究的四个环节做出恰当的调整。

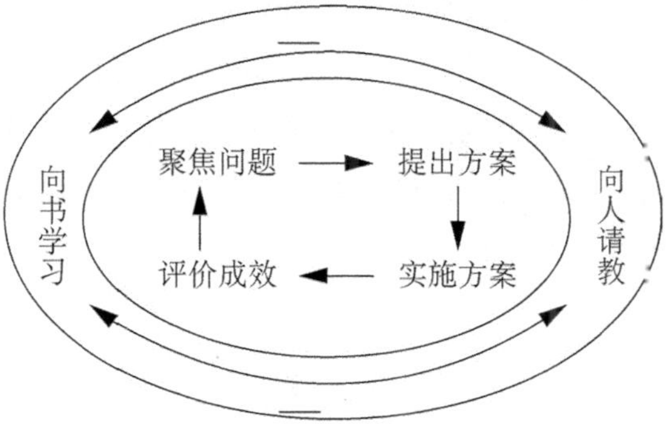

图1：行动研究示意图

4. 对我国“行动研究”的展望

教学研究应该成为教师的自觉行动。教师常年工作在教学第一线，和学生共生，与教学共长，是教学活动的组织者、引导者、实践者。作为一名教师，要想从敬业到精业，必须具备一定的教学研究意识和研究能力。行动研究是从事教学研究的主要方法。行动研究的对象是教师本身，是教师的实践，是教师所教的学生，是教师所用的教材与教学方法，是与教师朝夕相处的同事或朋友。教师边教学，边研究；边研究，边教学。教学与研究溶为一体，教师身份与研究者身份合二为一。简言之，行动研究指向教师的工作与生活实践；扎根于教师熟悉的教学场所；聚焦于教师渴望解决的教学难题。行动研究的目的是使教师行为更具反思性与理据性，给教师的工作与生活注入更多活力与创意，让学生的成长更健康、更全面、更高效。

“行动研究”首先由社会心理学家勒温（Lewin）于20世纪40年代提出，被介绍到中国已有许多年（韩淑萍，2009），但在我国高校外语界显现的时间比较短。2010年7月中国外语教育研究中心与外语教学与研究出版社合作，首次为全国高等学校英语骨干教师举办了“外语教学中的行动研究”研修班；2011年《中国外语教育》第一期上刊登了4篇北京外国语大学4位年轻教师从事行动研究的报告；《英语教学中的行动研究方法》(*Doing Action Research in English Language Teaching*)一书也将于今年引进出版；并且本书作者Anne Burns将于今年11月来到北京，参与高等学校青年骨干教师高级研修班“Doing Qualitative and Action Research in TESOL”的工作，担纲主讲教师。笔者相信在这一系列活动的推动下，行动研究的理念与做法必将被高校广大外语教师所接受，行动研究必将成为我国高校外语教师提高教学质量的自觉行动，成为提升外语教师自身专业化能力的重要手段。

参考文献

韩淑萍，2009，行动研究的历史与现状。《中国教育报》2009年4月24日第5版。

文秋芳、韩少杰，2011，《英语教学研究方法与案例分析》。上海：上海外语教育出版社。

文秋芳

北京外国语大学中国外语教育研究中心

2011年6月20日

Preface

In recent years, action research (AR) has become increasingly popular in second language teaching circles. Language teachers in many countries have heard about AR, either through formal courses of study, or in-service teacher education, and are interested in knowing more about it. Over the last two decades, I have worked with teachers all over the world, who are committed to their own professional development and attracted to the idea of doing AR in their classrooms. Many of these teachers have asked me challenging and insightful questions about the areas covered in this book. They have also told me they were looking for reader-friendly guidance to get themselves going along the AR pathway.

So, I have written this introduction to AR for all the reflective and dedicated language teachers I have met, and for language teachers around the world who want to get started in AR and are looking for a practical, hands-on introduction. My audience is pre-service and in-service teachers who want to try doing AR or, for one reason or another, are in the process of learning about it, either for formal study or for their own interest. My book is also written to be used by academic colleagues who see their work as centrally connected to teacher education, and who are already convinced that introducing teachers to AR and supporting them in their endeavours is a worthwhile thing to do. The audience for the book is not academic researchers whose interests do not lie in working with teachers, and whose research approaches are directed elsewhere. My hope is that this book makes a real contribution to the professional lives of language teachers around the world by introducing them to the excitement of doing AR in their particular teaching contexts.

Anne Burns
Macquarie University, Sydney
May 2009

Acknowledgements

I am very grateful to friends, colleagues and students from many different parts of the world who have contributed in more ways than they will ever know to the writing of this book. At various stages in its conception, development and birth I have been most fortunate to receive their encouragement to keep going. Melba Libia Cárdenas Beltrán, from the Universidad Nacional de Colombia, who visited me at Macquarie University, in 2006 responded enthusiastically when I asked her whether she thought a basic introduction to action research would be useful to teachers in the language teaching field. I ran this idea again past Randi Reppen from North Arizona University at the TESOL Convention in 2007. Randi was kind enough to give me further encouragement. After I wrote the first two chapters, Melba and her colleagues in Colombia gave me valuable feedback and many useful suggestions, as did Kazuyoshi Sato, from Nagoya University of Foreign Studies, who was a visiting scholar working with me in early 2008 at Macquarie. Yoshi sent me many materials and gave me access to the action research work he has conducted with many teacher colleagues in Japan.

At just the right moment in May 2008 when my enthusiasm for writing was flagging, Jenny Barnett from the University of South Australia listened patiently to my description of the project and urged me to go on. Jenny shared the material with her students whose comments helped to reassure me I was on the right track. As I wrote on, Sue Garton, from Aston University in the UK, was unflagging in her reading of chapters from the book and always offered insightful suggestions. She also shared the chapters with some of her students who willingly forwarded more material and suggestions as I went along. Jill Burton from the University of South Australia and Heather Denny from Auckland University of Technology were also kind enough to read and make suggestions about early chapters.

I'm grateful also to Diane Malcolm in Bahrain, Heliana Mello in Brazil, Sarah Springer in Costa Rica, Graham Crookes in Hawai'i, Rita Balbi, Philip O'Gara and Graziella Pozzo in Italy, Andrew Gladman, Simon Humphries, Tim

Marchand and Jerry Talandis Jr in Japan, Robert Dickey in Korea, Maria del Carmen Sanchez Chavez in Mexico, Antonia Chandrasegaran in Singapore, Frances Wilson in Sydney, Derin Atay in Turkey, Simon Borg and Steve Mann in the UK, and Jamie Gurkin in the USA for sharing their own work, or that of their students with me. I have been privileged to have contact with many teachers who were brave enough to try action research in their classrooms and schools and to open up their explorations and discoveries to their colleagues. Some of the work they have done is included in this volume. My particular thanks go to them, as well as to my doctoral students in Australia, China, Indonesia, Japan, Mexico, the Middle East, the UK, and the USA from whom I have learned much about doing qualitative and action research.

But this book would never have seen the light of day without the determination and enthusiasm of Naomi Silverman from Routledge and Eli Hinkel, the Series Editor. Whenever we met, they continued to insist that an introductory book on action research was needed. They fired my enthusiasm for this project and I am grateful that they kept it burning. My thanks also to Sophie Cox, who proved to be such a marvellous and careful copy-editor. Of course, none of it would have happened without the continuing support of my family and I thank Ross, Douglas and Catherine for their confidence in me over all the years.

CHAPTER 1

What Is Action Research?

Pre-reading questions

Before you read this chapter, think about the following questions. If possible discuss them with a colleague or write some brief responses to each one.

- What is action research?
- What do you already know about doing action research?
- What steps are involved in doing action research?

We will explore these questions in this chapter.

Language teachers all around the world want to be effective teachers who provide the best learning opportunities for their students. Action research (AR) can be a very valuable way to extend our teaching skills and gain more understanding of ourselves as teachers, our classrooms and our students. In this first chapter, we begin by looking at some of the key concepts in AR – what it is, what characterises it, how it relates to other types of research, and what basic steps are followed when we do it. We will consider what is different about doing AR from doing what all good teachers do – thinking about what is happening in our classrooms. But we will also explore a question you may have already asked yourself – why should teachers bother to do research when, after all, they are employed and paid to be teachers and not researchers?

Reflection point

What are your views about teachers doing research? In your opinion, what are the advantages and disadvantages of being a teacher researcher?

We will come back to these issues later in the chapter.

Action research (AR) is something that many language teachers seem to have heard about, but often they have only a hazy idea of what it actually is and what doing it involves. So, one of the first questions teachers new to AR usually ask is: *What is action research?*

1.1 What is action research?

AR is part of a broad movement that has been going on in education generally for some time. It is related to the ideas of 'reflective practice' and 'the teacher as researcher'. AR involves taking a self-reflective, critical, and systematic approach to exploring your own teaching contexts. By critical, I don't mean being negative and derogatory about the way you teach, but taking a questioning and 'problematising' stance towards your teaching. My term, *problematising*, doesn't imply looking at your teaching as if it is ineffective and full of problems. Rather, it means taking an area you feel could be done better, subjecting it to questioning, and then developing new ideas and alternatives. So, in AR, a teacher becomes an 'investigator' or 'explorer' of his or her personal teaching context, while at the same time being one of the participants in it.

So, one of the main aims of AR is to identify a 'problematic' situation or issue that the participants – who may include teachers, students, managers, administrators, or even parents – consider worth looking into more deeply and systematically. Again, the term *problematic* does not mean that the teacher is an incompetent teacher. The point is that, as teachers, we often see gaps between what is actually happening in our teaching situation and what we would ideally like to see happening.

The central idea of the *action* part of AR is to intervene in a deliberate way in the problematic situation in order to bring about changes and, even better, improvements in practice. Importantly, the improvements that happen in AR are ones based on information (or to use the research term, *data*) that an action researcher collects systematically. (Incidentally, data is the plural from the Latin word 'datum' meaning 'something known', so you will find me using it in the plural.) So, the changes made in the teaching situation arise from solid information rather than from our hunches or assumptions about the way we think things are. To understand what this means in more concrete terms, let's consider an actual classroom situation in Italy where a language teacher identified a problematic area in her teaching.

Classroom voices

Isabella Bruschi is a teacher of English language and literature in an upper secondary school in Turin, Italy. Isabella's starting point for AR was her negative feelings about the oral tests (*interrogazione oral*) she used in class. She had a whole cluster of questions and doubts about this aspect of her teaching and she was concerned to find out how she could improve things for herself and her students.

> What makes me feel so uncomfortable when I have to assess students' oral English? Do I know what happens during an oral test? Am I aware of the nature of the questions I ask and of their different weight? How do I react when students give me the wrong answers? When I intend to help students do I in fact help them? What do my students think of my way of conducting an oral test? What are their preferences?

To understand the nature of her problem, she collected this information:

- She kept a diary to explore her feelings of uneasiness.
- She gave students a questionnaire to investigate their preferences and difficulties in oral tests.
- She recorded a number of oral tests.
- She asked students for written feedback after the test.
- She asked a facilitator to interview students after the oral test.

The recordings gave her back an image very far from the ideal she had of herself as a teacher. There was a mismatch between her intention to facilitate students' responses during the test and what was actually happening. She saw a set of behaviours that did not please her. She became aware of her 'disturbing interventions'. These were the interruptions she made that were distracting students from searching their minds or following their trains of thought.

These are the patterns she found in the way she was questioning students:

1. Frequent interruptions while students were looking for the answer or for the right word.
2. Questions posed in a sequence, which often changed the original focus and resulted in students feeling embarrassed as they don't know which question to answer first.
3. Questions which suggested how students should answer.
4. Use of questions formulated as open questions, but treated by the teacher as if they were closed questions.
5. Subsequent use of negative reinforcement in spite of the intention to be helpful.
6. Use of feedback of the type, 'no, I actually wanted you to tell me …'

When she looked at the students' responses to the open questions in the questionnaire, she found that they confirmed these patterns, as these examples show:

> I don't like being interrupted all the time without having the possibility of carrying forward what I want to say.
>
> Being passive. When the teacher talks too much.
>
> The questions 'in bursts', without being given the time to answer.

As a result of this information, she set up three strategies to improve her teaching:

1. Giving students the questions for the oral test five minutes before answering so that they could have time to think and organise their ideas.
2. Restricting her interventions to a minimum.
3. When interviewing, paraphrasing what students say to help them keep the thread of their thoughts, search their memory or trigger off new ideas.

Her students' comments after the test show that these changes made a big difference:

> What I liked in the oral test was the fact that you didn't interrupt me while I was speaking. (Mara)
>
> I appreciate the fact that you didn't interrupt me while I was talking and that you tried to help when I had difficulties, and the fact that you were listening attentively to what I was saying, while encouraging me to go on. (Sabrina)
>
> I felt helped when the teacher repeated what I had said. This helped me reformulate my thoughts more clearly. (Francesca)

This is what Isabella writes at the end of the AR cycle. When she considers what it has all meant for her teaching:

> I have a neat perception of the changes I've been through, which doesn't mean that I have solved all my problems. I have certainly acquired new tools, and, above all, a greater awareness of my being a teacher. Observing and analysing ... have made me see more clearly the asymmetric nature of classroom communication. As a result I now feel more in control of what happens during an oral test.

She adds this comment on how the research will continue to have an impact on her teaching and how she intends to continue her investigations:

> I don't think my research ends here. I think the way I formulate and ask the [test] questions is open to further enquiry and reflection. The research on my 'questioning' of students has opened up new perspectives to my teaching. Now I know that the cycle of explanation – oral test – assessment is inadequate. What I need to investigate now are the opportunities I give my students to pose questions themselves and the space I give them to discuss ideas among themselves. In other words, what opportunities do I give them to practise such skills as selecting, ordering and organising information into a coherent speech before taking the oral test? Do I give them enough time to understand and learn in the first place? My new research will be on alternative ways to do assessment, keeping in mind that as a teacher I am not just a transmitter of knowledge, but a facilitator of processes so as to make students autonomous in the construction of their knowledge.

(Data translated and supplied by Graziella Pozzo)

Isabella's situation illustrates how AR can throw a light on our teaching practices and improve an unsatisfactory situation. It shows how she identified and improved a classroom dilemma by using *a reflective research cycle* of planning, acting, observing and reflecting.

Reflection point

Look back at the pre-reading notes you made for this chapter. Would you add anything to your statements about AR?

If possible, discuss your ideas with a colleague.

Here are some descriptions of AR that were suggested by three of my teacher researcher students located in different parts of Mexico. At this point, you may want to compare what you think with their ideas about AR.

Classroom voices

Action research is research carried out in the classroom by the teacher of the course, mainly with the purpose of solving a problem or improving the teaching/learning process. (Elizabeth, Sonora)

Action research is carried out by teachers in their context, in their classrooms. Teachers identify a problem or an area they wish to improve and based on theory or experience or a hypothesis they think of an intervention. They document the intervention and results of it. If the results are positive they could lead to the dissemination of the information. If not, the cycle may be started again. (Iraís, Tlaxcala)

AR is a reflective process that aims to solve a particular teaching-learning problem that has been identified. One of the aims of AR is to improve the teaching practice and in the long run the whole curriculum. In order to do action research it is necessary to carry out a rigorous study in which the problem has to be clearly specified, an action plan has to be described and carried out, and finally an evaluation has to be contemplated in order to show if the decisions taken were the adequate ones. (Carmen, Mexico City)

To follow up what these Mexican teachers stated, here are some definitions offered by writers on action research:

> 'self-reflective enquiry' undertaken by participants in order to improve the rationality and justice of their own social or educational practices as well as their understanding of these practices and the situations in which these practices are carried out.
>
> (Carr & Kemmis, 1986, p. 220)

> the study of a social situation with the view to improving the quality of the action in it.
>
> (Elliott, 1991, p. 69)

> a flexible methodology, not merely in terms of being eclectic in research methods, but more fundamentally in needing to adapt to the social and political situation in which it is employed.
>
> (Somekh, 1993, p. 29)

> small scale intervention in the functioning of the real world and a close examination of the effects of such intervention.
>
> (van Lier, 1996, p. 32)

> a self-reflective, systematic and critical approach to enquiry by participants who are at the same time members of the research community. The aim is to identify problematic situations or issues considered by the participants to be worthy of investigation in order to bring about critically informed changes in practice. Action research is underpinned by democratic principles in that ownership of change is invested in those who conduct the research.
>
> (Burns, in Cornwell, 1999, p. 5)

All these various definitions suggest that AR is not just a simple question of following a fixed pattern to solve a straightforward technical problem in an individual classroom. The aims and contributions of AR are multiple, overlapping, and varied. As Edge explains, using examples to illustrate the possibilities, AR may be:

- means oriented: *We know that we are trying to teach people to write English on this course. How can we improve the ways in which we do so?*
- ends oriented: *We know that these students want to become librarians. How sure are we about the importance of teaching them to write in English?*

- theory oriented: *As we investigate our teaching of writing, how can we articulate our increased understanding of what is happening here? How can we connect with other written records in order to theorise our practice and perhaps, contribute to the theory that informs us?*
- institution oriented: *To what extent is my writing course, through its goals, its topics, and my practice, contributing to an integrated educational program through which the institution mediates between its students and its social context?*
- society oriented: *To what extent is my writing course, through its goals, its topics, and my practice, promoting values that I believe in (e.g., contributing to a healthy dialogic relationship among students, teachers, institution and society at large)?*
- teacher oriented: *Where is my own personal and professional development in this? What is the contribution to collegiality and, thereby, the kind of society I want to live in?*

(Edge, 2001, p. 5)

1.2 Why should I do action research? I'm a teacher not a researcher!

At this point you may be thinking that the discussion so far is all very well, but it doesn't alter the fact that your role as a teacher is to teach. And, indeed, there is every good reason for you to think that doing research is beyond the call of duty. Teachers don't get paid or given time off to do research as academics do; they have full teaching loads which means that any time spent on research needs to be added onto a busy teaching schedule. Nor does any research they complete necessarily get acknowledged by their colleagues, head teachers or educational administrators – in fact, it may be opposed as something that is not the business of teachers. It's not particularly easy for teachers to find the resources, support or facilities needed, such as books or articles from the literature, or people who can offer advice about methods for collecting and analysing data. Many teachers have been put off research, and the theories about teaching they were taught in teacher training courses, because they find out that when they get into the classroom the theory does not match the reality. AR can also seem like a 'scary' thing to do if you are more used to classroom teaching; it takes time and it might mean making changes that take us out of our comfort zone.

However, for a teacher who is reflective, and committed to developing as a thinking professional, AR is an appealing way to look more closely at puzzling classroom issues or to delve into teaching dilemmas. For example, Linda, one of my Australian teacher colleagues, commented to me that AR encourages teachers 'to reach their own solutions and conclusions and this is far more attractive and has more impact than being presented with ideals which cannot be attained' (Burns, 1999, p. 7). Because this type of research is so immediate to our teaching situation, as we saw in Isabella's story, doing AR can reinvigorate our teaching, lead to positive change, raise our awareness of the complexities of our work, and show us what drives our personal approaches to teaching. So what kinds of benefits to their teaching have teachers who have carried out AR found? This question is best illustrated by an actual example.

Classroom voices

Heather Denny is one of my teacher researcher colleagues based in New Zealand. She worked with other colleagues in her teaching centre on a collaborative AR project that focused on new ways of teaching spoken discourse to adult learners. After working with them Heather surveyed four of the teachers in her research group. Heather says:

> Group members reported major benefits for both teaching and research skills development in this type of group action research activity. For teachers there was faster professional development, through basing teacher changes and decisions not only on reflection but also on reliable data collection and analysis. There was also more effective and focused teaching materials development, some of it very innovative and the generation and propagation of relevant and useful theory ...
>
> Research skills were learned in this project through individuals 'learning by doing' and also through the sharing of expertise and experience. The voluntary nature of group membership was also an asset, as was the fact that members of the group all saw the area of the focus as being of interest in their teaching ...
>
> Many teachers felt keenly a lack of research experience. However this was not an insuperable barrier as one of the most inexperienced had with support managed to carry a project to presentation state after 20 months in the group.

(Source: Denny, 2005, p. 8)

Time is one of the biggest problems facing teachers, as Heather's colleagues reported. But there is growing evidence that language teachers from all over the world get immense satisfaction from doing AR, especially when they can work collaboratively with other colleagues to explore common issues (see, for example, Burns, 1999; Edge, 2001; Edge & Richards, 1993; Mathew, 2000; Rochsantiningsih, 2005; Tinker Sachs, 2002; Wallace, 1998).

1.3 What are the steps in action research?

According to Kemmis and McTaggart (1988), who are major authors in this field, AR typically involves four broad phases in a cycle of research. The first cycle may become a continuing, or *iterative*, spiral of cycles which recur until the action researcher has achieved a satisfactory outcome and feels it is time to stop.

1. Planning

In this phase you identify a problem or issue and develop a plan of action in order to bring about improvements in a specific area of the research context. This is a forward-looking phase where you consider: i) what kind of investigation is possible within the realities and constraints of your teaching situation; and ii) what potential improvements you think are possible.

2. Action

The plan is a carefully considered one which involves some deliberate interventions into your teaching situation that you put into action over an agreed period of time. The interventions are 'critically informed' as you question your assumptions about the current situation and plan new and alternative ways of doing things.

3. Observation

This phase involves you in observing systematically the effects of the action and documenting the context, actions and opinions of those involved. It is a data collection phase where you use 'open-eyed' and 'open-minded' tools to collect information about what is happening.

4. Reflection

At this point, you reflect on, evaluate and describe the effects of the action in order to make sense of what has happened and to understand the issue you have explored more clearly. You may decide to do further cycles of AR to improve the situation even more, or to share the 'story' of your research with others as part of your ongoing professional development.

(Adapted from Kemmis & McTaggart, 1988, pp. 11-14)

This model of AR has often been illustrated through the diagram in Figure 1.1 to show its iterative or recursive nature.

There are several other models of AR and, indeed, Kemmis and McTaggart's model has been criticised by some authors for being too fixed and rigid. McNiff (1988), for instance, sees it as 'prescriptive'. She prefers a more flexible approach that allows action researchers to be creative and spontaneous. She argues that the processes involved should be adaptable, according to how teachers' personal ideas and theories about what is happening in their classrooms are developing. Ebbutt (1985) argues that AR cycles should be successive and open, and allow for as much feedback and interaction between the cycles as possible. He sees Kemmis and McTaggart's model as a 'one-way street', that moves forward only in one direction. In a similar vein, language teachers I have worked with in various locations have reported that AR processes involve many interwoven aspects – exploring, identifying, planning, collecting information, analysing and reflecting, hypothesising and speculating, intervening, observing, reporting, writing, presenting (Burns, 1999, p.35) – that don't necessarily occur in any fixed sequence. In addition, my teacher colleagues have emphasised the many

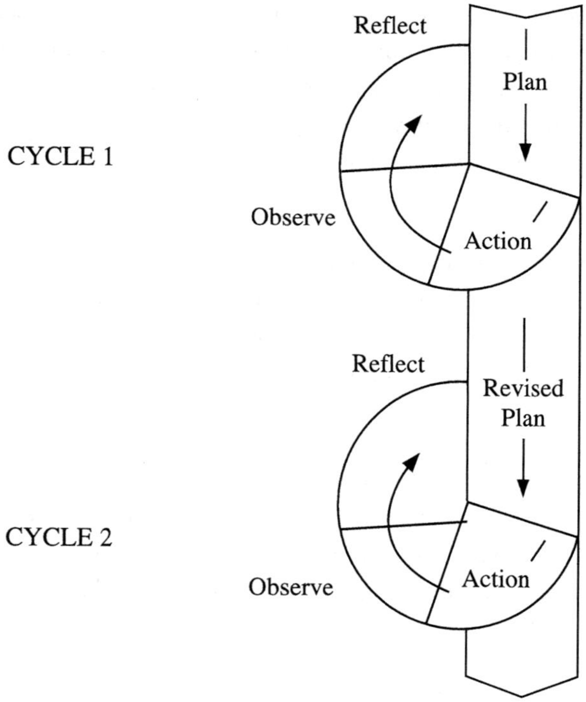

Figure 1.1 Cyclical AR model based on Kemmis and McTaggart (1988)

advantages of working collaboratively with other teachers as this allows for new ideas and insights to be shared. (Personally, I have never liked the way the cycles spiral downward rather than moving upward or sideways, which seem like more positive directions to me!)

Nevertheless, Kemmis and McTaggart's model is probably the best known. It's a kind of 'classic' and it appears often in the literature on AR. Despite the criticisms, it is a useful model as it summarises very succinctly the essential phases of the AR process. Therefore, I have selected it as a convenient way of structuring the discussion on AR in this book.

Classroom voices

Rita Balbi is a teacher educator who has worked with high school teachers conducting AR in Italy. She has this to say about using Kemmis and McTaggart's model:

> Adopting Kemmis and McTaggart's model as a reference framework does not necessarily mean a rigid division between the various phases but only that each aspect involved in the phases is part of the process. It is not a sort of lockstep and I would rather look at the four steps they recommend as necessary 'ingredients' of any AR process, interacting in a flexible way and not according to a rigid sequence.
>
> (Personal communication, 12 March 2009)

The four chapters that follow each take one phase of the cycle and discuss the decisions and steps that action researchers must make at that point. Chapter 2 looks at the steps involved in starting up an AR project, such as finding your focus, identifying your questions or issues, getting permission as necessary to address ethical issues, and considering the resources and materials you are likely to need. Chapter 3 introduces you to methods for collecting the information, or data, that you will need in order to find out more about the topic you have selected. We'll look at methods that involve observing and describing the situation and the participants, as well as those that can be used for asking questions and discussing the research issues and people's views about them. We will also discuss how you can check and strengthen the data to make sure that the information is resulting in insights that are accurate and well founded. In Chapter 4, we'll discuss how to analyse the data in order to make sense of them. We will look at how to prepare for data analysis as well as how both qualitative and quantitative data can be synthesised and presented. We will also look at issues involved in ensuring the data are trustworthy, which helps to strengthen the quality of the research. The final chapter,

Chapter 5, looks at reflecting on the research as a whole and planning for further action. This chapter discusses how to bring the AR process together, to consider the next steps, and to share the research with others.

Before we move on, this might be a useful point to summarise the essential features of AR raised in the discussion so far. First, it involves teachers in evaluating and reflecting on their teaching with the aim of bringing about continuing changes and improvements in practice. Second, it is small-scale, contextualised, and local in character, as the participants identify and investigate teaching-learning issues within a specific social situation, the school or classroom. Third, it is participatory and inclusive, as it gives communities of participants the opportunity to investigate issues of immediate concern collaboratively within their own social situation. Fourth, it is different from the 'intuitive' thinking that occurs as a normal part of teaching, as changes in practice will be based on collecting and analysing data systematically. Finally, we can say that AR is based on democratic principles; it invests the ownership for changes in curriculum practice in the teachers and learners who conduct the research and is therefore empowering.

Action point

Share with your colleagues what you understand about AR at this point. If you wish, you could use the overview in the sections above and the pre-reading questions as a starting point for your discussion.

Find out whether any of your colleagues are interested in collaborating with you to conduct AR on an area of teaching or learning that interests you all.

1.4 How is AR different from other kinds of research?

Teachers who are new to AR sometimes ask me how it relates to other ways of doing research. A set of questions posted by Dale Griffee in 2003 on the Action Research listserv of the Japan Association of Language Teachers' (JALT) Teacher Education Special Interest Group (SIG) raised some interesting issues that provide a good starting point for this discussion.

What is the difference between AR and other kinds of research? The answer has to be a characteristic that is not the case for applied research, theoretical research, or evaluation research. In other words, I don't think we can say that AR is done by teachers, and that is its defining characteristic, because applied research is also done by teachers all the time. What are the characteristics that set AR aside and mark it as different from other types of research?

Reflection point

How would you answer the two questions posted by Dale?

Discuss them with your colleagues.

These questions are useful and challenging as they get to the crux of the confusion that sometimes exists between applied research and AR. AR and applied research are in some ways similar and overlapping, but there are also important differences between them. Let's uncover some of the main issues a little more.

Most people have the idea that research is about investigating something in order to discover new information and that there are particular methods and procedures that must be used to collect the information. But there are many different ways of going about doing research. As McKay (2006) notes, 'research' is difficult to define because of the different philosophies, assumptions, theoretical frameworks, purposes, methods and sources of data associated with different approaches. Nunan (1992, p. 3) boils the idea of research down to its essentials. He suggests that any piece of research will have three core components: '(1) a question, problem or hypothesis, (2) data, (3) analysis and interpretation of data'. Similarly, Wallace (1998, p. 12) offers this synthesis of the key elements of research:

> The process of *data collection*, the setting up of a *database*, and the subsequent *analysis* of the data we have collected forms the core of what we call *research*. There are many aspects of research, and other procedures may also be involved, but this process forms its essence. We see that according to this definition, research is a special kind of inquiry, since not all inquiry is based on data collection and analysis.

These descriptions of research are a useful starting point for considering the essential bases of AR.

To illustrate how a researcher can undertake research in different ways, let's consider the following two accounts. As you read you might want to note the common features that these two situations share and the main ways that they differ.

Example 1

As part of the introduction of a new syllabus, a researcher wishes to know whether the use of group work will improve students' ability to speak English.

She first consults the literature on this area of research. She then decides on the approach and methods to be used. The researcher's hypothesis is: *group work will increase the development of both fluency and accuracy in oral tasks.*

She assigns one group of students in a school to an experimental group, where all classroom tasks are conducted through group work for a period of two months. An equal number of students (the control group) are taught using the same tasks through a whole-class teacher-fronted approach for the same period.

In order to ensure that the students in the experimental group are not at higher levels of language learning to begin with, the researcher first administers a test. She then assigns students to the groups on the basis of the test results. At the end of the two months, each of the groups is given a further identical test in order to see whether the use of group work has resulted in higher results for the experimental group.

The results show that the students assigned to group work have performed at a higher level in relation to fluency, but that their performance on some aspects of grammatical accuracy is lower than the control group. The researcher publishes the findings of the study in a journal.

Example 2

As part of the introduction of a new syllabus, a researcher decides to move away from using whole-class speaking activities in his classroom. He decides to introduce more group work for certain tasks and to observe how the students react.

He assigns students to groups and keeps a journal noting down his observations over a period of two weeks. At the end of this period, he notes that some students are not participating in the group tasks and are increasingly reluctant to work in groups. He decides that students are unused to this approach and need more practice.

He increases the use of group work and assigns students to the same groups. He also asks the students to complete a survey on their responses to group work. His own observation and journal entries, as well as the surveys indicate that students are becoming even more reluctant to do group work.

The researcher discusses the problem with some colleagues who suggest he tries letting students choose their own groups. He tries this strategy over a further period of one week and notes that students are less reluctant. He also observes that the groups do not remain static, but appear to change according to the task.

He decides to try a further approach of giving students a choice of tasks. This approach works even better and interaction amongst the students increases noticeably. The researcher presents the findings of his study at a professional development session and publishes the study in a journal.

The two examples I've presented here are, of course, simplified and idealised. But they serve to draw out some essential similarities and differences about different approaches to research.

The first thing to note is that both researchers adopt a 'scientific' approach (Cohen & Manion, 1994) to the group work topic they are investigating. In other words, they are both concerned to go beyond their intuitions or assumptions about the effectiveness of group work, and to use a systematic approach to asking questions, collecting information, analysing the data, drawing out conclusions, and interpreting their findings. These aspects of their approach form the 'special kind of inquiry' to which Wallace referred.

However, there are also noticeable differences in the way they go about planning and conducting the research. The first researcher adopts an 'objective' stance in which she attempts to control the variables (the factors in the research situation that do not remain constant) that may affect the findings – for example, differences in language proficiency. She is also attempting to identify the relationships between the treatment (group work) and the outcomes (increases in fluency and accuracy); in other words she is looking for a cause and effect (i.e., X causes Y) relationship. The second researcher, however, is not interested in establishing relationships of this type, but instead wants to explore the best possible ways of setting up classroom activities. This is a more 'subjective' approach, concerned with exploring different ways of teaching, and as a result of the information collected deliberately changing the conditions that exist in the classroom.

Second, both researchers are concerned with an area of language learning and teaching and their aim is to find answers to issues relating to practice in the classroom. However, their research differs in the way these answers may be applied. As one of her main goals, the first researcher will want to make a new contribution to a body of existing 'scientific' evidence about effective teaching and learning. It may be possible to apply the findings in language classrooms, but these applications are not likely to be immediate. Instead, they will be absorbed into what is known generally in the field of research about the use of group work and its contribution to language learning. In the second example, the researcher's main goal is directly focused on addressing an issue of immediate practical and personal concern. In other words, the researcher wants to know more about what works well in group work so that he can apply this knowledge immediately. His focus is on discovering more about a specific teaching issue which is important to him in relation to his own classroom and students.

Third, each researcher uses a different approach to selecting and using the research methods. The first researcher adopts a structured and controlled set of methods, using control and experimental groups of students and guarding against threats to the validity of the research through pre- and post-testing (validity is discussed in more detail in Chapter 4). She follows this approach because one aim of her study is to generalise beyond this specific research situation to other similar situations. The second researcher uses a much more flexible and open-ended approach, selecting and changing the methods as needed and as new insights emerge. His concern is with his own teaching situation and with resolving his practical classroom issues.

A fourth area to consider is the area of theory. Both applied research and AR may be concerned with theoretical ideas, but these will probably be viewed in very different ways. Applied research is usually concerned to connect with and test out 'grand' (that is well-known public or general) theory from the field. It draws substantially on the literature in a particular research area in order to lay out in detail what is already known about the topic and to provide a theoretical base for the study. This is why the researcher in the first example consults the literature thoroughly to provide a conceptual framework for the study. She then draws from a tried-and-tested set of methods for the research design. In contrast, the action researcher is interested in understanding what his explorations show him and what meaning for his teaching he can make from them. In other words personal knowledge (Polanyi, 1962) becomes the main basis for developing his theories about teaching and learning (we'll go back to Polanyi's ideas in Chapter 5). He is looking for a theory *for* practice rather than a theory *of* practice (Burns, 1996).

I should stress here though that, by emphasising that teachers develop their own personal theories through AR, I am not suggesting that theory from the literature is not acceptable or interesting to action researchers or that teachers will not use theories as a basis for their research. The literature may, in fact, be the starting point for AR, to test out in our own classrooms the more general findings from research studies (see Chapter 2). What I'm suggesting is that doing AR usually helps us to articulate and deepen our personal theoretical ideas about teaching.

This section has highlighted some of the major differences and similarities between applied research and AR. Each type could well be carried out by the same person, who may also be a teacher in a school. The main point is that the overall approach adopted in the examples is relevant in each case, but is used for different reasons and different purposes. The discussion you have read here is very brief and only begins to scratch the surface of the fascinating complexities of different approaches to research. If you want to deepen your knowledge and learn more about research in applied linguistics and English language teaching it would be very useful to consult some of the books listed at the end of this volume.

1.5 Is action research the same as reflecting on your teaching?

Action is the driving force in the classroom. Teachers are, on the whole, practical people and tend to focus on what needs to be done in the classroom to help their students learn. But talking about and reflecting on experiences are also an important part of our professional lives, as anyone who has been in a school staffroom during a morning or lunch time break will know (see Richards, 1999). Schön (1983) captures two essential concepts about how teachers reflect on teaching. The first he calls *reflection-in-action* and the second, *reflection-on-action*. Reflection-in-action is 'reflection on one's spontaneous ways of thinking and acting, undertaken in the midst of action to guide further action' (p. 22). This kind of reflection is what we do 'on our feet' in the classroom as we evaluate our own and our students' reactions to the moment-by-moment activities and interactions that are taking place. Reflection-on-action is after the event; it's a kind of 'meta-thinking' about what happened – reflecting on the decisions we made, on our students' and our own responses, and on our thoughts and feelings about the lesson, and working out our reactions to it all.

Telling stories or narratives about our classrooms is the stuff of daily teaching life, but simply talking or thinking about teaching does not mean that we are engaged in reflective teaching, or not, at least, the kind of reflection-on-action that Schön refers to. We can easily begin to think or talk about our teaching in a rather technical or automatic way (especially if we have been teaching for some time) without questioning our teaching routines, our assumptions about our teaching approaches, our learners, our teaching contexts, or the philosophies or values that motivate what we do in the classroom. Using a similar illustration by Zeichner and Liston (1996, pp. 2-3), let's look at a classroom situation that illustrates this point. This example shows two sides – how a teacher can adopt either a technical approach to teaching or a reflective approach.

Classroom voices

Margaret teaches in a 'low-intermediate' adult ESL class in Australia where most of the students are immigrants from different cultural backgrounds. The focus of the class is on literacy and writing skills as many of the students have higher oral than written skills. All of the students are literate in L1 and most have received 9–12 years of education. She notices that the students have varying degrees of confidence and independence as language learners, varied speeds in writing and that some are becoming frustrated when they are given writing tasks and don't seem interested in completing them. They are slow to get started, and don't seem to have any ideas about what to do. Often they take a very long time to produce anything and she feels that class time is being wasted. She is frustrated that these students are so unmotivated.

Margaret as technical teacher

In her TESOL graduate studies, Margaret learned about process writing and she decides to adopt a process writing approach. She believes this will motivate all the students and not just the ones who seem prepared to complete the writing tasks. She decides that she also needs to give the students writing tests mid-week and to publicise the results each Friday as a way of introducing some kind of competition among them. She expects that when the students who seem uninterested notice their low marks they will be 'pushed' into making a greater effort. As the students all received quite a high level of education before arriving in Australia, she senses that this approach will remind them what it is like to study in a classroom and reinforce the idea that they must try hard to achieve results.

Margaret as reflective teacher

Margaret uses a process writing approach in her classroom where she meets individually with a small number of students in a 'writing conference session'. These are sessions where they can go over the writing closely together and decide what needs more work through further drafts of the text. During a session with two of her students she discovers a little more about their lives and begins to think differently about her teaching 'problem'. Student A is young and single, with 12 years of education, but no family in Australia. She had never worked in her country of origin, but is very eager to learn. Student B is older, has 14 years of education, and lives with her husband and seven children. She worked as a teacher in her country. Neither of these students has much confidence in writing, but Margaret notices that A begins to make fast progress compared with B. As the teaching method is the same she asks herself: *What else is influencing their learning?* Margaret decides to find out more about their individual learning strategies and their approaches to writing tasks.

Student A is eager to talk and has clear ideas about how she should learn – 'not afraid anyone'; 'you give idea for me, must I try in my home'; 'interesting is necessary'. Student B is much less aware of how to learn and lists activities she does rather than learning strategies – 'I like to watch TV news'; 'I read from my children'. Their attitudes to the task of learning English are also different. A believes in her ability to make progress – 'I say, oh no, it's too difficult for me to [previous teacher] ... but it's not difficult'. B feels the task is overwhelming – 'I hope my English is very well, but too much problem'.

Margaret's new insights about these two students lead her to think about her teaching more generally. She realises that she is making her teaching of writing too limited by following a particular teaching approach and that she should also extend her students' awareness of learning and writing strategies. She also realises that she needs to let her students talk more in class about how they feel about learning English and how effective the strategies they are using really are. She feels it has taken weeks for her to see what should have been obvious! Margaret continues to use a process approach but she also introduces very explicit discussions about strategies for writing and for learning English more generally.

(Adapted from Quinn, 1997)

'Margaret-as-technical-teacher' believes that by adopting a particular teaching approach and using an assessment measure that will show up her students' results, she will fix up her students' inattentiveness and apparent lack of effort. She is operating from a number of assumptions about the students' lack of motivation. She doesn't look at their backgrounds or the wider context of their lives and ask what these might mean for their learning in her classroom. She also fails to question her own underlying theories about the methods she has chosen and the effects they have on her students. In short, she tries to change her students' behaviour rather than looking at the structure of the activities and the conditions in the classroom. 'Margaret-as-reflective-teacher' is beginning to show qualities that Dewey (1933, 1938) recognised as the difference between teachers who operate routinely and teachers who operate reflectively. First, she shows *openmindedness,* as she begins to listen to other points of view; second, she also exhibits *responsibility*, as she becomes more alert to the consequences of her own actions; third, she demonstrates *wholeheartedness* by putting the first two qualities at the centre of her actions. She questions her assumptions and begins to introduce new approaches that do not place the students at the heart of the 'problem'. She is moving from a 'deficit' view of the students ('my students are the problem') to a deficit view of the learning situation as a whole ('there are problems in my teaching set-up'). She is trying to find ways to restructure classroom activities that will lead to better outcomes for the students and more productive use of class time.

Zeichner and Liston (1996, p. 4) develop the idea of reflective teaching even further. They argue that the reflective teacher concept is a reaction against a view of teachers 'as technicians who narrowly construe the nature of the problems confronting them and merely carry out what others, removed from the classroom, want them to do'. In their view, reflective teaching is 'empowering'. In other words, it provides a way for teachers to become actively involved in articulating the nature of their work and extending the knowledge base of teaching. It also enables teachers to complement the work of educational researchers, involve themselves in curriculum development and school change, and take a leading role in their own professional development.

Burton (2009) points out that there are three central questions underpinning reflective teaching: *What do I do? How do I do it? What does this mean for me and those I work with?* She notes that strategies for teaching reflectively are wide-ranging. They include oral processes of stimulated recall (which is what Isabella Bruschi, in our first classroom voices example, did when she recorded the oral tests, played them back and reflected on what they meant), seminars and discussion groups, journal writing involving written narratives, reflective logs or teacher dialogues, as well as collaborative investigations through AR. Here, we see AR as part of the general 'reflective teacher' movement, but it takes the possibilities for reflection-in-action and reflection-on-action further into the realms of research. It also creates opportunities to link teachers' inquiries with 'public' academic theories. Griffiths and Tann (1992, cited in Zeichner & Liston, 1996) provide a very useful way of seeing these opportunities as a continuum of activities. Table 1.1 is based on the five dimensions outlined by these authors and I have added examples to show how the different options might work in practice.

You can see from Table 1.1 that becoming a reflective action researcher has many dimensions and possibilities. For some teachers it may not be attractive, necessary or possible to go into a 'full-blown' AR process. Indeed, Allwright (e.g., 1993) has argued that expecting teachers to do AR places a burden on them that may be impossible to fulfil. Instead, Allwright proposes the idea of 'exploratory teaching' which, he argues, gives teachers a way of exploring and understanding classroom 'puzzles' or 'dilemmas'. He suggests that exploratory teaching is a more practical way of bringing 'a research perspective' into the classroom without adding 'significantly and unacceptably' to teachers' workloads by requiring them to do research. These are the procedures he suggests for exploratory teaching:

Step 1
Identify a puzzle area

Step 2
Refine your thinking about that puzzle area

Step 3
Select a particular topic to focus upon

Step 4
Find appropriate classroom procedures to explore it

Step 5
Adapt them to the particular puzzle you want to explore

Step 6
Use them in class

Step 7
Interpret the outcomes

Step 8
Decide on their implications and plan accordingly

Table 1.1 Continuum of reflective teaching practices (adapted from Griffiths & Tann, 1992)

1. Rapid reflection Example: *I need to give the students instructions again as they don't seem to know what to do.*	**Reflection-in-action** (individual) In-class; immediate; automatic; intuitive; routine-based
2. Repair Example: *Mimi is asking me for help again, but if I don't react and let her work it out with her neighbour, she might realise she is very capable of doing this task herself.*	**Reflection-in-action** (individual) In-class; with pause for thought; adjusting; innovatory; non-routine
3. Review Example: *That new listening task I introduced doesn't seem to fit in with the current theme I'm teaching. The students were confused and the vocabulary was too difficult. How can I reorganise my unit of work to give them more practice before I introduce it again?*	**Reflection-on-action** (individual/ collaborative) After-class; distanced; thought-provoking; insightful; open; forward-looking
4. Research Example: *My students don't seem motivated in class. Why is this the case and what strategies can I introduce to change this situation? How do other teachers in my school manage this situation?*	**Reflection-on-action** (individual/ collaborative) Short-term; systematic; issue-focused; practically oriented; problematising; data-based; changing, evidence-using
5. Retheorising and research Example: *How do the findings of my action research relate to the broader literature on motivation? Do my findings lead to any new or different insights? How can I incorporate the literature into my teaching? What opportunities are there for me to pursue more research on this topic?*	**Reflection-on-action** (individual/ collaborative) Long-term/lifelong; literature-based; theoretical; academic; abstract; theoretically and/or practically oriented

For Step 4, Allwright suggests several interesting classroom procedures which allow for exploring puzzles, as well as being the basis for good classroom activities.

1. Group work discussions
2. Pair work discussions
3. Surveys
4. Interviews

5. Simulations
6. Role-plays
7. Role-exchanging
8. Diaries
9. Dialogue journal writing
10. Projects
11. Poster sessions
12. Learner-to-learner correspondence.

Exploratory teaching shares many characteristics with AR and it also fits perfectly within the continuum of reflective teacher approaches suggested by Griffiths and Tann. However, it keeps closely to the idea of exploring 'teaching', or more recently 'practice' (see Allwright, 2005 for an account of how the concept has developed), as the main focus. In this respect, it would be unfortunate if it discouraged teachers from contemplating that they, too, can enter the research community if they choose to do so. AR offers an inclusive and participatory perspective on the range of possibilities for research in the language teaching field and who should be involved.

Reflection point

What kind of reflective teacher are you? Where on the continuum of reflection are you now? Where would you like to be?

Discuss your ideas with someone you'd like to share your thoughts with and who can give you some professional feedback.

1.6 Summary point

We have covered several ideas in this chapter that should provide you with starting points for understanding AR. We looked first at what is meant by the term 'action research', a term that seems to contain a rather odd combination of two different kinds of behaviour – action and research. We saw that these behaviours come together in AR through cycles of planning, action, observation and reflection that problematise (in a positive sense) issues, dilemmas or gaps that concern us in our teaching situations. In the next part of the chapter the important question was raised of why teachers should, in fact, do research. Although, time is a major practical hurdle, we saw that there are distinct benefits that make AR attractive to many teachers and make a difference to the way they regard themselves as teaching professionals. We then discussed the main steps and processes in AR and considered how and why it overlaps with and differs from other forms of applied research in the classroom. Because AR contains such a strong notion of practical action, the next part of the discussion raised the question of its relationships to the idea of reflective teaching. We noted that AR could be considered part of a continuum of becoming a thinking and theorising professional.

By now you should have a clearer idea of your responses to the pre-reading questions at the beginning of this chapter. At this point, go back and think about them again. Now, use the list below to decide whether you understand more about the main concepts or whether you need to do further reading. Ideas for further reading are set out at the end of this book.

- The main characteristics of AR
- The steps in the AR process
- The pros and cons of being an action researcher
- The kinds of topics that are investigated in AR
- The main differences between AR and applied research
- The relationships of AR to reflective teaching.

References

Allwright, D. (1993). Integrating 'research' and 'pedagogy': Appropriate criteria and practical possibilities. In J. Edge, & K. Richards (Eds.), *Teachers develop, teachers research: Papers on classroom research and teacher development* (pp. 125-135). London: Heinemann.

Allwright, D. (2005). Developing principles for practitioner research: The case of exploratory practice. *Modern Language Journal*, 89(3), 353-366.

Burns, A. (1996). Starting all over again: From teaching adults to teaching beginners. In D. Freeman, & J. Richards (Eds.), *Teacher learning in language teaching* (pp. 154-177). Cambridge: Cambridge University Press.

Burns, A. (1999). *Collaborative action research for English language teachers*. Cambridge: Cambridge University Press.

Burton, J. (2009). Reflective practice. In A. Burns, & J. C. Richards (Eds.), *The Cambridge guide to second language teacher education* (pp. 298-307). New York: Cambridge University Press.

Carr, W., & Kemmis, S. (1986). *Becoming critical: Knowing through action research*. London: The Falmer Press.

Cohen, L., & Manion, L. (1994). *Research methods in education*. 4th edition. London: Croom Helm.

Cornwell, S. (1999). Interview with Anne Burns and Graham Crookes. *The Language Teacher*, 23(12), 5-10.

Denny, H. (2005). *Reflective practice and action research as a source of pre-service and in-service professional development and classroom innovation: Burden or benefit? Myth or reality?* Auckland: The Centre for International Education, AIS (Auckland Institute of Studies), St Helens. Available at www.crie.org.nz (Research Paper Series).

Dewey, J. (1933). *How we think*. Buffalo, NY: Prometheus Books.

Dewey, J. (1938). *Experience and education*. New York: Collier Books.

Ebbutt, D. (1985). *Educational action research: Some general concerns and specific quibbles*. Cambridge: Cambridge Institute of Education.

Edge, J. (2001). Attitude and access: Building a new teaching/learning community in TESOL. In J. Edge (Ed.), *Action research* (pp. 1-11). Alexandria, VA: TESOL.

Edge, J. (Ed.). (2001). *Action research*. Alexandria, VA: TESOL.

Edge, J., & Richards, K. (Eds.). (1993). *Teachers develop, teachers research: Papers on classroom research and teacher development*. London: Heinemann.

Elliott, J. (1991). *Action research for educational change*. Milton Keynes: Open University Press.

Griffiths, M., & Tann, S. (1992). Using reflective practice to link personal and public theories. *Journal of Education for Teaching*, 18(1), 69-84.

Kemmis, S., & McTaggart, R. (Eds.). (1988). *The action research planner.* 3rd edition. Geelong: Deakin University Press.

Mathew, R. (2000). Teacher-research approach to curriculum renewal and teacher development. In R. Mathew, R. L. Eapen, & J. Tharu (Eds.), *The language curriculum: Dynamics of change. Volume I: The outsider perspective* (pp. 6-21). Hyderabad: Orient Longman.

McKay, S. L. (2006). *Researching second language classrooms*. Mahwah, NJ: Lawrence Erlbaum Associates.

McNiff, J. (1988). *Action research: Principles and practice*. London: Routledge.

Nunan, D. (1992). *Research methods in language teaching*. New York: Cambridge University Press.

Polanyi, M. (1962). *Personal knowledge*. Chicago: University of Chicago Press.

Quinn, M. (1997). 'Ah … writing … it's OK now': Perceptions of literacy learning. In A. Burns, & S. Hood (Eds.), *Teachers' voices 2: Teaching disparate learner groups* (pp. 43-49). Sydney: National Centre for English Language Teaching and Research.

Richards, K. (1999). Working towards common understandings: Collaborative interaction in staffroom stories. *Text*, 19(1), 143-174.

Rochsantiningsih, D. (2005). Enhancing professional development of Indonesian high school teachers through action research. Unpublished PhD thesis, Macquarie University, Sydney.

Schön, D. A. (1983). *The reflective practitioner: How professionals think in action.* New York: Basic Books.

Somekh, B. (1993). Quality in educational research – the contribution of classroom teachers. In J. Edge, & K. Richards (Eds.), *Teachers develop, teachers research: Papers on classroom research and teacher development* (pp. 26-38). London: Heinemann.

Tinker Sachs, G. (Ed.). (2002). *Action research: Fostering and furthering effective practices in the teaching of English.* Hong Kong: City University of Hong Kong.

van Lier, L. (1996). *Interaction in the language curriculum.* London: Longman.

Wallace, M. (1998). *Action research for language teachers.* Cambridge: Cambridge University Press.

Zeichner, K. M., & Liston, D. P. (1996). *Reflective teaching: An introduction.* Mahwah, NJ: Lawrence Erlbaum Associates.

CHAPTER 2

Plan – Planning the Action

Pre-reading questions

Consider the following questions:

- Is there something in your teaching situation that you would like to change?
- What 'burning questions' do you have about your students' learning?
- Have you ever tried out a new teaching idea in your classroom and wondered whether it really helped your students to learn?
- Are there aspects of the way you teach that you would like to improve?

Make some brief notes to record your ideas. If you can discuss them with another teacher or a mentor so much the better.

At the end of the chapter you can go back to your responses to see how your ideas are developing.

In this chapter we will explore the first steps in starting up an AR project. You may already have some questions, ideas, puzzles, conundrums, or 'what ifs … ?' about teaching and learning that you have been wondering about for some time. Alternatively, you may not be too clear at this stage what it is you want to focus on, even though you feel keen on the idea of looking into the practices and behaviours in your classroom in more detail. The starting point for AR is identifying a problem you want to focus on. 'Problem' is the research term for the issue under investigation (but as I said in Chapter 1 it doesn't mean your teaching is 'the problem'). Exploring your AR problem doesn't necessarily mean that you will find the ultimate solution; but it does mean that you've recognised areas you want to examine in more depth and you want to find possible answers for them.

The chapter will first cover ways of finding and narrowing your focus and developing your questions. We will also consider what key ethical issues are involved in doing action research – issues that are important in the sound conduct of any research project. Another aspect of planning for AR is considering the resources and materials you will need, such as access to literature you might want to read or participants you might want to include.

2.1 Finding your focus

Many of the teachers I've worked with say that finding a starting point for their research is not easy – in fact, it can be very frustrating trying to narrow things down so that the focus is clear and the research is manageable. Sometimes, finding a focus is difficult because the characteristics and processes of AR are themselves not yet clear to you. Alternatively, there could be a number of areas that suggest themselves but it is tricky to identify exactly which focus you want to select. Clarifying your focus may require some time and a lot of careful thought, as well as opportunities to synthesise your ideas by talking or writing about them. The nature of AR is such that some teachers find the focus becomes clearer only when they begin the research. It is not uncommon to find that the real nub of your focus area only emerges as you proceed and your initial hunches give way to deeper understanding.

Classroom voices

Jane, a teacher from Melbourne, Australia, found that her real understanding of her focus happened gradually:

> My experience of action research is that it is difficult to grasp or explain the concept until one is in the process of doing it. It is in the doing that it starts to make sense and become clear.
>
> (Jane Hamilton, cited in Burns, 1999, p. 20)

Yasmin and her colleagues, from Surakarta in Indonesia, made these comments:

> Firstly, it was difficult to grasp the idea of AR, but it became easier when I started identifying and focusing research problems.
>
> I found it easier when I did it.
>
> AR made sense after I put it into my teaching context.
>
> (Cited in Rochsantiningsih, 2005, p. 144)

But, one has to begin somewhere and identifying your general area is the usual starting point. These kinds of questions can help guide your thinking in these early stages:

- What do you feel passionate about?
- What do you feel curious about?
- What new approaches to learning or teaching are you interested in trying?
- What will make you a more effective teacher?
- What gaps are there between your current teaching situation and what you would like to see happening?
- What needs of your students are not being met?
- Why are some of your students not achieving in the same way as others?
- Why are your students behaving the way they do?
- What do you want your students to know, understand, or do better than they currently do?
- What language skills would you like your students to improve?

Some teachers find that keeping a 'freewriting' journal helps ideas to come to the surface. Alternatively, fixing a time to have an open-ended and relaxed conversation with an interested colleague about your teaching ideas or philosophies can help to clarify a focus that is not immediately obvious. Here are some other suggestions that I discussed with a group of Thai teachers at a workshop in Bangkok (see Burns, 2002, p. 6):

- Keep a diary or brief notes of teaching, learning or administrative activities in your workplace over a chosen period of time (e.g., a week, month). Read over the diary at the end of this time and identify some of your key thoughts, ideas or concerns.

- Brainstorm some starter statements:

  I don't know enough about how my students …
  My students don't like … Why is this?
  I'd like to find out more about what my students do when they …

- Make a list of questions about things in your workplace that have puzzled you for some time. Ask other teachers for their 'favourite puzzles'. (Do they compare?)

- Observe (preferably over a period of time) a typical situation in your place of work. What stands out for you from your observations? What research questions or issues do they suggest?

- Find a favourite article (for example, from the *ThaiTESOL Newsletter*). Think about how the issues it presents can be related to your classroom. What questions or issues does the writer address? What questions or issues does the writer leave out that you would like to know more about?

The possibilities for AR are endless and could include any of the following broad areas, which teachers have suggested to me in workshops:

- Increasing learner autonomy;
- Integrating language skills;
- Focusing on language form;
- Understanding student motivation;
- Developing writing skills;
- Promoting group work;
- Making classrooms more communicative;
- Trying out new materials;
- Finding new ways to do assessment;
- Integrating technology into class activities;
- Helping students to develop self-study techniques.

Fischer (2001) says that typically there are four broad areas of teachers' interests that provide a focus for AR. These are: a) your teaching and making changes in teaching; b) your learners and how they learn; c) your interaction with the current curriculum and with curriculum innovation; d) your teaching beliefs and philosophies and their connections with daily practice.

Reflection point

How would you categorise the following questions in relation to Fischer's four areas?

1. *I'm interested in the concept of teacher expertise. What should be the balance between learner-centredness and teacher-centredness in my classroom?*
2. *What can I do to make the syllabus required by my school more appealing to my learners?*
3. *How do my learners respond to my teaching of pronunciation?*
4. *What kinds of activities are most effective in motivating my students in writing class?*

Develop your own question(s) for each of the areas. They could become the basis for your research.

2.1.1 Where do your teaching philosophies and beliefs fit in?

The fourth area identified by Fischer highlights the teaching beliefs and philosophies that underpin teaching. As Fischer notes, this area can be a basis for focusing your research topic and questions. In the list above it is reflected in question 1. But it is also an important area to think about if we want to be sure that our personal beliefs or assumptions about our teaching situation don't blind us to what our research is really telling us.

The assumptions that underpin the way we conduct an AR process are connected to the issue of *research validity*. Validity in research raises important questions, such as: *How can you ensure the methods used for collecting data are trustworthy? How can you be sure that your conclusions are solidly based on the data you have collected?* We will explore validity in more detail in other chapters (especially Chapters 3 and 4) as we go through the various steps in AR. In the meantime it is worth commenting on it here in relation to teaching philosophies and beliefs and how they might influence our research.

There is a growing body of research on teacher beliefs and philosophies in language teaching (that is sometimes called *teacher cognition*). It shows that they play a substantial and complex role in influencing our behaviours, actions and interactions in the classroom (see, for example, Borg, 2006; Borg & Burns, 2008; Burns, 1996). Our beliefs and philosophies are not always obvious to us; they are not usually at the forefront of our consciousness as we teach – especially when we are relatively new to teaching and our main focus is on 'surviving' in the classroom. Nevertheless, they form networks of assumptions that lie underneath our practice. During the research process, they create the lenses through which we will perceive, analyse and interpret what is going on in our classrooms. So, before beginning your research it is useful to consider how your personal beliefs might influence the attitudes you have about instruction, activities, classroom management, teacher-student interaction, assessment and so on. For example:

> What do you believe about your role in the classroom? (facilitator, guide, director, expert, friend, disciplinarian, mentor, authority?)
>
> How do you want your students to behave towards you? (equal role, subordinate role, 'knowledgeable learner' role, 'empty vessel' role?)
>
> What do you believe is the purpose of your students' language learning? (have fun, pass exams, increase knowledge about grammar, gain cultural

sensitivity, increase employment prospects, fulfil syllabus requirements, develop intercultural awareness, appreciate global diversity, develop critical thinking, become citizens of the world?)

What attributes or attitudes do you believe your students have about learning languages? (few or none, enthusiasm, no motivation, teacher-dependent, limited attention span, openmindedness, lack of relevance, commitment, rigour, helplessness, lack of interest?)

What kind of instructional techniques do you believe work best in your classrooms? (games, rote-learning, dialogues, role-plays, puzzles, quizzes, substitution drills, dictations, grammar tests, interactive tasks, translation?)

What kind of materials or resources do you consider to be the most effective? (course books, 'realia'/authentic texts, newspapers, websites, teacher-prepared handouts, CD/DVD/TV recordings, board games?)

Reflection point

Take 10-15 minutes to think about your philosophies and beliefs about teaching. If you wish you can take some of the questions listed above and examine your personal views on them.

If there are other questions important to you, add them to the list and think about your responses.

If you have time, make brief notes or write about them in a journal. Even better, discuss your ideas with a colleague. You could post them on a blog or interactive discussion list too to see what responses you get.

Examining our personal beliefs and being aware of their inevitable presence in the research process is valuable. It is to do with being aware and openminded. It helps alert us to any built-in assumptions we might have about what actions to take and what our data will reveal. This is especially important in AR as you have to play the dual role of researcher and teacher. As your research proceeds you may find that the strong beliefs you bring to your classroom practice are not borne out by the evidence emerging from your data. In this situation you may need to overturn or rethink the things you take for granted to find more effective ways of dealing with the issue you are investigating. Being aware of your assumptions, keeping an open mind, and acknowledging what your data are telling you are ways to increase the validity of your research.

To illustrate this point, an example from my experience of working with teachers of adult learners in Australia shows how initial assumptions about a research area can become misleading.

Classroom voices

A group of eight Australian teachers of adult ESL students were attending the first of five AR workshops spread out over six months. They had volunteered to be part of a collaborative project where we were investigating the teaching of 'disparate' (mixed-level) classes. They had all joined the project because they were concerned that the very different language backgrounds, pace of learning, and learning skills of their students would impede their progress. In fact, one teacher said she had joined because she was a 'desperate' disparate class teacher!

They all saw their disparate classes as problematic. They reasoned that: i) weaker students would hold back more able students; ii) finding different materials to meet all the students' needs was difficult and time consuming; iii) students had very different interests and skill levels; iv) some students would resent having to work at a different pace from others; v) it was impossible to give adequate attention to all the students; and vi) conflicts would arise because of the great diversity of cultural backgrounds and learning expectations.

During the first workshop, each teacher identified a focus area for research. Some wanted to investigate materials development to cater for mixed levels, others decided to examine various student groupings. Two of them wanted to see how they could promote student self-study and independent learning. During the next two workshops each teacher described the actions they were putting in place in the classroom and their methods for collecting data on what happened. The discussions ranged constantly across the problems and challenges they were experiencing in teaching their disparate classes. They supported each other by providing reflections, suggestions, and feedback on each project.

During the third workshop, Linda suddenly exclaimed, 'You know, we've all been talking about the problems of disparate groups, but has anyone asked their students what they think?' They all looked around the group, and then agreed that they hadn't. Sue said, 'No, but it's a really good idea. I'm going to have a class discussion on what they think about being in a disparate group.'

At the fourth meeting, to everyone's surprise, almost all the teachers reported that their students thought being in a disparate group was really positive. Sue said, 'All the students liked being in [a class] of various levels. They saw no problem in this at all.' Others said that their students were more concerned about being able to work with friends and people they liked. As Sue said, 'They've come to have a very positive attitude to the class and to the other members of the group. When one of the students said his time at high school had been bad, others said the same. When one said she had trouble with [numbers], another offered to help her.' 'Hmm,' said one of the teachers, 'we're the ones with the problem, not the students.'

The teachers agreed that their assumptions about disparate groups were leading them in the wrong direction. They were looking at their student groups in 'deficit' terms rather than seeing the positives identified by their students. This realisation completely changed the teachers' viewpoint and led to some very novel approaches to teaching disparate groups.

(See Burns & Hood, 1997 for accounts of what these teachers did in their research)

2.1.2 Identifying broad areas

By now you should be getting some ideas about the broad area(s) you are interested in researching. They could be ones that have been your 'burning questions' for a while. Or they might at this point be just 'hunches' you have about ways to do things better in your classroom or school. Maybe you are experiencing a pressing classroom problem that you want to do something about immediately. Alternatively, your ideas may be only hazy thoughts, or musings based on something you read or heard about at a teachers' workshop. You may have been trying new strategies for a while and want to get some evidence about how they are working. Teachers doing AR have experienced all these ways of getting going.

Action point

Select one of the following strategies to begin identifying your possible research areas.

1. Get together with one or more teacher colleagues at your school or form a group with others in your teacher development course. Brainstorm areas for AR that your group would be interested in. Alternatively, ask each person to identify a 'puzzle' or dilemma they have about their teaching.
2. Use Table 2.1 to begin mapping out broad ideas. Before you complete it you might want to look back at your pre-reading responses. Or you could discuss the questions in the table with colleagues who are also interested in AR.

Table 2.1 Finding a focus area

What is my broad topic area?	
Why am I interested in this topic?	
What do I want to know about this topic?	
How will it improve my students' learning or my teaching?	
What am I likely to learn about by focusing on this topic?	

3. Ask a teaching mentor or your course tutor to recommend one or two journal or newsletter articles that could provide practical ideas. Make notes as you read about possible research areas.
4. Use the Internet – enter descriptors like 'action research', 'language teaching' and 'finding a focus' into a search engine such as Google. Make a note of anything interesting that strikes you.
5. Attend a teacher workshop or conference where teachers will be discussing AR. Take the opportunity to discuss your own ideas with the workshop presenters and other teachers who are attending.

Do not be put off if you are not too clear at this point how to proceed. Often good AR experiences come about through feeling your way into the research, as Alison's experience highlights.

Classroom voices

Alison Perkins, a teacher at Portland Adult Education in the USA, tells how she gradually evolved an AR process that helped her to survive as a new language teacher.

> I am a novice teacher. There are moments of uncertainty, hesitation, and rejoicing every single class. I have waited patiently for the feelings of trepidation to be replaced by confidence. It has not happened … Most times I have felt like a technician …
>
> I have found teaching in the TESOL world to be incredibly complex. Faced with the multitude of decisions that all teachers are faced with, I began to realise that most are not dichotomous. Each classroom dilemma is a multifarious, bewildering mix

> of value clashes and theoretical options. As a new teacher, I am often stymied by the goings-on in my 10-ft by 10-ft square ...
>
> What I have needed is a model through which I can fight my private battles and uncover my personal values, theoretical assumptions, and gaps of knowledge. Action research is providing such a model ...
>
> My primary motives in undertaking this action research model were twofold: to improve the situation in my classroom and to foster my own professional development as a teacher. The guided process of inquiry and reflection provided me with unexpected insights and paths that I would have otherwise left unexplored ... The action research model ... gave me the courage to cross the border from technician to professional.

Alison describes how first of all she used a diary to gain initial ideas, identify important classroom themes and to 'reach deep inside and attempt to bring to the surface underlying assumptions and values so that they could be better examined' (p. 16). She went on to develop a series of action strategies and to evaluate their implementation in her classroom. She reflects that what she did is just 'the story so far' (p. 19) in her quest to make better sense of her teaching environment.

(Excerpts from Perkins, 2001, pp. 13-14)

2.2 Developing and refining your questions

It is not at all unusual to find that the problems or issues you first come up with are too broad. Having to narrow the initial focus area is a common experience in most research. It involves developing more specific questions that should help lead you logically to the most appropriate ways to collect your data and analyse your findings. The more focused and 'answerable' the questions, the more they are likely to bring you good results. 'What, why and how' questions are probably the most important in forming the kind of qualitative questions used in AR (cf. Mason, 2002) as they allow us to ask about puzzles and seek explanations.

In these early stages you might find you have quite a number of research questions. There is nothing wrong with having several questions, but your research will be more manageable if you can keep it focused. It is better to have one or two questions and investigate them thoroughly than to have several that you can't go into in enough depth. It's also likely that the form of your questions keeps changing in your mind. I should stress that, even though you want to have some fairly clear questions in mind to start off, it is quite 'normal' for questions to change as you proceed. One of the key aspects of AR is that it centres squarely on change over time. In fact, it is not unusual to find that the questions you first start with are not getting to the real issues at the heart of the research. As Lenn, a teacher from the Philippines, once said to me 'my research raises more questions than it answers'. This sentiment also underlies Alison Perkin's comment earlier that her AR was 'the story so far'.

I usually suggest shaping the questions along the following lines (see Burns, 1999, p. 55). First, avoid questions you can do little about. For example, choosing a question that has to do with changing the whole of the required syllabus in your school or district will not take you far – although you might be able to change the way you teach some of the compulsory activities (Lems, 2007 is a good example of how a teacher working within a very rigid grammar-based curriculum was able to introduce language arts activities). Second, tailor your questions to fit within the time limit you have available. Trying to track students' progress across a year, for example, might take you beyond the bounds of the time and resources you have available. Also, focus on one issue to see where it takes you rather than trying to look at multiple aspects. Attempting to investigate how to teach grammar more effectively, how to promote your students' autonomy in learning grammar, how to select or develop grammar exercises, and how to integrate grammar into a range of speaking and listening activities all at the same time is likely to lead to 'AR burn-out' and give you mixed and unclear outcomes. Finally, choose areas of direct relevance and interest to you, your immediate teaching context, or your school. For example, one of my students, Andrew Gladman, is currently investigating teachers' perceptions about team teaching in the college in Japan where he teaches. The college has a long history of subject and language teachers working together. Little research has been done on this topic and his research aims to discover more about effective ways for team teachers to work together in his immediate context.

There are several other techniques that can be used to help shape your thinking and focus your questions.

Classroom voices

Steve Mann is a teacher educator who has worked extensively with teachers from all over the world doing AR as part of a postgraduate programme. For many years he taught at Aston University in the UK, where he developed two very useful techniques for focusing and refining his students' research questions.

> I advise (Mann, 1997) the complementary use of focusing circles (Edge, 1992) and mind mapping (Buzan & Buzan, 1996) as techniques for this kind of decision

making. Subsequent feedback from teachers confirms the usefulness of this combination. My experience of working with teachers on the Aston Master's in TESOL is that teachers have little problem in finding a general issue but that this issue or problem is often too big and, therefore, daunting and demotivating. Achieving a focus, small enough to manage, which does not balloon up and become overwhelming, is where focusing circles and mind mapping might be useful.

- Focusing circles: This is a technique from Edge (1992, pp. 37–38) through which you can narrow your focus by drawing a small circle at the centre (inside) of a larger one. The issue, topic or problem is written in the small circle and the larger [circle] is divided into four segments. In each of these segments an aspect of the topic is written. One of these four segments then becomes the center of the next circle and so on.
- Mind maps: Most teachers have, at some time, used mind maps or spider webs. Probably the most comprehensive guide to the use of mind mapping is provided by Buzan & Buzan (1996). Here the issue is written at the centre of a piece of paper and related factors branch out from the center.

Teachers at Aston reported that there is a different kind of thinking involved in the two techniques. The thinking in focusing circles is selective, you are involved in decid- ing, and you need to make choices and justify them. In mind maps, the main thinking goes into making connections, one thing leads to another. Most of these teachers felt that of the two, focusing circles was more productive in finding a focus for AR. There was a feeling that once a decision had been made, that is, a focus found, then mind mapping could be used to trace back the connections and see the small focus within the bigger picture. Significantly, a number of these teachers report that using both during the AR process had helped them.

(Mann, 1999, p. 12 and personal communication, 7 August 2007)

Without doubt, there is something of a dilemma for action researchers at this particular stage in the process. On the one hand, action research requires flexibility so that you can refine your questions as you go along. On the other hand, you need a question that is sufficiently clear to be doable. This means that 'research questions need to be general enough to permit exploration but focused enough to delimit the study – not an easy task' (Marshall & Rossman, 2006, p. 39). As you develop your questions it is useful to check them out from time to time to make sure that they are taking you along the right track – they need to be relevant and useful and also able to provide you with good outcomes. The question checklist in Table 2.2 may help to provide you with some guidance.

Table 2.2 Question checklist (adapted from Schwalbach, 2003, pp. 18-21)

Question type	Sample questions	Comment
1. Does the question have the right scope?	*What improves motivation in my class?*	The first question is too broad and there will be too many learning and teaching factors to point to any particular reasons for improvement.
	What kind of speaking activities will motivate my students?	The second question allows for a focus on a particular skill area.
2. Is the question closed or open-ended?	*Can group work be extended in my classroom?*	The first question invites a 'yes/no' response.
	How can group work be extended in my classroom?	The second question allows for a range of possibilities to be identified.
3. Is the question biased?	*How will using electronic dictionaries lead to higher test scores in my students' writing?*	The first question already assumes that the dictionaries will make an improvement.
	How will using electronic dictionaries influence my students' writing?	The second does not assume there will be an improvement. Finding that something doesn't work may be as important as finding that it does.
4. Does the question allow for a logical connection between the action and the outcome?	*How will observation of my students carrying out listening tasks increase my understanding of how best to develop their listening skills?*	Observation alone is unlikely to result in comprehensive findings about how students develop their listening skills.
5. Does the question lend itself to data collection?	*What is task-based language learning (TBLL)?*	The first question is a very general one that should be answered by reading the literature on TBLL.
	What kinds of reading tasks work the most effectively in my classroom?	The second allows you to try out different kinds of tasks for teaching a specific skill and collect data on what happens.
6. Does the question relate to current research?	*How can I develop students' reading skills by using a phonics-only approach?*	Although teaching phonics is a part of developing reading skills, current research indicates that reading development requires attention to a variety of other complementary skills and strategies.

(to be continued)

(continued)

Question type	Sample questions	Comment
7. Is the question ethical?	*How can I stop beginner low-achieving Chinese students from using their first language (L1) in my class?*	This question assumes first that beginner Chinese students are not able to achieve well, and second that using L1 is a negative aspect of early language learning – an assumption that is not supported by current research.
8. Is the question stated clearly and concisely?	*What kinds of listening tasks based on contemporary theories of communicative language teaching used in a seventh grade classroom at Au Bord de la Mer Secondary High School in the Region of Normandy, France, can best be applied to increase the listening skills of EFL students in that class?*	The first question is full of redundant information and is very wordy. Some of the information relates to the context and to current widely used teaching approaches and should be placed in a report of the research.
	What kinds of listening tasks will assist my EFL seventh grade students to develop their listening skills?	The second question indicates specifically what kinds of tasks will be investigated and what the aim of the research is.

2.3 Getting permission and covering ethical issues

One of the question types in Table 2.2 was *Is the question ethical?* (Q7). We look more closely at this issue in this section. As I have already suggested, the goals of AR are to work towards educational improvement and more effective outcomes for our students by reflecting on and observing current classroom practices. These goals are underpinned by core AR ideologies which can be summed up briefly as:

- promoting the effective learning and best interests of students;
- working towards more inclusive, democratic, and just educational goals;
- enhancing teacher professionalism;
- empowering teachers professionally, educationally, and politically by giving them a stronger voice in matters of teaching and learning.

The goals that stand out in AR are connected more broadly to conducting research ethically and it is important to be aware of the fundamental ethical standards. Ethical research practice has its roots in a principle widely taught to doctors before they enter the field of medicine, which is sometimes summed up in the expression: *First, do no harm*. Essentially, research ethics are to do with conducting research in a moral and responsible way.

Classroom voices

Rob Dickey tells me he has been teaching English (and assorted other courses) to university learners of English in Korea since 1994. Here is his summary of what ethics is about, based on his professional involvement with ethical issues in language teaching and language teaching research.

> Ethics in action research is actually pretty simple to understand. First, you treat others as you wish to be treated. Basically, we don't risk the safety, privacy, or dignity of our learners or collaborating researchers. Second, we are role-models for our learners in everything we do ... so how we set about research is a message to them about how they should do research.
>
> We can't complain about plagiarism – which is a kind of intellectual theft, you could say – if we 'steal' from learners by not getting their informed consent for participation. When our learners understand what we are trying to do, how we would like them to be involved, what we expect to do with the information we gather from them, and they agree to participate, then we are satisfying these two concerns. Of course, then we have to live up to our end of the bargain!
>
> (Personal communication, 10 August 2007)

The requirements for ethical standards involving human participants vary in different research studies. They depend on the scope of the project and the methods to be used, the number of researchers, the participants involved, the location of the research, and how the results will be distributed. Typically, AR is small-scale and carried out by an individual, or a group of colleagues working collaboratively together. For AR projects, you should keep at least three important issues in mind:

1. Whose permission do you need for your research?
2. Who will be affected by your research?
3. Who should be told about your research when it is completed?

2.3.1 Whose permission do you need for your research?

Two kinds of permission must be considered. First, depending on the requirements in your organisation you may need to obtain permission from the school board, district, or the individual school to undertake the research. Gaining permission ranges from informing the principal or head of department about the research and obtaining approval to go ahead, to supplying full details of the rationale, focus, questions, methods, recruitment procedures, participants, and benefits of the research. Each organisation will have its own perspectives on what needs to be done so you need to find out before you begin what the requirements are. In some countries, organisations, particularly universities or education departments, have stringent rules about applying for permission that involve completing comprehensive forms outlining the procedures in detail. At my university, for example, action researchers cannot begin their research until all the aspects of the project have been described in detail and approved by a Human Ethics Committee. The website for my university listed at the end of this book will give you an example of the kind of procedures you might have to follow. If you are doing AR for a tertiary qualification, you should ask your tutor for advice.

Action point

Find out the requirements for conducting research in your organisation. If you are enrolled in a pre- or in-service course, discuss them with your lecturer or professor.

The other type of permission is to do with: i) informing people that you are conducting research; and ii) gaining their consent to participate. This is usually referred to as *informed consent*. Informed consent goes further than just letting your participants know you are doing research. It means giving them sufficient information about the research so that they can decide whether to be involved. Participants have a right to know about the purpose, the procedures, possible effects of the research on them, and how the research will be used, and should not be deceived or tricked about the aims of the research. You should be confident that your participants fully understand what you are doing and how it affects them. Informed consent also means assuring your participants about their rights, specifically:

- their identities will not be revealed (you will use pseudonyms or labels, S1, S2 or A, B, C, etc., to refer to individuals when you report the research);

- their participation is voluntary (they can decide whether to be involved or not; they should also know that if they don't participate there will be no repercussions);
- they can withdraw from the research (they can decide at any time that they no longer wish to be involved; again there should be no fear of repercussions).

Classroom voices

Lucy Valeri was one of the teachers who participated in the Australian disparate learner project mentioned earlier. She used a great deal of group work but had never thoroughly investigated what her students thought about the way she grouped them. As her class was very diverse, she wanted to ensure that working in groups really did facilitate her students' learning. She describes how she took account of ethical issues before she began her research:

> Both my co-teacher and the learners themselves were collaborators in my research. All were informed about the project and happy to participate. One student suggested, 'We must be special to be chosen!' I took some time to explain what action research was and I said it was not unlike what they did in the classroom when they undertook a task and then evaluated it and tried to improve on it next time by changing the way they did it. I also discussed the kind of data I would be collecting.
>
> (Valeri, 1997, p. 38)

In cases where you are working with children or young adults, rather than adults, you may need to seek written permission from their parents or others responsible for their welfare. In primary school situations in particular, participants may be too young to understand the implications of giving permission. It is important to find out from your school or department what the procedures are for making sure parents are informed and have given permission. Preferably, you should ask participants, or their parents, to sign a consent form (a copy of which they keep) that sets out the terms of their agreement to be involved. A written agreement has advantages over verbal agreement, as McKay (2006, p. 26) points out:

> First and most importantly, it is one way of demonstrating respect for the individuals involved in a research project. Second, most institutions involved in research projects require it. And finally, it is necessary for publication of the findings in a refereed journal.

Written consent also helps to ensure that your participants are clear about the procedures you will undertake and can easily refer back to them. It also means you can be more confident that they are willing to be involved in your research. You can find a sample consent form based on Lucy's AR in Appendix 2.1. You can see from this form that, at a minimum, written consent requires statements about:

- the purpose and goals of the research;
- the benefits that are anticipated for the participants;
- the procedures to be followed;
- the participant's roles in the research;
- the assurance of confidentiality and withdrawal without penalty;
- a section for the participant to provide written agreement.

2.3.2 Who will be affected by your research?

This is the second key ethical area you need to consider. Research should not involve any risk, harm or disadvantage to the students by being involved in the actions you take. Neither should it invade their privacy by touching on personal, sensitive areas. If you work with ethnically diverse groups it's important to realise that students may not be familiar with the concept of research or its procedures, or understand why they are being observed or asked for information. For example, some of the refugee students who were involved in AR with Australian teachers I've worked with did not understand why they were being asked to sign consent forms, or were suspicious about signing. Often these students have escaped oppressive regimes or war-torn countries where being questioned, watched or asked to sign something carried high risks. In AR involving such students it is particularly important to ensure that participating will not cause them psychological distress. Explaining carefully why you are asking people to participate, what methods you are using and how the research will be used for positive purposes is essential. For example, being video-recorded means that students can immediately be identified on-screen (although there are now techniques available to blur faces on digital videos; Sue Garton, personal communication, 28 November 2008). You should always ask permission if you think you might eventually be showing the recordings in presentations to colleagues.

In this second area, you should also be aware of the power differences that exist simply because you are the teacher of the class. Inevitably, you are in a position of authority. Be sensitive to the fact that students might not want to refuse to participate if they feel that it will displease you or that there are consequences for them. One way to offset this possibility is to outline the benefits you expect from your research, both for your teaching and for their learning. Another way is to reassure them that participation is completely voluntary and that they can change their minds at any time. It is also important to tell your participants who will have access to the data you collect and how you will make sure their confidentiality is respected if the data are shared with others. Usually, it is best to store the data in a secure location where you know the information will be available only to you and to others directly involved in the research.

2.3.3 Who should be told about your research when it is completed?

Here, there is a need to explain who will be informed about the research and how it will be publicised. Participants have a right to know whether they will be given information about the outcomes and in what form, as well as who else is likely to be told about the research. It is good practice to provide some kind of feedback to the participants. One way of ensuring the validity, or trustworthiness of your analysis, which we will discuss in much more detail in Chapter 4, is to provide a summary of it to your participants. Their feedback on whether you have interpreted the situation accurately from their perspective helps to strengthen the findings. Also, it is a courtesy to provide information at the end of the research about what came out of it, in a form that your participants will understand. This could mean holding a discussion with students about what you found out, giving participants a shortened version of a longer written report or article, or providing a class poster which displays your data visually. Some teachers I know have sometimes involved their participants in presenting the research at teacher workshops or conferences so that they can give their perspectives.

Your participants will also want to know whether they will be able to be identified as individuals when your research is presented to others. Clearly, it can be embarrassing to be easily singled out and possibly compared (unfavourably) with others. If you are presenting to colleagues in the same school or district this is quite likely. So you should weigh up whether the local nature of your research could lead to easy identification of your participants, even when you didn't anticipate it. As we've already seen, in the case of recordings you intend showing you should get permission first.

In all aspects of doing AR, ethical issues present teacher researchers with decisions, challenges and choices. Following the procedures I've outlined is not always clear-cut or easy, but knowing about the basic principles means that you are in a position to adopt an ethical stance as you proceed (see also Flick, 2006). Also, because AR is flexible and changeable your decisions might need to change over time. The main thing is to use ethical concepts to put yourself in the position of your participants and be open to thinking carefully about the type of data you really need to collect. Not only will this enable you to conduct the research in the reflective spirit of AR, but it will also help to focus and strengthen it.

Finally, it is highly likely that the ethical requirements I have outlined have raised a number of issues in your mind as you think about your own project. Below are the most common questions I get asked by action researchers concerned about ethical issues.

Classroom voices

'If I tell my students the focus of my research won't that change the outcome?'

It might, but people need to be informed as fully as possible so that they are not left concerned or puzzled. When collecting your data and reporting the research you can show you are aware of this possible limitation on your research. Students are in your class to learn, so learning is likely to be more important to them than the fact you are doing research. Students often feel pleased to be 'chosen' as in Lucy's class and keen to be 'insiders' in the research.

'What if my students are young learners?'

Depending on the age of the students and the requirements of your institution, parents' or guardians' permission may be necessary. In any case, you should also explain (or have someone else explain) to the students in terms they can understand what your research involves. It will probably be necessary to do this in the students' first language.

'My students don't understand English yet so what do I do?'

If students are beginner learners, you may need to get the consent forms translated or have them explained by someone proficient in the students' language. Explaining in first language is also necessary if students have limited literacy in English and/or their first language.

'Do I need informed consent if I am using data collection tools where I don't need to know the identity of the participants?'

If you are using something like written surveys where it is not important for participants to identify themselves you don't need written permission.

'What if there are one or two students who don't want to be involved?'

You can still proceed with the research, but those students should not be included in your data collection or in reports on your research. For instance, if you are doing interviews you should not approach students who do not wish to be involved. If you are video- or audio-recording your classroom you should avoid recording those students.

2.4 Preparing your resources and materials

As you begin your research you need to consider what resources, materials and support you should access. I will touch on three areas I have found action researchers to be most interested in.

1. Consulting the literature
2. Involving others
3. Identifying and using equipment.

2.4.1 Consulting the literature

It is not absolutely essential to do a literature search before you begin your AR. In fact, some action researchers take the view that going to the literature takes them away from seeing things as they really are. They believe the literature moulds their research towards 'received' ideas, theories and approaches (e.g., see Naidu *et al.*, 1992). They argue that local knowledge and practice is more relevant for AR than generalised research conclusions that recommend applying a certain approach uncritically.

Nevertheless, many teacher action researchers have found consulting the literature very helpful and I strongly recommend that you do this at some point for several reasons. First, reading the literature can help give you ideas for your focus area and questions. Next, it helps you connect what you are doing with a larger body of work in language teaching and learning. You can find out more about whether what you are investigating is already of interest to others in the field, whether or not it has been researched recently, and how much or how little research has been done on it. Also, you can get ideas about how to design your research and collect data, as well as suggestions and examples for analysing your data. Another reason is that you get a better feel for the value that doing this research will have for yourself and for others in the field. Referring to the literature allows you to strengthen the validity of the research by comparing your findings and outcomes with what others have done, and basing your research in a broader theoretical framework.

Next, the literature can help you to crystallise your ideas about the terms you are using and what they mean. For example, how are you defining 'motivation', 'pronunciation' or student 'attitudes' in your research? *Operationalisation* is the research concept that means ensuring your terms are defined; it is an important issue in research if you want the concepts you are working with to be clear to yourself and others. We will look again at this issue in Chapter 3. Finally, going through the literature helps you refine your own personal theories about teaching, re-evaluate your teaching practices and identify what you have found out about them by doing your research.

Classroom voices

In the classes they taught at the Instituto de Idiomas in Barranquilla, Colombia, Angela Bailey, Lourdes Rey and Bayibe Rosada decided to do AR to investigate what was causing disappointing student achievements in reading and writing at the end of the programme.

To start off they looked for literature on literacy research in Latin America in contexts that related to theirs. They consulted Seda-Santana's report (2000) on approaches to literacy teaching in Latin American primary schools, Smith, Jiminez and Martinez-Leon's (2003) research in primary schools in Mexico, and Barletta *et al.*'s (2002) investigation into first year students' reading competencies in Spanish courses at 10 UniNorte programmes. They discovered that these studies showed that all the students seemed to read texts at literal sight and sound levels. Critical, inferential, and meaning-based reading comprehension were lacking, both in how teachers taught and in how students read.

They linked these insights to international literature by Devine (1993), who highlighted the challenges for EFL and ESL students of developing reading and writing comprehension. The Latin-American literature they read and Devine's comments that students needed to be deliberately taught the skills and strategies for academic success provided a start for their AR. They realised they needed to 'determine some of the major challenges our students faced and make necessary adjustments ... we needed to enter the classroom to be certain what the problems were'.

(Based on Bailey, Rey, & Rosada, 2007, pp. 8–9)

Of course, there is an immense choice of literature that might be relevant to your area of research and it can be daunting deciding where to look. Here is a very brief overview of where to start.

2.4.1.1 Books

Perhaps the first step is to ask for recommendations – from your tutors if you are enrolled in a course, or from experienced mentors or colleagues, especially if they have done AR. They might even be able to lend you personal copies or advise on where and how to borrow them, especially if they are not held in your library. It can also be useful to go to edited collections that provide overview chapters of different topics in language teaching research. Recent collections, at the time I am writing, such as *The Cambridge Guide to Teaching English to Speakers of Other Languages* (Carter & Nunan, 2001), the *Handbook of Research in Second Language Teaching and Learning* (Hinkel, 2005), *The International Handbook of English Language Teaching* (Cummins & Davison, 2007) and *The Cambridge Guide to Second Language Teacher Education* (Burns & Richards, 2009) offer a vast array of discussions of recent research in the field by authors knowledgeable in their areas of expertise. The reference lists in collections such as these will be helpful in pointing you to key authors in your area of interest. You should look for the most recent collections to get up-to-date overviews.

2.4.1.2 Journals

There are now numerous journals in the language teaching and applied linguistics field and more are started each year, some available free online, such as *TESL-EJ*, or *Reading in a Foreign Language*. Not all journals specialise in classroom, teacher or action research or are focused on how research is applied in the classroom. You should look for ones that actively encourage teacher research submissions or publish articles which stress links between theory and practice, for example *ELT Journal* in the UK or *Prospect* in Australia. They will give you ideas of what people have researched and the literature they used for different topics. Some journals, such as *Language Teaching*, provide state-of-the-art papers and short abstracts of recently published articles which give useful leads. Also, as Angela, Lourdes and Bayibe did, look for journals in your country or region that show examples of how others have dealt locally with the topics that concern you. An example of a journal from their country, Colombia, that is dedicated to publishing good articles on AR is *Profile*.

2.4.1.3 Databases

There are a number of educational databases (some of which are listed at the end of the book) which provide lists of written resources for different research areas. For searches in language teaching, a widely used one is the Education Resources Information Center (ERIC) which is available on the Web. To use ERIC, or any other database, you need to be aware of the idea of *keywords*. These are the main content words or concepts in your research question. Another concept to be aware of is Boolean searching, which allows you to narrow or widen your search. Boolean searching involves three options: AND which narrows the search by linking keywords, OR which expands the search by alternating the keywords, NOT which narrows the search by excluding a keyword. To see how this all works in practice, let's take one of the questions in Table 2.2 above: *How will using electronic dictionaries influence my students' writing?* The keywords are *electronic dictionaries* and *writing*. Here, step by step, is how to find some of the relevant literature for this question on ERIC:

1. Enter www.eric.ed.gov to get to the main website.
2. Click on Search ERIC at the top of the screen to get to Basic Search.
3. Type in *electronic dictionaries*; this gave me 79 results.
4. To narrow the search to include writing, go to Back to Search. Click on Advanced Search.
5. You now have a number of options for narrowing the search. Click on Publication Types and you can choose from Journal Articles, Books and so on. When I limited my search to articles I got 41 results.
6. To bring in your other keyword, go back to Advanced Search. There you will see boxes where you can enter more keywords. This is where the Boolean search comes in, which you can access by changing the boxes on the left-hand side of the screen. When I entered AND *writing*, I got 7 results but when I entered OR *writing*, there were 31,067 results! As you can see, how you use the Boolean options considerably changes the results.
7. If you want to widen your search beyond the results for a certain type of publication – in my case articles – go back to Publication Types. When I clicked on Any Publication Type for electronic dictionaries and writing, my results increased from 7 to 12. I could then scroll through the abstracts displayed to see which were likely to be relevant.

One thing to be aware of is that ERIC results are listed chronologically from the most recent. ERIC also offers a very valuable AskERIC service where you can email questions about searching to askeric@askeric.org to which you get replies within two working days.

2.4.1.4 Internet

The Internet is a wonderful resource for researchers. But it is also both a treasure trove and a trash bin, so you need to evaluate what you find. To search the Internet you need to use a Search Engine (such as Google, www.google.com or Google Scholar, http://scholar.google.com) or a Directory (such as Yahoo, www.yahoo.com). Via an Internet Browser, such as Netscape Navigator or Mozilla Firefox you can conduct a search using keywords. Here are some basic hints that can help you search the Internet effectively.

Classroom voices

Frances Wilson was the resource librarian at the National Centre for English Language Teaching and Research (NCELTR) in the Department of Linguistics at Macquarie University, Sydney. Frances worked for many years with language teacher researchers all over the world. She offers the following suggestions for good searching.

> Develop your search strategy by creating a list of key research terms first. Ask yourself these kinds of questions:
>
> > *What type of information is required? Do I need scholarly information or practical information? Should it be current or do I need a historical perspective? What time frames should I choose? What extent of coverage do I need? What formats am I looking for (full journal articles, helpful hints)?*

The next thing is to be as specific as possible in your search, by using the *Advanced Search* options, and the *Help* link. Also, think about using more than one search engine. My suggestions for using the *Advanced Search* option are these:

- Use the *Exact Phrase Search* or place 'quotation marks' around search terms.
- Limit your search by using: date; format; domain (e.g., site au will only return Australian websites, so try domain addresses for other countries); *Define* option (searches for definition of a word); *Search Within Results* (narrows your results).

Finally, here are some keyboard shortcuts that help make the search faster: CTRL+F finds a word on a web page; ALT+D selects the text in the address bar; CTRL+ENTER adds 'www.' to the beginning and '.com' to the end of the text typed in the address bar.

(Personal communication, 17 September 2007)

2.4.1.5 Some criteria for evaluating literature resources

Whether you are using print-based sources or sources from the Internet, it is important to evaluate the quality and reliability of the information you have found. Schwalbach (2003) suggests that there are four criteria to consider when weighing up the literature and they apply equally well to Internet sources. They are listed below with some key questions to ask yourself:

Quality: How good is the literature you are reading?
Key questions: Are you reading someone's opinion or does the article have a research base? Does the author provide evidence for the assertions? Does the author provide an accurate reference list? Is there an adequate depth as well as breadth of information?
Objectivity: How balanced is what you are reading?
Key questions: Does the author provide several different perspectives on the topic? Is there a sense of where the theory/research fits historically? Does the author argue for a particular approach after he or she shows that others have also been considered?
Timeliness: How recent is it?
Key questions: Is it written within the last five years/ten years/longer? Does the author use up-to-date information and references? If you (or the author) are using older literature, is this because they are the leading works in the area?
Quantity: How much should I read?
Key questions: Have you read enough to become more familiar with the area? Are you beginning to recognise key ideas and author names? Are you getting a sense of the current main trends in teaching or researching the area? Is the reading providing you with clearer ideas about your research topic?

(Adapted from Schwalbach, 2003, pp. 36-37)

It is worth spending some time collecting and reading several pieces of literature on the topic you are interested in. Perusing several sources of information on the same topic will enable you to become familiar with the key writers and the research already conducted. This is likely to give a better sense of the 'hot issues' than relying on only one or two sources.

2.4.1.6 Scaffolding your reading of the literature

You may or may not end up writing about the literature when you report your AR (see Chapter 5). However, Barkhuizen's (2002, p. 22) helpful guide, called QUEST, which aims to scaffold the writing of a critical review, is also valuable when reading the literature. Scaffolding in the QUEST analysis takes the form of leading questions:

Q	What Questions do you have after reading the article? For example: anything you don't understand? any issues you'd like to debate further? anything you'd like to know more about?
U	What in the article are you Unhappy about? For example: any weaknesses in the article? any problems in the arguments? anything you disagree with?
E	Are there any Excellent points that got you Excited? For example: any points you agree with? anything that satisfied a gap in your knowledge? anything that sparked off a research idea for you?
S	What are the Strengths of the article? For example: is it well written? is it critical? does it confirm some of your beliefs and experiences?
T	What are the important Themes in the article? For example: what is the main message in the article? are there useful recommendations related to these themes? what can YOU take away from the article?

(Adapted from Barkhuizen, 2002, p. 22)

The QUEST task should help you to critique the ideas and concepts presented in literature you read. But as Barkhuizen notes this outline is 'not a model method for writing a critical review' (p. 21) of the sort required for formal study. To do this you should follow guidelines provided by your lecturer or professor.

2.4.2 Involving others

Another aspect of the resources you need for your research is identifying the people you will involve. One essential group is the research participants themselves. These are usually you as the teacher, of course, and the students in your classroom, but others such as co-teachers, team-teachers, bilingual support teachers, cooperating practice teachers, classroom aides, parents, school librarians, school principals, administrators, university-based mentors, or volunteers assisting your students might also be included. Of course, you will need to ask permission if they are to be directly involved in your data collection.

Apart from these direct participants, you may wish to encourage other teachers to be co-researchers who work collaboratively with you. Collaboration could involve a colleague who comes into your classroom to collect data on your behalf, or a 'critical friend' who simultaneously observes your classroom with you, but then provides a complementary perspective to yours on the area in question. In addition, a group of colleagues working on a common research topic or area can create a very supportive way of doing action research that allows you to extend and challenge your own reflections and findings through ongoing dialogues (see also Chapter 5).

Classroom voices

Joko Priyana is a teacher who conducted AR in a primary school in Yogyakarta, Indonesia. As the curriculum documents in Indonesia had just changed to an approach using task-based teaching, Joko wanted to try out different tasks in the classroom to evaluate their effectiveness for students in Grade 4.

Because task-based teaching was a new approach for him and he would be fully occupied in teaching the children the language items and then trying out the tasks, he asked a 'critical friend' to observe him in the classroom and to take notes on various aspects of his teaching. At the end of the lesson, Joko and the observer got together to compare their observations of how a particular task had worked. This is how Joko described it:

> The observation had three parts. The first part was the description of the task. In this part [I described] the task being evaluated. The second part was a task evaluation rating scale ... that rated different aspects of task completion (e.g., input, activity, learner role). The observer was asked to rate his extent of agreement by circling 1 (strongly disagree), 2 (disagree), 3 (neutral), 4 (agree), or 5 (strongly agree). The third part was open questions about the changes that could be made to the original task for some reason. This part also allowed the observer to write general comments on the task completion.

(Adapted from Priyana, 2002, p. 121)

I have written extensively on the benefits of collaborative research elsewhere (see Burns, 1999). My aim in this book is to encourage you to understand and get going with AR; so I have not specifically focused on collaboration. However, for me and for many teachers I have worked with, collaboration is a much preferred way to do AR. This is because it gives action researchers great support and increases your ability to deepen your insights through dialogue with others. In my personal view and experience, it also gives teachers a very welcome opportunity to get out of the isolation of the classroom and find time to interact with their colleagues on topics of much common interest. If you have opportunities to get together with like-minded colleagues I would certainly encourage you to do AR collaboratively. On the other hand, we cannot just assume that collaboration is the best way to do AR. Interestingly, Steve Mann (1999), whose classroom voice you read earlier in this chapter, and who I know is very supportive of collaborative research, also provides some good counter-arguments to collaboration. He notes that working in groups can be a mixed blessing as members may not always get on. Also someone from outside your teaching context may be able to offer more unbiased advice. Finally, collaborators could short-circuit insightful thinking by offering surface advice or suggestions rather than deep, genuine cooperative understanding (see Edge, 1992). Clearly, in the end the choice of how you proceed with AR is up to your personal preferences and depends on the circumstances you are in.

Other forms of input and support on a whole range of AR issues can come from professional mentors or academic researchers to whom you have access. Teachers I've worked with have found that senior colleagues, directors of study, principals, tutors, parents, students, lecturers, professional development officers, teacher developers and teacher colleagues experienced in action research have all been sources of encouragement, insights, information and helpful hints. Even when you don't have direct access to such support at a personal level, it can still be found on the Internet. For example, some professors maintain lists of publications about action research or offer reflections on projects they have conducted themselves or with teacher colleagues (for an example see the homepage of Graham Crookes, who works at the University of Hawai'i, at http://www2.hawaii.edu/~crookes/ – cited with permission). These resources are in the public domain and can be invaluable ways of getting moral and practical support.

2.4.3 Preparing equipment and materials

In addition, you need to plan for the equipment or materials for your research and have them ready for use. We will consider this issue from two perspectives: software and hardware. In Chapter 3, we will explore in more detail how some of these software and hardware materials can be used during data collection.

2.4.3.1 Software

Obviously, the software materials you use depend on the types of data you decide to collect and your own preferences for documenting information.

When you are actually in the classroom it might be easier, for example, to capture some of your data through hand-written notes. Teachers I've worked with have used notepads, diaries, day books, post-it notes, the margins of lesson plans, notelets, different coloured paper for different kinds of observations, index cards, squared paper for map drawing, overhead transparencies, electronic notebooks, memo pads, preprepared observation/interview/survey sheets, and electronic whiteboards. The possible uses of these materials is only limited by your imagination – it's a question of what works for you.

2.4.3.2 Hardware

Modern technology means that hardware equipment is developing at a rapid rate. This is a great bonus for action researchers as there are now numerous ways to capture what your participants say and do which were not available in previous decades. The possibilities are only limited by the technology you have available and your confidence in using it. Recordings of classroom interactions and behaviours can be made using video-recorders, audio-cassettes, MP3 players, mini-disc, digital cameras, and mobile phones. Recordings can now be downloaded from most of these tools straight onto your computer which, of course, you are also likely to use to write up your notes and reflections in more detail. The widespread use of these forms of technology in daily life means that participants in your research are also less likely to be distracted by them or 'play to the camera' as participants might have been 10 or 20 years ago. Before we leave this section a word or two should be said about recording your data.

2.4.3.3 Hints on recording

When I first started recording people in classrooms in the late 1980s, I lost some of my recordings because I didn't follow a few simple rules. The following points may seem rather obvious, but checking them could save you quite a few headaches (and heartaches) when it comes to replaying your recordings. These guidelines were developed during an action research project I was involved in several years ago that focused on teaching speaking.

- Test your equipment before you begin using it by recording yourself and playing the recording back.
- Make sure you have spare batteries (and tapes or film if needed).
- Ask your participants to try to minimise noise or movement that might reduce the recording quality (e.g., tapping pens on a table or touching the microphone).

- Have the microphone as close as possible to the speaker(s) (e.g., MP3 players can be suspended around the neck; lapel microphones can be used if available).
- Record in an environment that is as quiet as possible (not always straightforward in a classroom, but be aware that incidental noise such as traffic or people talking loudly next to your classroom can distort your recording).
- Set up your microphone at an equal distance from the speakers if you are recording more than one speaker.
- Use a cloth or foam mat under the microphone to minimise surface noise.
- Remember to turn your recording equipment on (this is not a joke – I know teachers who forgot to do this, and I have done it myself!) and check from time to time that it is still recording.

(Adapted from Burns, Joyce & Gollin, 1996, p. 40)

2.4.3.4 Taking stock of your planning

Before we leave this chapter it is worth pausing to take stock of where your AR plan is up to. As I mentioned in Chapter 1, AR is not a lockstep process; it is dynamic and recursive and new decisions and plans will constantly arise as you develop your research. Having an overall sense of the 'map' of your investigation as you take the first tentative steps in your research journey helps to anticipate what the whole process might look like. Following Fischer (2001, pp. 44-45), two outline guides are presented in Appendices 2.2 and 2.3. The first is for teachers working on AR plans for professional development purposes. The second is for those studying in university programmes who might be asked to submit a more formal proposal. As Fischer explains AR plans can be 'less or more elaborate, depending on your intent, audience, time, and resources. The differences are mainly in the specific purposes of individual teacher researchers, school districts and university degree programs' (p. 46).

Action point

Use the outline guide that best relates to your situation as a basis to develop an action plan or proposal for your research.

Remember this is just your first pass at the plan. Don't be afraid to modify and refine it as you go along. It is meant to be a 'living' plan that is dynamic and open to change as your research unfolds.

2.5 Summary point

The focus of this chapter has been on planning your research. We have seen how AR starts by identifying a broad area which fits with your interests, passions, curiosity, or a pressing teaching need. Having identified an area, focusing your investigation helps to refine the questions or issues. We noticed that although focusing can be difficult and may only occur gradually or after the research begins, it is an essential part of clarifying what your research is really about. With clarification, you are then in a position to define the terms you are using and what they mean. You can also begin identifying who you will involve in the research and how you will collect your data. These decisions raise ethical considerations. You need to reflect on how you will conduct the investigation in a morally responsible way that meets the requirements of your organisation and of research more generally. At these initial stages, you also begin scanning your plans over the longer term to make decisions about what resources you will need – whether you will consult the literature and if so how, who you are likely to involve, who can provide support, and what software and hardware you are going to require.

By now your responses to the issues you were asked to think about in the prereading questions should have a firmer foundation. You may even have been modifying them as you read this chapter. Go back to them now and spend some time thinking over your ideas. Also, scan the list below to see whether you feel more confident about planning your research, and making decisions about each of these areas. If you want to read more on any of these points, the sources at the end of the book will start you off.

- Finding a focus area for your research;
- Developing and refining your questions;
- Getting permission;
- Addressing ethical issues;
- Searching the literature;
- Identifying participants;
- Finding support;
- Organising equipment and materials.

Appendix 2.1: Sample consent form

< Name of institution >

Research project informed consent

Title of project: Adult ESL students' perceptions of group work

<Your name> of <name of your institution> (Telephone: ______) is conducting research on the above topic.

The aims of the research are to explore my students' responses to group work in a mixed-ability class. The purpose of the research is to investigate what kinds of groupings work most effectively in my classroom from the students' point of view.

If you agree to participate in this study, you will be asked to complete a written survey and be part of a focus group interview with other students to discuss how you respond to group work. The focus groups will be audio-recorded. These recordings and the notes I take during the interview will be used as information for the project.

Your participation in this research is voluntary and you can withdraw at any time. You do not have to give a reason for withdrawing from the research and there will be no negative consequences if you decide to withdraw. Before the final report for the project is prepared, I will send you a summary of what I have written about the surveys and interviews and will ask you to comment on any descriptions or interpretations that you believe are inaccurate or mistaken.

When I report on the research, I will ensure that you are not identified. No reference to personal names will be used. I am the only person who will have access to the data collected for the project. Any data I use in reports or publications will be for illustration only. If you wish to have a copy of the final report sent to you, I will arrange for this to be done.

Participant consent

The participant has been given a signed copy of this form to keep.

I agree to participate in this research.

Signed: ______ Date: ______

The ethical aspects of this study have been approved by the <name of institution> Ethics Review Committee (Human Research). If you have any complaints or reservations about any ethical aspect of your participation in this research, you may contact the Committee through the Research Ethics Officer (Telephone: ______ Fax: Email: ______). Any complaint you make will be treated in confidence and investigated, and you will be informed of the outcome.

Name of researcher: ______ Date: ______

Appendix 2.2: Outline guide for professional development

1. Context
   Briefly describe your school and class. Do you have to work within any specific syllabus or school goals? What issues within this overall context does your research hope to address?
2. Focus and questions
   Outline your broad focus area and specific questions.
3. Rationale
   Summarise why you are doing this research. What is its importance to you/your students? How does it support your class/school goals and your professional development?
4. Benefits to students
   Identify what differences you want to make for your students and their learning. What benefits do you want the research to offer them?
5. Evaluation of outcomes
   List the ways you will know whether the research has been successful. What indicators will tell you that the research has produced results (e.g., better test scores, more positive attitudes to group work)? What data will you use to support your evaluation (e.g., samples of student writing, survey responses, journal entries)?
6. Action plan
   Describe the steps you anticipate taking. What will you do now? What do you anticipate doing in future? What data will you collect? How will you analyse it? How will you present your research to others? How long will you continue the plan?
7. Resources needed
   Itemise the support you need to put the plan into action. What kind of literature would be useful? Who could assist, collaborate or advise you? What equipment and materials do you need?

(Adapted from Fischer, 2001, p. 44)

Appendix 2.3: Outline guide for university study

1. Focus
   Describe the context of the research and your research problem. What are the main issues embedded in your research problem? Where does your problem fit in the wider scheme of second language teaching in your context?
2. Questions
   Outline the main research questions. How are the questions logically related to your focus area? (Remember that your questions are likely to change as you proceed, but should be clear enough to provide a good starting point.)
3. Rationale
   Describe your reasons for undertaking this project. What is its relevance to your context, your students, your own professional development? How will it benefit your teaching and your students' learning? What outcomes do you expect from the research? How will the project contribute to the field of second language teaching and learning?
4. Review of literature
   Provide a brief summary of the key works on your topic and questions. Who are the main authors and what are their key ideas? How do they reflect your own classroom experiences? How much research seems to have been conducted on this topic?
5. Research methods
   Outline the main methods you will use. What actions and strategies will you use in the classroom? What involvement will your students have? What types of methods will be appropriate (e.g., case studies, narratives, course evaluations)?
6. Data collection
   Describe how you will document what happens. What data collection tools will you use (e.g., observations, surveys, class discussion, student portfolios, videos)?
7. Data analysis
   Summarise how you will analyse the data. How will you identify themes and categories in open-ended comments? What tools lend themselves to quantitative analysis? How will you display the information?
8. Timeline
   Set out the timelines for the research. How long will you continue the research? What are the different phases of the research? How do the different steps break down in terms of months/weeks/days? What additional phases or steps do you anticipate might be needed?
9. Resources needed
   Identify the resources, equipment and materials you need. To what extent are they readily available? What limitations to doing your research can you foresee?

10. References

List the references mentioned in your proposal. Use recognised conventions for referencing, advised by your tutor or ones such as the American Psychological Association or Harvard systems. Present an additional bibliography of other references you intend consulting.

(Adapted from Fischer, 2001, p. 45)

References

Bailey, A., Rey, L., & Rosado, N. (2007). Understanding practices: Bridging the gap between what teachers do and what students know. In H. M. McGarrell (Ed.), *Language teacher research in the Americas* (pp. 7-24). Alexandria, VA: TESOL.

Barkhuizen, G. (2002). The quest for an approach to guided critical reading and writing. *Prospect*, 17(3), 19-28.

Barletta, N., Bovea, V., Delgado, P., Del Villar, L., Lozano, A., May, O., et al. (2002). *Comprehensión y competencias lectoras en estudiantes universitarios* [Reading comprehension and competences in university students]. Barranguilla, Colombia: Ediciones UniNorte.

Borg, S. (2006). *Teacher cognition and language education: Research and practice.* London: Continuum.

Borg, S., & Burns, A. (2008). Integrating grammar in adult TESOL classrooms. *Applied Linguistics*, 29, 456-482.

Burns, A. (1996). Starting all over again: From teaching adults to teaching beginners. In D. Freeman, & J. Richards (Eds.), *Teacher learning in language teaching* (pp. 154-177). Cambridge: Cambridge University Press.

Burns, A. (1999). *Collaborative action research for English language teachers.* Cambridge: Cambridge University Press.

Burns, A. (2002). Action research: Some questions from Thailand. *Thai TESOL Focus*, 15(2), 5-11.

Burns, A., & Hood, S. (Eds.). (1997). *Teachers' voices 2: Teaching disparate learner groups.* Sydney: National Centre for English Language Teaching and Research.

Burns, A., Joyce, H., & Gollin, S. (1996). *I see what you mean: Using spoken discourse in the classroom. A handbook for teachers.* Sydney: National Centre for English Language Teaching and Research. Available at http://www.ameprc.mq.edu.au/docs/research_reports/I_see_what_U_mean.pdf

Burns, A., & Richards, J. C. (Eds.). (2009) *The Cambridge guide to second language teacher education.* New York: Cambridge University Press.

Buzan, T., & Buzan, B. (1996). *The mind map book: How to use radiant thinking to maximise your brain's untapped potential.* London: Plume.

Carter, R., & Nunan, D. (Eds.). (2001). *The Cambridge guide to teaching English to speakers of other languages.* Cambridge: Cambridge University Press.

Cummins, J., & Davison, C. (Eds.). (2007). *The international handbook of English language teaching.* Norwell, MA: Springer.

Devine, J. (1993). The role of metacognition in second language reading and writing. In J. G. Carson, & I. Leki (Eds.), *Reading in the composition classroom: Second language perspectives* (pp. 105-127). Boston: Heinle & Heinle.

Edge, J. (1992). *Cooperative development.* Harlow: Longman.

Fischer, J. C. (2001). Action research, rationale and planning: Developing a framework for teacher inquiry. In G. Burnaford, J. Fischer, & D. Hobson (Eds.), *Teachers doing research: The power of action through inquiry* (pp. 29-48). 2nd edition. Mahwah, NJ: Lawrence Erlbaum Associates.

Flick, U. (2006). *An introduction to qualitative research.* 3rd edition. London: Sage.

Hinkel, E. (Ed.). (2005). *Handbook of research in second language teaching and learning.* New York: Routledge.

Lems, K. (2007). The motive, means, method and magic of using the arts in a grammar-based adult ESL program. In A. Burns, & H. de Silva Joyce (Eds.), *Planning and teaching creatively within a required curriculum for adult learners* (pp. 177-188). Alexandria, VA: TESOL.

Mann, S. (1997). Focusing circles and mind mapping. *IATEFL Newsletter*, 136, 18–19.

Mann, S. (1999). Opening the insider's eye: Starting action research. *The Language Teacher*, 23(12), 11-13.

Marshall, C., & Rossman, G. B. (2006). *Designing qualitative research.* London: Sage.

Mason. J. (2002). *Qualitative researching.* 2nd edition. London: Sage.

McKay, S. L. (2006). *Researching second language classrooms.* Mahwah, NJ: Lawrence Erlbaum Associates.

Naidu, B., Neeraja, E., Ramani, E., Shivakumar, J., & Viswanatha, V. (1992). Researching heterogeneity: An account of teacher-initiated research into large classes. *ELT Journal*, 46(3), 252-263.

Perkins, A. (2001). Here it is, rough though it may be: Basic computer for ESL. In J. Edge (Ed.), *Action research* (pp. 13-19). Alexandria, VA: TESOL.

Priyana, J. (2002). Developing EFL task-based language instruction in an Indonesian primary school context. Unpublished PhD thesis, Macquarie University, Sydney.

Rochsantiningsih, D. (2005). Enhancing professional development of Indonesian high school teachers through action research. Unpublished PhD thesis, Macquarie University, Sydney.

Schwalbach, E. M. (2003). *Value and validity in action research: A guidebook for reflective practitioners*. Lanham, MD: The Scarecrow Press.

Seda-Santana, I. (2000). *Literacy research in Latin America: Context, characteristics, and applications*. Available at http://www.readingonline.org/articles/handbook/seda/

Smith, P., Jimenez, R., & Martinez-Leon, N. (2003). Other countries' literacies: What US educators can learn from Mexican schools. *Reading Teacher*, 56, 772-781.

Valeri, L. (1997). What do students think of group work? In A. Burns, & S. Hood (Eds.), *Teachers' voices 2: Teaching disparate learner groups*. Sydney: National Centre for English Language Teaching and Research.

CHAPTER 3

Act – Putting the Plan into Action

Pre-reading questions

Before you read this chapter, think about these questions. Talk about them with colleagues who are also interested in doing AR.

- What are some ways of collecting information (data) in your classroom?
- What materials or equipment would you need to prepare before you collect it?
- Apart from you, who else might be involved when you collect data?

We will explore these questions in this chapter, so you might want to make notes on your thoughts and ideas as we go along.

In this chapter we'll be looking at ways of collecting information, or to use the research term, *data*, for AR. You might say that all good teachers are interested in information about their classrooms and students but, remember, in AR it is important to collect data in a *systematic* way. By reflecting on the data – the information or evidence you have before you – your understanding and insights about teaching issues will get much deeper. Also, collecting data in AR is always mixed in with the strategies or actions you put in place to change or improve the situation you have decided to focus on. And since these strategies change as you test them out in practice, so too could the ways you collect the data. As we shall see, it's all a question of matching your data collection methods with what you want to find out.

3.1 Collecting your data

If you have never done any research before, the thought of collecting data can seem very daunting (I well remember my first attempts!). However, teaching lends itself naturally to data collection. For example, surveys conducted by your students about their views on various aspects of language learning can provide you with good sources of information. Asking students to note in a journal what they feel or think during a new kind of activity is another rich data source. Table 3.1 demonstrates how some of my teacher colleagues have used classroom activities to collect AR data.

Table 3.1 Combining classroom activities and data collection

Regular classroom activities	Action research data collection
• Teaching new grammar items	• Audio-record classroom interaction or students' group work responses to see how students are using them
• Teaching aspects of writing (e.g., structuring the essay)	• Collect students' texts over a set period of time and monitor the improvements and gaps in their writing
• Using different materials	• Discuss with students their reactions to new materials compared with previous materials
• Teaching vocabulary	• Give students a survey asking them for their responses to different vocabulary activities
• Encouraging students to take more responsibility for learning	• Ask students to write a letter to a class partner to explain their most effective strategies for learning English
• Extending students' motivation	• Get students to interview each other about what they like/dislike about various activities and ask them to record their responses

Reflection point

Think about two or three activities you often do in class. Discuss them with a colleague.

Brainstorm some ways you could turn them into data collection activities. To focus your brainstorm, use one of the topic areas or questions you identified for your research in Chapter 2.

Classroom voices

Here is an example of how one action researcher used class activities focused on his AR issues to begin collecting information.

Salah Troudi taught EFL to female undergraduates preparing for entry into an English for Specific Purposes course as part of their studies in a university in the United Arab Emirates. His class contained a lot of 'multiple repeaters', or students who had previously failed, and had low morale and motivation. Salah says:

> I must admit that when I found out that my Level 2 [low intermediate] class was a mixture of repeaters and multiple repeaters I was not thrilled, to say the least. The year before I had taught a similar class, and it was an experience in frustration and even exasperation at times. It was hard to work with students who simply refused to study ... The action research I conducted was partly to find a more efficient way to help my students and partly to challenge accepted labelling and definitions of multiple repeaters.

To begin the process:

> I ... collected written samples of language problems my students had. They were mainly in the form of grammatical or functional errors.
>
> ... we [had] a group chat ... With 15 minutes left at the end of the fourth class session, I asked the students about their problems in English and why they were multiple repeaters ... There was some hesitation ... but then one student asked if she could reply in Arabic ... therefore many more were encouraged to take part in the conversation. I had to allocate turns ... What the students said in this session convinced me that I needed to allocate more than just a 15-minute chat ... I then asked their permission to interview them [individually] for 15 minutes after class.

This classroom information led to other methods that Salah decided to use to take his action research further – observation, interviews, and questionnaires.

(Troudi, 2007, pp. 162-164)

In the next sections we will look at a range of observation and non-observation methods commonly used by action researchers. Before we do, though, it is important to be aware of a few things about data collection in AR. First, the techniques you use should be well matched to what you are trying to find out. There's no point, for instance, in observing someone doing a classroom writing activity if you want to know how they go about planning what vocabulary to use. You need to ask them! Similarly, asking someone what they said when they did a speaking activity will not give you reliable information, as people usually cannot recall their exact words. You would need to record them as they actually do the activity. Second, you should weigh up how to balance data collecting with teaching – the 'cost-effectiveness' of data collection, if you like. In AR, the one should not outweigh the other – so choose manageable and doable techniques that you are comfortable with and do not take excessive amounts of time. However, third, don't be afraid to use data techniques in creative and adaptable ways. Doing AR does not mean following a recipe-like approach. You can adjust the cycles, processes and methods to meet your needs creatively in your teaching context. Finally, remember that data are not an end in themselves but a way to link action, observation and reflection as your knowledge and understanding get deeper. Knowing more about our actions helps to develop them and developing them leads to greater knowledge.

Two major questions underlying data collection are: *To answer my questions: What do I need to see?* (observation); and *What do I need to know?* (non-observation). In Table 3.2 I've listed the main methods used in AR.

Now that we've seen some of the broad possibilities in data collection methods, let's look at each of these approaches in turn.

Table 3.2 Methods for action research

Observation: What do I need to see?	Non-observation: What do I need to know?
Examples: • Observation by teacher or colleague on particular aspects of classroom action • Brief notes or recorded comments made by the teacher while the class is in progress • Audio- or video-recordings of classroom interactions • Transcripts of classroom interactions between teacher and students or students and students • Maps, layouts or sociograms of the classroom that trace the interactions between students and teacher • Photographs of the physical context	Examples: • Interviews • Class discussions/focus groups • Questionnaires and surveys • Diaries, journals and logs kept by teacher or learners • Classroom documents, such as teacher-made or textbook materials used, samples of student writing, speaking tests, assessment portfolios, or self-evaluations

3.2 Observing and describing: What do I need to see?

Observing and describing have a key role to play in AR. Collecting data through observation is to do with 'making familiar things strange', or in other words, seeing things that are before our eyes in ways we haven't consciously noticed before. As teachers we are so used to being in classrooms we don't always really 'see' what is interesting, unexpected, unusual or just plain routine, even when we think we are 'looking'. Good AR observation is about becoming 'strangers' in our own classrooms. It is about asking self-reflective questions like: What is *really* happening here? What role(s) am I taking up in my class? What role(s) are my students taking? What happens if I change the set-up of the classroom in some way? What happens if I communicate differently with my students? What happens if I use my materials in a new way? What will my students do if I give them more choices about class activities?

AR observation is different from the routine kind of looking/seeing that teachers do every day. It is much more self-conscious because it is:

- focused: you are seeking specific information about something, rather than looking in a general way;
- objective: you are aiming to see things as they really are and not just through a personal, subjective or intuitive lens;
- reflective: you are observing in order to see things from a position of inquiry and analysis;
- documented: you deliberately make notes or records of the information;
- evaluated and re-evaluated: you check out your own interpretations again later by yourself or collaboratively with others

Action point

This is a kind of pre-reading activity for this section that asks you to start practising 'making familiar things strange'. It works even better if you can do it with a colleague and talk about your impressions afterwards.

- Choose a setting in your teaching context that interests you – your classroom, the staffroom, the school office, the playground, the lab, the school corridors, the library, the canteen and so on. Take five or ten minutes to observe it very closely.
- If it helps, imagine that you have just arrived from another planet and everything you see is unfamiliar, intriguing or puzzling and you need to make sense of it. Make as many notes as you can about this context – either during or immediately after observing it.
- What language use, activities, patterns of behaviour, interactions between people, or use of materials did you notice about this context? Were there any other things you noticed? What was the physical set-up like? What was the most memorable or striking thing about this context?

3.2.1 Observation roles and approaches

Observers can take on a variety of roles, or *modes* of observation, for example:

- 'Other'-observation: observations by you of others (students, team-teachers, pre-service practicum teachers, classroom aides, bilingual assistants, parents).
- Peer observation: observation of other teachers by you, or of you by other teachers (acting as mentors, influencers, critical friends, supervisors).
- Self-observation: observation of your own behaviours, thoughts, actions, ways of communicating as a teacher.
- Collaborative observation: observation with other observers (your own observations of your classroom are compared and contrasted with those of others you have asked to observe you, such as students, colleagues, team-teachers, classroom aides).

Classroom voices

Anparo and Marco, two teachers from Venezuela, decide to use collaborative observation. Anparo is teaching a class of beginners who are very shy about speaking English and reluctant to interact. She wants to increase confidence and communication among her learners. She asks Marco to observe her and give her feedback on her teaching. Here is part of their conversation after class:

Anparo: I was trying to get good group dynamics ... to make a supportive environment ... I know I spent a lot of time ... perhaps too much time ... organising the getting-to-know-you activities and getting students to move around a lot in pairs and meet new people.

Marco: Well, I actually I thought this was a very good aspect ... you were like a driving force in the class ... you made your voice very clear ... with a high volume ... your body language was quite exaggerated, you were really energetic! Is this a personality thing?

Anparo: No, I was using that as a deliberate teaching strategy ... to get good classroom energy and get them talking ...

(Author's data)

It can be difficult at first to focus your ideas about what and how to observe. You could begin by just observing quite generally as you go about your work, perhaps using the action point task above to help you focus your ideas. Also, the questions in the list below could be useful as you start to link your observations to the issues you are trying to investigate.

1. Which particular setting do you want to observe?
2. Which key players do you want to observe?
3. What kinds of learning activities should you focus on?
4. What aspects of language learning are of interest?
5. What kinds of events are you interested in?
6. Which kinds of behaviours should you target?
7. Which kinds of interactions are of interest?
8. What techniques in your teaching do you want to change?

These questions are all about *what* to observe. McKay (2006, p. 81, following Richards, 2003) suggests four approaches about *how* to observe:

> (1) ... observe and record everything, which gives the observer a broad look at the environment ... (2) observe and look for nothing in particular, which may lead the observer to notice unusual happenings ... (3) look for paradoxes so that observers might notice a student who is generally very quiet in the classroom suddenly becomes ... talkative ... (4) identify the key problem facing a group.

Action point

From the set of eight questions above, select *what* to observe. Now think about *how* to observe using one of McKay's four approaches.

Try out a short observation in your classroom or the classroom of a colleague. If you have time during the week alternate the approach you select in different lessons.

What did you learn from the approach you chose? What did you learn from using different approaches to observation?

Discuss your ideas with a colleague, preferably a partner who has also used this action point.

3.2.2 Planning your observation

Before deciding to observe you need to think about whether observation is the most appropriate way to answer the questions you have in mind. Let's look at some AR issues explored by teachers I've worked with and decide which would lend themselves to observation.

As you can see from Table 3.3, some issues are not appropriate for observation, so it is worth thinking things through when it comes to your own AR.

Reflection point

Go back to the issues and questions you developed in Chapter 2. Will observation be the most appropriate way to collect data for your research? If so, why? Discuss your ideas with colleagues and get their views too.

Once you have decided on your focus and reviewed your questions – the *why*, *what* and *how* of your research, that we discussed in Chapter 2 – you are ready to observe your classroom. You need to think about *who* or *what* you will observe, *how many* people or events will be involved, *when* and *how often* you will observe, and *where* and *how* you will do the observation. Some of the decisions will become clearer as your research goes on, but you need a starting point.

3.2.2.1 Who? How many?

Try to focus on the range of people who will provide the data you need to answer your questions. In Q2 below, you would be interested in observing yourself and all the students in your class. You might also want a colleague to observe you and give you feedback.

3.2.2.2 What? Where?

Consider the specific behaviours and locations you are interested in. Look out for any 'critical incidents' or unexpected events too. For example, you can learn more about what is going on for the students in Q5 by observing what they do during the activities, noting what they say and who they talk to, and focusing on how and where they locate themselves within the group and in the classroom.

Table 3.3 Issues and questions for observation

Issues and questions	Should observation be used?
1. *My colleagues and I are concerned about the quality of our students' writing. We've heard about the genre-based approach. Will explicit instruction on genre and text structure help to improve students' writing?*	This question focuses on the quality of the texts produced by following a particular teaching approach. Therefore observation is not going to be useful. You need to focus on analysing the language in students' written texts.
2. *I want my classroom to be more learner-centred. How much talking do I do in the classroom compared with my students?*	This question lends itself well to self-observation and student observation. You can begin to note who speaks, but the best way to find out is to record the classroom interaction.
3. *My students seem to have difficulty with listening but I don't know much about how they approach it. What strategies do my students use during listening comprehension activities?*	Strategy use in listening is more a mental (cognitive) activity than a behavioural or observable activity. So you need to find a way of asking what people are thinking, or mentally processing. Using questionnaires where students indicate their thinking or asking students to say what they are thinking as they do a listening task would be more appropriate.
4. *My team-teacher and I are concerned that one female student in our class is disruptive and does not join in well with others. What are some of the reasons for this?*	Observing the student and the way other students interact with her over a period of time could throw some light on the students' patterns of behaviour. It could lead to discussing teaching strategies for better interaction. You might need to combine observation with discussions or interviews with students.
5. *Some of the students in my class are a difficult group and they seem unmotivated. What are they actually doing during the group activities I set up?*	More specific information about the students' behaviour and their actual use of language can be found through observation. This information would allow for some new teaching strategies to be developed.
6. *I am really keen to improve oral skills but the tasks I have been using don't seem to have helped. What are my students' views about the speaking tasks we use in class?*	This question asks about what the students think. It would be better to use questionnaires or interviews.

3.2.2.3 When? How often?

Decide on which parts of the lesson or event you need to focus on. It may be that you select certain activities only, or you may get more information by observing the whole lesson. You will also want to decide whether the observation should happen over a number of lessons or events, and in what sequence you observe them. For Q4 above you would need to decide whether to observe the student concerned during certain activities, a whole lesson, or a period of a week or more.

3.2.2.4 Where? How?

In addition to these decisions, you also need to think about *where* you will observe and *how* you will position yourself. For example, if you are involved in Q2, you will most likely take up your usual positions as the classroom teacher. For Q5 you will need to position yourself where you can best see and hear the students concerned as they do the group tasks. In the next section, we will consider *how* you will record your observations.

3.2.3 Doing your observation

Classroom voices

Hamed Mohammed Al-Fahdi is a deputy headmaster in a boys' school in Oman. He was interested in the types of oral feedback he and six of his colleagues gave in their Grades 4–6 primary and Grades 1 and 2 secondary classrooms. A further interest was whether he and the other teachers gave feedback to individuals or groups. Each class consisted of 35–40 students. He describes how he set up his observations and recorded the data:

> Data ... were collected through audio-recordings and observations. In one of my own lessons and in one each of the other six teachers', two oral tasks were chosen for analysis. These were recorded, transcribed and the teachers' use of oral feedback in them analysed. The recordings were also supplemented by notes I made during the lessons of my colleagues (which I observed). During these observations I used a simple observation sheet to record information about the type of feedback the teachers were using and how often.

(Al-Fahdi, 2006, pp. 41-42)

Hamed's description captures the essential elements of the decisions he needed to make in planning his observation: the decisions about who (*teachers*), how many (*himself and six colleagues*), what (*oral feedback*), where (*primary and secondary classrooms*), when (*during two tasks*), and how often (*once*) outlined above. In addition, he outlines the tools he used to collect his observation data: observation sheets, notes, recording and transcription. We will consider all these tools in this section.

3.2.4 Observation sheets

Observation sheets are used in what is sometimes called systematic or structured observation. This type of observation involves using a coding system or checklist prepared before the lesson begins. The observer records the things he or she observes as categories of events, for example behaviours, or types of interaction. Observation sheets collect data which can be treated quantitatively and summarised in numerical forms (see Chapter 4). Some of the best known systems for language teaching observation are the Communicative Orientation for Language Teaching (COLT) (Spada & Fröhlich, 1995) and FOCUS (Fanselow, 1987). They are very comprehensive checklists that contain many different categories that capture aspects of teaching, learning and classroom interaction. However, not many of the teachers I have worked with have used them for AR, since they are quite complex and are more likely to be used in larger-scale and more extensive classroom observation research. If you are interested in these types of coding systems it is best to consult the books by the original authors that will introduce you to these systems.

More likely, you will use a simpler checklist that you develop yourself in order to focus on the particular issue you have in mind. Before we look at examples, here is some advice from a teacher researcher about using a checklist:

Classroom voices

For me a classroom observation checklist must not contain too many items. This is a lesson I learned from a few observations I conducted. Some time back, in order to appear very professional and show off my newly acquired knowledge I developed wonderfully detailed checklists divided and subdivided into many topics. The checklist looked very well done and highly useful but in practice that was not the case. I ended up with too much to look for in too little time. So now, when I design checklists I restrict myself to looking at one or two aspects of my teaching and I do not devise too many questions nor do I have too many categories. If you keep your checklist concise and stick to the most important points, your observation will be 'good'.

(Amna Khalid, cited in Richards & Farrell, 2006, p. 90)

What are the different types of checklists you might consider using? Some (adapted from Simpson & Tuson, 1995, p. 95) are listed and illustrated here.

3.2.4.1 Behaviour checklist

A list of behaviours is set out and events are recorded as they occur. The observer uses a particular period of time to note the behaviours and tally them. This one could be used for Q4 in Table 3.3 where the teacher wants to find out more about a student who is disruptive and not joining in well during class activities. Table 3.4 shows what it might look like filled in.

The information from this kind of checklist allows you to see which particular type of behaviour the student keeps repeating most (*interrupting neighbour's work*), as well as the kind of tasks that seems to interest the student more than others (*vocabulary game*). This information could provide you with insights into a student's preferred patterns of learning, or the behaviours most irritating to other students and, with some reflection, could lead to developing strategies to integrate the student better into the classroom dynamics. This kind of tally checklist allows you to capture 'snapshots' of classroom events and to say what patterns of behaviour are emerging.

Table 3.4 Behaviour checklist

Student: MP	*Date: 12/6* *Time: 10.00–10.30* *Task: silent reading*	*Date: 13/6* *Time: 2.00–2.30* *Task: vocabulary game*	*Date: 14/6* *Time: 9.30–10.00* *Task: grammar exercise*	*Etc.*
Interrupts neighbour's work	卌 III	卌	卌 卌 卌 IIII	
Attempts to get other students' attention	IIII		卌 卌	
Teases neighbour physically	卌 III	IIII	卌	
Etc.				

Table 3.5 Events checklist (Mendoza López, 2005, p. 36)

	TIME											
TL												
TQ												
TR												

(to be continued)

(continued)

	TIME											
PA												
PV												
PR												
PW												
PRA												
PSA												
PWA												
SWA												
TRP												
S												
U												

3.2.4.2 Events checklist

An events checklist is similar but this time focuses on recording specific phases or activities in a lesson. Table 3.5 presents one that was devised by Edgar Mendoza López (2005) who wanted to observe how process writing was being taught in Grades 10 and 11 at six high schools in Colombia. To fill in the checklist, Edgar used a key that indicated different interactions taking place in the classroom at specific times.

Key

TL:	teacher describes, narratives, explains, directs	**PRA**:	pre-reading activity
TQ:	teacher questions	**PSA**:	post-reading activity
TR:	teacher responds to pupil	**PWA**:	pre-writing/planning activity
PA:	pupil responds to teacher's question	**SWA**:	post-writing/revising activity
PV:	pupil volunteers information, comments, or questions	**TRP**:	teacher revises pupil's work
PR:	pupil reads	**S**:	silence
PW:	pupils writes	**U**:	unclassifiable

Classroom voices

Edgar comments on why he devised and used this checklist:

> to record the class activities, focusing especially on pre-writing/planning, writing/formulating and post-writing/revising activities and also on pre-reading, reading and postreading activities ... It is important to note that these observations provide only a snapshot of the activities taking place ...

As a result of using the checklist, he observed that:

> in general, the English class gave priority to listening and speaking over reading and writing ... reading activities were more frequent than writing activities and were focused mainly on reading comprehension of short texts. Writing was done mainly at home which supports the idea that process-oriented writing is rarely done in class.

(Mendoza López, 2005, p. 28 and 32)

This type of checklist gives you an objective picture of the patterns of activities occurring in a classroom and to identify how well they relate to a particular, or desired, teaching approach. Obviously, the checklist used by Edgar contains quite a large number of items and, as Amna suggested above, you may want to focus on fewer events. In addition, it is not easy to record a large number of event types as you are actually teaching your class. In this case, you might use this kind of checklist after first audio- or video-recording your classroom. Alternatively, you might ask a colleague to use it to observe your class and to give you feedback on the events she observed. Or, you might first select the main ones you want her to focus on at different times. As a result, you should be able to identify patterns of classroom events or activities you would like to change.

Of course, the kind of checklist that will be useful in your classroom depends on the focus of your research and the questions you are asking. In one of the examples above, Hamed said that he used a simple observation sheet. This helped him to analyse his feedback patterns. Here's the table he produced to summarise the types of oral feedback he was using in his classroom. 'Evaluative' feedback involved commenting on student performance (e.g., *Good*, *Yes*, *OK*, *thank you*), 'corrective' meant identifying and correcting errors (e.g., S: *A limp*; T: *No, a lamp*), while 'strategic' was to do with reminding learners to monitor and check their performance (e.g., checking that they use plural verbs for plural nouns).

Classroom voices

Types of feedback in my teaching

Feedback type	*Task 1*	*Task 2*	*Total*
Evaluative	23	25	48
Corrective	8	6	14
Strategic	5	3	8

Hamed says:

> it is clear from these figures that most of my oral feedback was evaluative ... Such an attitude might frustrate learners and create in them negative attitudes towards learning.
>
> (Al-Fahdi, 2006, pp. 42 and 45)

Action point

Select a particular type of behaviour or set of events that you want to observe in your classroom. Use some of the ideas above to devise a simple checklist that will categorise and count them. Show your checklist to your colleagues and get their feedback on how well it captures what you want to observe. Keep in mind things like:

- Do the categories adequately cover the range of behaviours you are interested in?
- Are there too many for you to observe while teaching?
- Are the descriptions of categories clear so that someone else using it would know what you mean?
- Are the categories objective or do they rely too much on your personal judgement?

If possible try out the checklist in one of your lessons, preferably asking a colleague to observe the same lesson. Discuss whether you end up with similar counts for each category. This increases the reliability of your data – an issue we'll look at again in Chapter 4.

If you found your descriptions of your categories were not clear, ask your colleague how they could be improved.

3.2.5 Observation notes

Not all observation data are counted. Some are produced using a descriptive and narrative style and are not as structured as observation checklists. These kinds of data are recorded in the form of notes made by the researcher or other participants. They are used to note descriptions and accounts of what happened in the classroom, including – depending what you are focusing on – the physical layout, verbal and non-verbal information, the structure of the groups, or the sequences of activities and tasks.

Classroom voices

Duong Thi Hoang Oanh was interested in whether and how learner autonomy operated in her two speaking classes, which focused on the oral presentation activities of fourth-year university students. Observation was one of the techniques she used for her AR:

> I observed my two classes, which consisted of 99 students who were studying at the upper-intermediate level of English. Ten 90-minute sessions were videotaped. I used an unstructured class observation method to observe the classes (not to follow any fixed plan or structure), with a detailed record of observational notes that included reflective and analytical observations. I kept daily teaching logs and aimed to describe the classes' activities objectively and in detail. The videos were of great use as I reviewed specifically what the students and I had been doing in class, focusing on elements related to independent learning. They helped me make insightful reflections about my own classroom practices.

(Oanh, 2006, p. 38)

In this description Duong highlights two ways that notes can be prepared – through reflective and analytical observations. We'll next look at each of these tools in turn, as well as some others used for observation. She also refers to the use of recording to capture the events and behaviours of the classroom as they happen, and to complement the notes and teaching logs. We'll look at these other two methods later in this chapter.

3.2.5.1 Reflective observations

Reflective observations are notes written about classroom events with the researcher's comments placed next to them. Alexandra Aldana, a teacher of Grade 9 students in Colombia, used this kind of observation tool for her research on improving her students' writing skills.

Classroom voices

Lesson Plan Two

Topic: Pre-writing

Date: July 29th	
1. Teacher asks students questions about what writing is, its importance and how they write.	Students show low interest in the class. They do not want to answer the teacher's questions. Only five students participate actively.
2. Students and teacher brainstorm about Love and Friendship Day. Students brainstorm individually.	Some of them are doing other things and some are copying again.

(Aldana, 2005, p. 57)

As you can see, Alexandra recorded the events on the left side of the page and then added her reflections about what was happening during these events next to each one. Although this is not shown in Alexandra's layout, another column is sometimes added to this kind of table to show the time when each event began. Adding the time gives you a sense of how long each event took, but you can decide whether this is necessary for your own research.

3.2.5.2 Analytical observations

Analytical observations take the process of recording reflective observations one step further by getting you to think about the main elements or features of their meanings. To provide an example, let's look at Aldana's observation chart again, but this time with her analysis of what she is observing.

Classroom voices

Date: July 29th

Lesson Plan Two

Topic: Pre-writing

Sequence of actions	*Student responses*	*Analysis*
1. Teacher asks students questions about what writing is, its importance and how they write.	Students show low interest in the class. They do not want to answer the teacher's questions. Only five students participate actively.	Attitudes of class: • Low interest • Lack of response • Little participation
2. Students and teacher brainstorm about Love and Friendship Day.	Students brainstorm individually. Some of them are doing other things and some are copying again.	Engagement of class • Individual • Passive • Off-task

(Aldana, 2005, p. 57)

3.2.5.3 Narrative observations

A narrative observation is another way you can make notes. It's a bit like telling the story of the events you observe as they happen. Narrative observation usually requires a great deal of freehand writing, even if you are using a computer, so it can be useful to develop a personal 'shorthand' to record things quickly as you watch. The abbreviations used in the following example are selected from Bailey (see Bailey, 2006, p. 102 for the full list), but you can easily develop your own versions. Let's go back to the disruptive female student in Q4 in Table 3.3. Previously I showed you how to tally, or count, behaviours for this student but a narrative account of some of the same behaviours might look like this:

Classroom voices

Student: MP   Date: 12/6   Time: 10.00-10.30

All Ss at T1 silent. Y rdg quietly to Rt of M. B moves, holds bk at angle to M. M knocks B on LKn. B frowns bt keeps still & ignones M. M bnies to dr on Y's bk cover. Y pushes M's RA away. M taps Y on LA and pulls hair. Other Ss at table lgh but do not make EC. M carries on rdg T comes to T1 & tells M mst be quiet.

Key to abbreviations

Ss = students	T1 = Table 1	lgh = laugh
LKn = left knee	bt = but	Rt = right

RA/LA = right/left arm	rdg = reading	dr = draw
mst = must	& = and	EC = eye contact

3.2.5.4 Shadowing

A shadow observation, as the name suggests, is where you set aside blocks of time, maybe during a whole day or week, simply to follow and observe what an individual or group does as they go about their regular routines. It focuses on tracking their movements, interactions or behaviours, while taking in and noticing the main features. This kind of study can be useful in certain situations to shed light on what is happening more generally in the lives of your students, either inside or beyond your classroom walls. It allows you to get an idea of what things are like 'from the other side of the desk'. Stevenson (1998, p. 29) comments that the main skill needed for a shadow study is 'attentiveness'. The first action point in this chapter asked you to undertake the kind of observation that is used in shadowing.

To do a shadow observation you will need to make sure you can position yourself close enough to the participants without becoming directly involved in their activities so that you can observe carefully what they do and say. It is common to supplement your observations by summarising them through descriptive notes made as soon as possible after your observations. Your notes are unlikely to be as fine-grained as those for a narrative observation. But, as with a narrative observation, you are aiming to tell a 'story' by focusing on the events that are of most interest for your research topic.

3.2.6 Recording and transcribing

Making a video-recording of her class was another tool Duong used. Recording the situation you want to observe has the advantage of capturing oral interactions exactly as they were said. It's pretty well impossible to record verbal exchanges accurately through notes alone and recordings are usually used to complement direct observations. You may decide to record a complete lesson or focus on particular segments that you are especially interested in investigating (e.g., how students react to a particular activity, or how a small group works together).

Audio-recording is usually easier to set up than video-recording and is less noticeable to the participants. It's great for recording what was said, but it doesn't allow you to observe gestures, facial expressions, body movements and the general look and feel of the classroom. These features are useful if you want to examine the classroom more holistically, as Duong pointed out. Whichever type of recording you choose, one thing to remember is that your participants may become distracted by the recording equipment, and this means they may not act or speak as they would normally. To overcome this problem, it's useful to record several sessions so that they get used to having the equipment present. As far as the practicalities of recording are concerned, we already looked at the main issues in Chapter 2 when we discussed the materials, resources and equipment you might need for AR.

Reflection point

Re-read the section in Chapter 2 where we discussed recording equipment and hints for making recordings in your classroom.

If you intend recording your classroom, check that you are well prepared for the practical aspects of making a classroom recording.

Altrichter, Posch and Somekh (1993, p. 97) say, 'it's easy to make a tape-recording and it actually takes very little extra time. The problems only start afterwards, when you try to make use of the information'. This is very true! You will need to allocate time to go through the recordings, probably listening more than once to get a really deep understanding of what it all means. Also, although it can give you very interesting and useful insights into what is happening in your classroom, transcribing is time consuming, so you will need to make decisions about how much to transcribe. It's often enough to transcribe just short extracts where there is something that strikes you as noteable, important, or even 'normal', and illuminates the issue you are researching. For example, for his research described earlier, Hamed Al-Fahdi transcribed typical segments from the recording because they illustrated the types of oral feedback he had detected in his and his colleagues' lessons. This allowed him to supply qualitative examples to support the numerical data from his tables.

Classroom voices

Hamed says:

> An example of corrective feedback from my work is the following where the learners were naming objects in their books:
>
> T: No. 11
> S: A limp
> T: No, a lamp
> S: A lamp
> T: Okay ...

My colleagues also used corrective feedback in a similar way that I did, i.e., by providing the correct answer and asking learners to repeat. Here is an example from Teacher 2:

T: (name) Read the sentence
S: Waleed caught a some fish
T: Waleed caught a small fish
S: Waleed caught a small fish
T: Okay

(Al-Fahdi, 2006, pp. 42-43)

The next action point aims to give you some practice in recording and also suggests steps for selecting which data to transcribe.

Action point

Record a short segment from your lesson – maybe up to 10 minutes or more if you have time.

1. Listen to the complete recording to get the gist of what you recorded.
2. Listen a second time and make notes about the structure of the events – the phases in the activity or the sequences of that part of the lesson. Give each different part of the structure a label and make a note of the number on the tape counter for easy identification.
3. Go back over your notes and select the sections that are of interest for the research topic you are developing. Transcribe them in full.

(Adapted from Altrichter *et al.*, 1993, p. 97)

As you transcribe you will probably realise that you need to note who is speaking or that some of the talk is unclear or that you need to insert a note about non-verbal details. It's useful to develop a list of conventions that you can stick to in order to make your transcription systematic. I have used various versions of the one below with teachers I've worked with, but you should go ahead and adapt it to suit your own purposes.

1, 2, 3, etc.:	Line numbering (for ease of reference)
T:	Teacher
S(s):	Unidentified student(s)
P:	Pseudonym of student
(??):	Inaudible words (not clear because or recording quality)

(on the last page??):	Best guess about unclear words
(...):	Pause
(laughter):	Non-verbal sound
(T writes on board):	Non-verbal actions
THIS word:	Capitals used to show word emphasis

3.2.7 Maps and photographs

For some people images are more powerful than words and you may prefer to document your observations through visuals. Photos, diagrams, maps, drawings, sketches, video images and other visual data are an excellent way of supplementing your observation notes. They can:

- remind you of the location and what was happening in it;
- capture a specific teaching moment;
- track a sequence of events or behaviours;
- record non-verbal aspects such as physical expressions or body positions;
- capture facial expressions that might reflect aspects of people's attitudes, thinking and ideas;
- identify who places themselves where in the classroom.

If the idea of taking photos yourself seems disruptive to your teaching, students can be enlisted to take them instead – you may need to brief them beforehand about what to focus on. Of course, digital cameras, including those available on mobile phones, are easy to use and the photos can be displayed quickly, but disposable cameras could also be handy and inexpensive alternatives for you or your students to use. If you introduce photography as a regular classroom activity, this avoids the risk of your participants 'playing to the camera' and you are more likely to capture regular behaviours. You can use photos as a stimulus for collecting more data – for example, in interviews (*Tell me what you were doing/thinking when this photo was taken*) – or a starting point for concrete discussions with students about their general behaviours or feelings (*You look happy here. Did you like this activity?*).

Maps or diagrams of the classroom can be used to note the social set-up and interactions of the classroom. Recording where students seat themselves or tracking their movements during the day can be very illuminating. You can work out where they usually position themselves, note who likes to work together or document which individuals are 'liked' or 'disliked'. Here's a very basic map of a classroom I made myself while I was observing a teacher in Mexico, who was teaching a group of adolescent beginners in a general English course. We were exploring together the way the teacher taught grammar and her views on why she taught grammar in the way that she did. This map shows the physical set-up (door, cupboard, etc.), the teacher's (T) position in the room as the lesson started, where each male student (MS) sat, where each female student (FS) sat, and where I (AB) sat as I observed the class.

Door	Cupboard	Table	Whiteboard		Poster
					T chair
		Separate table with cassette	T		T desk
			FS1		FS2 FS3
				FS5	FS4
					MS1 MS2
AB		FS6 FS7	FS8 MS3		MS4
	Window	Window		Window	

Classroom voices

Pam McPherson, a teacher of adult ESL students in Australia, has this to say about how she used diagrams to understand the social interactions of the students in her classroom.

> And drawings I found really, really useful ... In the particular class I had, the problem was with people not interacting with each other and not wanting to be involved with each other and I found it really useful to draw diagrams ... to see who typically worked together and who didn't work together and to try and gain some understanding of why this was going on.
>
> I began to realise that the patterns of interaction that the students were setting up in the arrangement of the desks and who they talked to allowed them to minimize interaction with some students and to barricade themselves into certain groups.
>
> (Burns, 1999, pp. 111-112)

You can read more about the AR that Pam was doing in the 'Planning the next steps' section in Chapter 5.

Now that we have considered the main ways of collecting information through observation, let's look at methods involving what can't be observed – people's thoughts, experiences and opinions.

3.3 Asking and discussing: What do I need to know?

The flip side of what you need to see (observation) is what you need to know (non-observation). This type of data is to do with what people think, believe and perceive and also the way they explain their personal histories, experiences and actions. Narrating and telling stories about experiences is an age-old way for humans in a particular social situation to make sense and meaning of their actions – and essentially this is what these kinds of methods are all about. Also, as I've already suggested above, the tools that aim to reveal what lies below the surface of classroom actions are often combined with observation methods to give a more rounded picture of what you are investigating. In the sections that follow, we'll look at four different methods that are commonly used – interviews, questionnaires/surveys, journals/logs, and classroom documents.

3.3.1 Interviews

Interviews are a classic way in research to conduct a conversation that explores your focus area. Indeed, Burgess (1984, p. 102) has described them as 'conversation with a purpose'. The number of people you choose to interview will depend on the time available as interviews can be more time consuming than, say, observations or surveys. One solution to overcoming the time issue is to use an interview as a class discussion activity, or a small group task. In this way, interviews very usefully double as classroom tasks – you could get your students to interview each other, for example, using a set of questions that relates to your research topic.

The types of interviews generally used for AR are:

- Structured interviews
- Guided, or semi-structured interviews
- Open-ended, conversational-type interviews.

3.3.1.1 Structured interviews

These are the most controlled kinds of conversations, where the researcher wants to get the same specific information from each person. The advantage is that you can then compare responses to the same questions across all the people interviewed. Usually the questions are all set out in advance – in a similar way to a survey or questionnaire, which we discuss in the next section – and the interviewer goes through them in the same order with each person. The interviewer may use a 'tick-the-box' kind of coding scheme to record the answers. This means that many of the results of this type of interview can be turned into numerical data as some questions will involve closed, factual kinds of responses. If you have ever been interviewed by a market researcher in a shopping centre you have probably experienced this kind of interview.

3.3.1.2 Guided, or semi-structured interviews

As the name suggests, these types of interviews are still structured and organised but also more open. Usually you have a set of topics in mind that you want to explore and you may also have developed some specific questions, but you will allow for some flexibility according to how the interviewee responds. For example, you may want to 'probe' to get more details about some of the answers that crop up or make allowances for unexpected responses that will lead you into new discoveries. In general there will be a more exploratory and conversational feel to this interview than in the first type. The aim of a semi-structured interview is to enable you to make some kind of comparison across your participants' responses, but also to allow for individual diversity and flexibility. For new interviewers this kind of interview can be more difficult to manage as it requires some skill in following the lead of the participant. The advantage over the structured interview, however, is that you are likely to find out about some things in more depth and so will get richer information.

3.3.1.3 Open interviews

A third type of interview is an open one where there are no pre-planned questions. These interviews are unstructured and individualized – though this does not mean they should become aimless or shapeless because, of course, their purpose is to bring out issues related to your research. Usually you will have a set of questions or topics in mind but will allow the direction of the interview to be determined by the participant. You will be trying to get as much in-depth information as possible about the speaker's experiences, views, perspectives and beliefs. Here your role will be to acknowledge, probe and encourage the interviewee to say more about the overall topics you are interested in, but not to intervene in where the speaker decides the conversation should go.

Classroom voices

Felix Banda teaches a Year 2 English Communication course to students at the University of the Western Cape in South Africa. His AR focused on his isiXhosa speaking students. Despite 12 years of English tuition at school, they 'showed little or no English proficiency as determined from the quality of their spoken and written English communication'. He noticed 'a particular group of students that kept doing badly' and three of them 'had already repeated the course twice' (p. 8).

Felix discovered that the problems 'could in part be explained by the fact that they belonged to study groups, which they had formed to improve their chances of passing the course by pooling their knowledge'. However, he says 'there was no doubt in my mind that there was a negative influence in the groups and that without my intervention the whole group would keep failing' (p. 11).

His research aimed to find out what went on in these groups and why they seemed to be preventing the students from achieving. He focused on two groups involving 10 students in total and used a number of data collection tools: 1) students' writing samples; 2) one-on-one interviews with the students whose writing he had analysed; and 3) focus groups, which involved discussions with small groups of students. This is what he says about why he chose to use open interviews:

> Because some students had difficulties expressing themselves in English, I decided to have an unstructured interview with open-ended questions. My classroom experiences had shown that tightly focused and structured questions would restrict students' capacity to formulate answers. During these unstructured interviews, even those with limited English vocabulary had something to say because the open-ended question allowed them to qualify and clarify issues. The loose interview schedule also allowed students to talk freely with minimum interruptions ... this technique proved useful in tapping into the students' thinking processes and hence the strategies that they used in their academic writing. (p. 12)

Felix discovered that in their schooling the students had experienced teaching practices that did not help them to develop academic English. Most of the teaching had been conducted in informal isiXhosa or a mixture of isiXhosa and English. It had involved discussing essays in L1 and then translating them into English. Translation made things worse because the students had not been taught how to tell the difference between everyday dictionary meanings and the formal meanings used in writing essays.

Felix says that his research made him much more aware of the reasons for his students' writing problems and the strategies he needed to use to help them. He sensitised his students to the differences between formal and informal English, gave them a greater number and variety of written assignments, told them what was expected point by point, helped them with grammar, assisted them with dictionary use, and warned the students and other lecturers about 'the dangers of unregulated study groups' (p. 20).

(Banda, 2009)

Although it sounds as though they don't need much preparation, these kinds of interviews are actually the most demanding. They require a high level of trust between interviewer and interviewee and careful handling because of the unpredictability of the conversation. It's unlikely that you will be able to make comparisons across your interviews as easily as in the other two types because of the highly individualised nature of the responses. Also, while the information you gain will probably be rich and may give you unexpected insights, it needs a cautious and sympathetic analysis. You need to make sure you are not basing your insights on your own interpretations rather than those of the speaker.

3.3.1.4 Issues to consider when interviewing

If you decide to interview your students you need to be aware of the problem of the power-relationship. You are, after all, their teacher and students may say only what they believe their teachers want to hear! In essence, you are dealing here with an ethical issue (see Chapter 2) where you must take care to ensure that your status as their teacher does not affect the students' willingness to be involved. McKay (2006, p. 55) has some useful advice about how to handle this problem:

- Explain the purpose of the interview, what will be done with the information, and the benefits to participants.
- Be sensitive to students' responses and any awkwardness or nervousness that might arise.
- Provide feedback and reinforcement to responses throughout the interview, using thanks, praise and support.

You will also need to consider how to record the responses you get; usually a recorder or notes are the main ways. Audio-recording gives you an accurate record of what people say, but can seem intimidating and make the interviewee nervous. Note-taking is less intrusive but you will not be able to record word for word and having to write diverts your attention away from the speaker. Whichever technique you decide to use it's useful to be aware of the advantages and disadvantages and also to explain to the speaker beforehand which approach you will use and why.

Not all interviews are conducted with individuals and you may prefer to set up focus group interviews which involve using any one of the above approaches with groups of six to eight participants (see Krueger & Casey, 2000). Focus groups have the advantage of taking the individual spotlight off one speaker, who may get nervous or anxious about being interviewed, and allowing ideas and thoughts to be triggered by what others in the group say.

You will need to take quite a number of practical steps and decisions in carrying out interviews. The discussion below outlines these steps and provides you with checklists.

STEP 1: PREPARING

You will need to think about what you want to achieve in the interview – its main aims and purposes. Having done this you need a list of the topics to be covered. It's useful to break the list down into sub-topics so that the various issues are grouped together logically. Then you can develop more specific questions to ask about each issue. For example, you may want a range of question types that cover things like i) background/experience, ii) actions/events, iii) reactions/interpretations, iv) feelings/emotions, v) values/beliefs or vi) knowledge/information (see Patton, 2002). It's then very valuable to try out the questions with a friend or colleague to make sure they are easily understood and work well in getting you the kind of information you are looking for – the research term for this is *pilotting*. Pilotting is also one way of increasing the validity of your findings (see Chapter 2). Don't worry if you have to change or rewrite the questions – it's all part of the process of refining your ideas and making sure your interview eventually goes smoothly.

Action point

Prepare for your interview. Have you:

• thought about the general aims/purpose of the interview?	☐ Yes	☐ No
• decided on the main topics and sub-topics to be covered?	☐ Yes	☐ No
• developed questions for each topic?	☐ Yes	☐ No
• tried out the interviews with a colleague?	☐ Yes	☐ No
• adjusted your questions as necessary?	☐ Yes	☐ No

STEP 2: ORGANISING THE INTERVIEW

Richards (2003) has a useful set of pointers for this step in the process. He asks us to consider:

- who? (who will you select to interview, how many, in what order?): think also about whether the people you select cover all the perspectives you need to include;
- when? (how does the timing fit in with the requirements of your

research, how does it best suit your interviewees?): think about the best times in the research cycle when you will need the data and the best times when the speakers will not be busy or tired;

- where? (how quiet and private does the setting need to be, how is the setting likely to influence the interview?): think about how you can make the setting as appropriate, comfortable and attractive as possible to put the interviewee at ease;
- how long? (how much time does your interviewee have available, how much time do you require to get the information you need?): think about a feasible amount of time for what you are trying to find out (half-an-hour to an hour is probably about right);
- under what conditions? (what do you tell your interviewee about their ethical rights, how you will record the interview, what you will do with the data, and how you will check the information with them later?).

(Adapted from Richards, 2003, pp. 66-67)

Action point

Organise your interview. Have you:

- identified the range/number of people to interview? ☐ Yes ☐ No
- clarified when you will interview them? ☐ Yes ☐ No
- located where you will interview? ☐ Yes ☐ No
- decided on the length of the interview? ☐ Yes ☐ No
- thought through the conditions of the interview? ☐ Yes ☐ No

STEP 3: CONDUCTING THE INTERVIEW

One of the things I learned very early on was that interviewing is not always as easy as it sounds, even when you have prepared carefully and organised what you need to do to get going. The main things to watch out for are how you listen, how you ask questions, and how you go about asking your interviewee to clarify or expand what he or she says (based on Altrichter *et al.*, 1993).

- *Listening*: Remember it's the interviewee's comments and ideas you are looking for and not your own! Listening carefully not only shows you are interested in what the speaker has to say but gives them as full an opportunity as possible to say it! It's important not to interrupt but to give people time to get their thoughts together and express their ideas completely. (Sometimes as teachers we are not so good at doing that as we don't usually wait too long for students to reply!) It's also important not to evaluate or judge what people say, even when it might not be what you want to hear. If interviewees think you disagree with their opinions they are not likely to tell you the truth.

- *Asking questions*: Depending on which type of interview you decide to do, you are likely to be asking four different types of questions (by the way, 'questions' will not always take a question form but might be statements that get the interviewee to start talking).

  - *Warm-up questions* aim to establish a good rapport with your interviewee and to start off the interview with some gentle and familiar openings (e.g., *Tell me about the reading activity you like best*).
  - *Open questions* are ones where you are genuinely unaware of the possible replies and want to find out about the interviewee' s behaviours or opinions. These questions usually begin with how, what, why, when, where (e.g., *How did you go about planning the activity? What kinds of books do you like to read?*).
  - *Closed questions* are ones that expect yes/no answers (e.g., *Do you like learning English?*). Unlike open questions, they don't really invite a conversational style and if you overuse them the interview can begin to sound more like an interrogation. These kinds of questions are best used when you are likely to know the answer but want to check your assumptions.
  - *Closing questions* are ones used to wind down the interview. They give your interviewee a chance to put the final word (e.g., *Is there anything else you'd like to add? Is there anything else I should have asked you about this?*). Sometimes these kinds of questions can result in a surprising amount of extra information.

- *Clarifying/Expanding*: Because we can't control conversation-style answers in advance it is useful to have some probing strategies ready that ask interviewees to clarify, expand, rephrase and so on as the interview unfolds. Using these strategies not only ensures you get more detailed answers but also tells your interviewee you are interested in what he or she says. Probing strategies take different forms: confirming (*So what you are saying is ...*); exemplifying (*Can you give me an example of how ... ?*); interpreting (*Why do you think ... ? What do you think was meant to happen about ... ?*); clarifying (*So was it X or Y that happened?*); reviewing (*So can you summarise that ... ?*).

Classroom voices

One of my students, Simon Humphries, teaches in a college in Japan. He wanted to interview other teachers in his language centre about their attitudes towards the textbooks they were using. He was interested because the college had just changed its books and he wanted to compare his colleagues' reaction to the changes with his own. He asked his colleagues if he could observe them and then interviewed them afterwards.

> Before I began, I wrote some basic questions for semi-structured interviews, based on literature that covered people's reactions to change. Also, I examined the textbooks to highlight some areas that I thought might cause problems for my colleagues. A practical thing that I did during the observations was to use a three-colour pen. I wrote in red for questions that could be asked in the interviews. Some of these questions were simple ones relating to the content of their teaching, others related to their opinions. It was easy to spot these questions in amongst the other scribblings.
>
> I interviewed the teachers using a digital voice recorder. I recommend investing in one of these. Unlike placing a huge tape recorder between you and the respondent like a kind of barrier, these things are very small and unobtrusive. Two further advantages came from the portability and the digital side. I could carry it with me everywhere and listen to the recordings whilst I commuted to work and also record ideas when I had no pen or notepaper at hand. The digital side of the recording meant that I could transfer the audio files onto my computer. This freed me for another method of developing ideas and questions—'rough transcription'. I typed this on my computer whilst listening to my audio files as soon as I could after each interview.
>
> (Personal communication, 18 August 2008)

Now that we've looked at interviewing, let's turn to another major non-observational way of gathering information often used in AR.

3.3.2 Questionnaires/Surveys

It's best to use a questionnaire (also sometimes called a survey, checklist or schedule), rather than interviews, when you want to get responses from several people and you don't have time to interview. Dörnyei (2003, pp. 8-9) notes that questionnaires can get you three types of information: *factual or demographic* (who the interviewees are and their background/experiences); *behavioural* (what they do, or did in the past); *attitudinal* (attitudes, opinions, beliefs, interests and values).

Reflection point

Here is a list of 20 items that might be included in a questionnaire. Classify them into factual, behavioural or attitudinal. When you have finished compare your answers with a partner:

1. How often do you practise English outside the classroom?
2. Which activity did you like best from today's lesson?
3. How old are you?
4. Identify five characteristics of a good teacher.
5. What is your highest level of qualification?
6. Which part of this exercise did you complete first?
7. What was the main aim of today's lesson?
8. How many years have you been learning English?
9. Did journal writing help you to improve your learning?
10. I have written a journal before.
11. How many students are in your speaking group?
12. Were the computer-based activities easy for you to complete?
13. How well do you know the students in Group B?
14. Please add any other comments on how you teach grammar in your classroom.
15. What are your three most effective strategies for teaching listening?
16. I usually complete grammar homework immediately after school.
17. Note the thing you found most difficult about completing this exercise.
18. I plan what I am going to say before I speak.
19. Name (optional): ______________
20. Reading English is more important than speaking English.

You probably noticed that five of these items are factual (3, 5, 8, 11, 19), six are behavioural (1, 6, 10, 14, 16, 18) and nine are attitudinal (2, 4, 7, 9, 12, 13, 15, 17, 20). Maybe you also noticed other things about these items. First, several are presented as questions (e.g., 1-3), but others are statements (e.g., 16) or commands (e.g., 4). Second, the way the questions are phrased would attract different kinds of responses.

Some ask for concrete facts (3, 19), others suggest a choice from a range of possibilities (2, 13), some invite yes/no answers (10, 20), and some ask for a longer and more personal written response (14, 15). As you can see from this list there are different ways of going about designing items for your questionnaire and we'll consider some of these next. To do so we will look at two types of items: closed- ended and open-ended.

3.3.2.1 Closed-ended items

Closed items are probably the ones most frequently used in questionnaires. These are items for which there is a limited choice of answers. The main types are yes/no (or true/false); rating scales; numerical scales; multiple choice; and ranking scales. Analysing the data you get from closed-ended items involves calculating overall quantities and scores (see Chapter 4).

YES/NO

Going back to the list above, we can see that Q10 assumes a 'true' or 'false' answer. These kinds of items are used when the interviewee may not have advanced language abilities, is very young, or where the researcher wants to reduce the risk that too many shades of judgement may be required. A third option may be added where the choice between yes and no is too extreme:

I have written a journal before. Yes☐ No☐ Sometimes ☐

RATING SCALES

Rating scales give you a broader range of responses than yes/no. Likert scales (named after their inventor) are the most common and ask people to give the degree to which they agree with something usually by circling or ticking the responses. Let's take Q20 from our list as an example:

(Please tick ✔ the answer you agree with most)
Reading English is more important than speaking English
Strongly agree ☐ Agree ☐ Neutral ☐ Disagree ☐ Strongly disagree ☐

Some researchers prefer to use a four- or six-point scale to avoid responses from the middle option. For example, if you wanted a six-point scale you could replace 'neutral' with two items, something like 'somewhat agree' and 'somewhat disagree' or 'partly agree' and 'partly disagree'. There are different ways of formatting these kinds of responses, depending on who you are surveying, their age, and how they will best be able to understand the question and provide a response. The examples below provide some alternatives and you should select the one you think will be most suitable for your participants and your research.

Example 1

Please circle your view about each of these statements (1 = strongly agree; 2 = agree; 3 = neutral/neither agree nor disagree; 4 = disagree; 5 = strongly disagree).

1. Reading English is more important than speaking English	**1 2 3 4 5**

Example 2

For each statement below mark the ONE number which best reflects your view.

	Strongly disagree	**Disagree**	**Neutral**	**Agree**	**Strongly Agree**
1. Reading English is more important than speaking English	1	2	3	4	5

Example 3

Please circle the answer you like best.

Reading English is more important than speaking English	☺	😐	☹

(Here, instead of circle, you could have tick, cross or colour in, for example.)

Example 4

Please tick the box/ ✍ ✔ ❐

Reading English is more important than speaking English

☺ 😐 ☹

❐ ❐ ❐

A variation on the Likert scale is a *semantic scale* where you can avoid writing statements at all. You ask people to answer by providing their evaluations along a continuum, as I show here for Q12 above:

Please mark your opinion with a ✘

Were the computer-based activities easy for you to complete?

easy ____: ____: ____: ____✘ ____: ____difficult

Dörnyei (2003, p. 40) says that these kinds of scales can be used to get at various meanings (hence the name semantic): evaluation (overall positive or negative meaning, e.g., good➔bad); potency (overall strength or importance, e.g., helpful➔unhelpful); activity (overall level of action involved, e.g., quiet➔ loud).

NUMERICAL SCALES

These scales require giving a score about how you would evaluate something. Typically, you ask for a score out of five or ten, depending on the shades of difference you would like to find. For Q13 above, participants can be asked to do this kind of rating:

Give a score from 1 to 10 in the space below (1 = not at all; 10 = extremely well).
How well do you know the students in Group B? ______

One problem with this more open-ended scoring is that it's hard to tell whether one participant's 7 is more like another one's 9. To get a more exact picture, you can set out this item by specifying more exactly what the various scores indicate.

1= not at all 2 = a little 3 = fairly well 4 = very well 5 = extremely well

Another kind of numerical item is one where you can anticipate the range of answers and participants can select the one that applies to them. For example, Q8 in our list can be answered by giving the exact number of years.

How many years have you been learning English? _______ years

However, if you think participants are not sure of the exact number, you could ask them to complete as follows:

Please place a cross (X) in the appropriate box
How many years have you been learning English?

0–4 ❒	5–9 ❒	10–14 ❒	15–19 ❒	20–24 ❒	25+ ❒

MULTIPLE CHOICE ITEMS

These kinds of items are often used in tests or exams so are quite familiar to teacher researchers. Participants are usually asked to mark one option. But sometimes you might want a range of items that allow participants to mark more than one option, to indicate where something does not apply (or where the participant may not be sure), or provide an opportunity to add options not on the list. A question on our list that lends itself to multiple choice is Q7.

Please circle ONE number that best reflects your answer.

What was the main aim of today's lesson?

1. To improve speaking
2. To improve reading

3. To improve listening

Here the participant is asked to select one response from three items. To extend this item to include other options, it could be set out as follows:

Please circle ALL the numbers that best reflect your answer.
What was the main aim of today's lesson?

1. To improve speaking
2. To improve reading
3. To improve listening
4. To improve pronunciation
5. None of the above
6. Not sure
7. Other (please specify): ______________________________

RANK ORDER ITEMS

Sometimes we want participants to let us know about their preferences, values or opinions from a list of possible alternatives. These items ask them to say what is most important to them – the *order* rather than the *extent* of importance. For example, if Q17 related to a writing exercise, we could turn it into an item like this:

Note the things you found most difficult about completing this writing exercise. (Indicate 1 for the most difficult and 5 for the least difficult)
Finding a topic ________
Researching the information ________
Making a plan or outline ________
Deciding where different information should go ________
Developing the arguments ________

Ranked items are not that straightforward to develop as we may include things that are not at all important to participants and exclude others. Also, if we include too many items it will be difficult for participants to select the order among lots of alternatives. Dörnyei (2003) notes that ranked items are not easy to process statistically, because they only indicate the order and not the extent or value in relation to other items. "That is, if something is ranked third, the value '3' does not necessarily mean that the degree of one's attitude is 3 out of, say, 5" (p. 45).

The *value* of the third item could be a long way from 2 or 4 in the ranking, or even not important at all. For example, on the above list, a participant might indicate *finding a topic* as 5, but its value to completing the exercise would be zero if the activity requires that you write on a particular topic anyway. (We'll discuss issues to do with numerical or statistical analysis in more detail in Chapter 4.)

Now that we've considered some of the main ways to develop closed items, let's move on to open-ended items which are an alternative way of presenting survey questions.

3.3.2.2 Open-ended items

In contrast to the closed type, these are items that look for a free-form response. You could, in fact, have a questionnaire that consists only of open-ended items, but more usually these items complement closed items and take the responses further. It is often very useful to ask the same kind of question using an open-ended form because then you get a different perspective. Usually, the responses are fairly short but give you information that may not be easily captured numerically. Open-ended items are analysed by describing the trends, themes or patterns of ideas you find in them (see Chapter 4). In AR reports they are often used to give examples of quotes from participants. Open-ended questions can be constructed along a continuum from completely open to guided to structured.

OPEN ITEMS

These items can either ask for concrete information or be very open to a variety of answers. Q19 'Name (optional): _______' in our list is an example of a concrete item. An example of an open item is Q14. A box or lines for comments is usually supplied beneath the question.

Please add any other comments on how you teach grammar in your classroom.

In this type of question, the participant is completely free to provide a personal, free-ranging kind of response. These questions are especially useful in giving the participants an opportunity to say things they feel might have been missed out in the survey.

GUIDED ITEMS

A guided item is less open as it suggests the kinds of things that you want participants to comment on further. Here is an example about grammar:

> If you rated your students' knowledge of grammar 'poor', please explain why:
>
> ____
>
> ____

This kind of question asks your participants to clarify or expand on a response and can give you information that is not obvious from the numerical response. Another kind of guided item is when you ask respondents to expand on an item they have selected as *Other*:

> Grammar is important in language learning because it:
>
> ❒ Provides students with rules
> ❒ Helps them to become more fluent
> ❒ Gives them a language to talk about language
> ❒ Helps them to self-correct
> ❒ Enables them to become more accurate
> ❒ Other (please specify and explain your response) ______________
>
> ____
>
> Reasons: ______________________________________
>
> ____

STRUCTURED ITEMS

Sometimes we want to provide participants with a set of structures for responding to the question – a kind of skeleton for the types of things we want them to select for comment. Items that ask them to complete the sentence are useful for this purpose, as in this modified example of the grammar item:

> Please provide comments on teaching grammar by completing the sentences:
>
> The thing I like best about teaching grammar is ________________
>
> ____
>
> The thing I like least about teaching grammar is ________________
>
> ____

My most difficult challenge in teaching grammar is ________________
____

Action point

Select up to three to four items from the Reflection point list on page 96. Alternatively, write three different items that would fit in with your own research.

With a partner, develop a format for each one that would fit into a questionnaire. Discuss whether there are different ways of setting out these items to get different kinds of responses. Use the ideas from the examples in this section.

3.3.2.3 Questionnaire layout

It's useful to think about how you will lay out your questionnaire so that it flows in a clear sequence and the respondents know what to do. Here is a skeleton outline of the structure that a questionnaire usually follows:

Title of project:	Clear and succinct name of project.
Researcher:	Name and role of researcher(s) and who they are.
Purpose of project:	What the project aims to do and to find out, what outcomes are expected.
Instructions:	General instructions on filling in the questionnaire (specific instructions are also included for sections or individual items).
Time:	Approximately how long it should take to fill in.
Items:	The open, closed or mixed questions that make up the questionnaire and specific instructions for filling them in.
Other information:	Contact name/email address for returning questionnaire.
Ethical statement:	Where necessary, a statement about meeting ethical considerations and/or indication of the confidentiality of the responses.
Thanks:	Last but not least! A statement of thanks to the respondent (written or symbol ☺).

Classroom voices

Eliana Santana-Williamson worked with students in Brazil to develop critical and reflective approaches to teacher professional development through journal writing. She saw these approaches as a way of introducing her students to current ideas about their development as teachers.

> Doubting that I would be effective by simply asking my students to reflect, I decided first to get to know their experience with reflection. In order to collect this information, student teachers responded to a survey on their first day of class. (p. 36)

Eliana's survey provides a useful example of a mixture of closed and open-ended items that can be included in a short questionnaire.

1. Name (optional): ______________________________
2. Age: ____________
3. Are you a teacher? YES NO
4. If yes, how many years of experience do you have? ______________
5. Have you had any previous training as a language teacher YES NO
6. If YES, describe your previous experience:

   ____

   ____

   ____

7. Have you ever had any experience writing class journals as a student or a teacher (consider elementary and high school)? YES NO
8. If YES, how difficult was it?

   VERY DIFFICULT DIFFICULT NOT EASY EASY
9. Do you think that writing journals helped you somehow? YES NO
10. If YES, how?

    ____

    ____

    ____

(Santana-Williamson, 2001, p. 44)

Action point

Use Eliana's survey as a model to start constructing your own questionnaire items. When you have finished, try out the questionnaire on a colleague to see how easy he or she finds it to answer the questions. Get feedback on what could be changed to make the questionnaire as clear and user-friendly as possible.

Designing a questionnaire may sound easy – and indeed it may be the first method that comes to mind when you think about doing research – but it needs some careful thought and planning if you are to get the information you need in a useable form. There is a lot of trial and error involved in getting to a good final version so to make sure you get the answers you want you should pilot the questionnaire before using it. This means trying it out on the type of participant who is likely to be answering it, but who won't eventually be involved in your research. Piloting usually alerts you to some of the most common problems and pitfalls in questionnaire design:

- Ambiguous questions: *Which class do you teach?* (this is not much good if the participants teach a number of classes in a number of schools).
- Multiple questions: *Do you enjoy reading, and how skilled are you in listening?* (there are too many aspects to the question – it is actually two questions, one requiring a closed answer and the other, an open answer).
- Knowledge: *How frequently do you use the subjunctive in writing*? (if your participants do not know what a subjunctive is, they can't answer this question).
- Language level: *What are your expectations of this introductory course?* (this will not work if your students are beginners or of a young age).
- Literacy level: *What complexities of controlling grammatical knowledge emerge in your learning?* (replies will be difficult if the language of the question is too dense and complex, and/or if the respondents have limited first or second language literacy. You may need to use the first language – see Appendix 3.1 for an example from Japan).

You can get some way in sorting out these problems if you sit down and try the questionnaire out on yourself too to see whether you could answer it!

3.3.3 Journals and logs

Keeping a journal, diary or log is common in AR. Duong, whose research we looked at in the section on observation, refers to using a teaching log. And this is another way of capturing the events that occur in AR. In general, journals and logs are unlikely to be used by themselves. Usually they are combined with other methods such as observations or interviews. They are extremely useful though as a way of capturing significant reflections and events in an ongoing way. Table 3.6 presents some of the most common types of journal, their aims, entry timings, and the general questions or issues they typically answer.

Journal writing is something of a 'classic' tool in AR as it allows you to record the events and happenings in your location, your reflections, beliefs and teaching philosophies, your ideas and insights about your practice, and your personal histories as a teacher researcher. However, it is not something that appeals to everyone (to be honest, it's not my preferred option!), so consider whether you want to include it in your investigation, and if so, how and when you will write the entries.

Table 3.6 Using journals in action research

Type of journal	*Aim*	*Timing of entry*	*Question(s) addressed*
Factual journal	To record observations, incidents or events in a factual way	Immediately after the lesson/events	*What is happening here?*
Descriptive journal (sometimes 'double-entry' – factual events on one side of page, and reactions on other)	To note factual events and personal reactions to them	As soon as possible after the lesson/events	*What is happening here? What are my perceptions/ attitudes about the happenings?*
Reflective journal	To capture 'stream-of-consciousness' ideas, thoughts, reflections, insights, feelings, reactions to lesson/ events	Quite soon after the lesson/events, and after thinking about and processing what occurred	*What are my responses to/ interpretations of what has happened? What meanings can I make about these happenings?*
Daily/Weekly log	To construct an ongoing record of daily or weekly events	At the end of the period of time when the events took place	*What happened in sequence over my teaching day/week?*
Memoir journal ('stepping stones' (Progoff, 1975) or 'significant moments')	To develop an account of your development as a teacher and theories about your teaching	At a time in the research process when you want to articulate your values and theories as a teacher	*What and who influenced my development as a teacher and my teaching philosophies?*

Classroom voices

Isabella, the teacher from Italy, who gave us the first classroom voice in Chapter 1, says this about diary writing:

> Going back to my diary and reading it again brings back the flavour of those days, the difficulties as well as the pleasure I used to derive from my students' feedback on the efficacy of the new procedures I had set up.

On the other hand, her colleague Giancarlo points out some of challenges of keeping a journal:

> Every time I missed the opportunity to write (because of laziness or lack of time) I would later on realise that I had lost something essential as it prevented me from understanding other data I had collected, something that I could no longer recover.

(Data translated and supplied by Graziella Pozzo)

3.3.4 Classroom documents

Classrooms are full of all kinds of written documents – syllabus guidelines, lesson plans, textbooks, readers, students' written texts, exercises, illustrations, maps, dictionaries and so on. Any of these can become a means for collecting data and identifying key issues – or even being confronted with some surprising feedback, as this example shows.

Classroom voices

Ponsawarn, a teacher originally from Thailand who teaches in Australia, was teaching an adult ESOL evening class and wanted to explore the best use of commercially produced teaching materials to support her students' reading development. Her specific question was:

> Do activities around reading such as vocabulary work, silent reading, syllabification practice, language games and dictation support the development of reading skills?

She says:

> In my enthusiasm to start the project I was oblivious to the fact that my learners lacked the language skills needed to tackle the reading texts. The initial outcome was rather negative and one evening two Chinese students, a husband and wife, with no basic education in first language came to me with this letter.

> Dear teacher
>
> Would I give you some advice for this course? Would you mind slowing down the speed of the class, and teaching us step by step. Because our English are poor. We cannot understand some you teached.
>
> Thank you

The students' letter caused Ponsawarn to re-evaluate the way she was teaching the materials and to break down the activities related to them into more manageable and achievable chunks.

(Brawn, 2005, p. 55)

Try some of the following ideas to collect data through classroom documents:

- Get your students to write a letter to the class you will teach next semester or year. Ask them to tell the new students about the best way to learn in your class. Identify the main strategies and tips your students mention.
- Collect copies of your students' writing once a week over a whole term. Identify the main improvements that the students have made, and diagnose what areas you need to focus on to assist them further.
- Collect your lesson notes for a logical period of time (e.g., a whole unit of work, a whole week, a whole term). Analyse them to see what kinds of activities, skills materials (or any other aspects) you tend to focus on. Think about the strengths and weaknesses in the patterns of your lesson planning.
- Collect a portfolio or dossier of students' work from one individual, a group, or all of your students over a period of time. Identify some obvious signs of learning development in these documents and discuss them with your students.
- Get your participants to draw pictures that represent how they feel about different aspects of learning (e.g., learning grammar, reading stories, practising listening tasks, learning vocabulary, doing practicum teaching). Identify what the messages in the pictures are telling you about their learning.

Let's focus in a little more on one of these ideas. In recent times, portfolio assessment, where students' work is collected and kept in a portfolio over a period of time, and student self-assessment, where students evaluate their own progress, have become popular ways of tracking student progress, and diagnosing areas for further development. As part of an ongoing process of curriculum development they can be a very valuable alternative to the more traditional forms of testing or examination.

Classroom voices

Here's how a high school teacher in Japan, Keiko Takahashi, used portfolios to deepen her understanding about teaching and revitalise the curriculum she taught. In her account of her research, she refers to 'the power of portfolios' (p. 216).

> In the writing class for 2nd-year students, I asked the students to write a report assessing their portfolios at the end of the school year in March. When they looked over all the worksheets in their file, they noticed improvements. By reflecting on their learning history, students gained confidence.
>
> However, slow learners seemed to make so little improvement that I often did not notice the improvement in class. For example, I was discouraged that the slower learners were unable to have 3-minute conversations, even in December, and to see them spending an entire period writing only 10 sentences. Thus, I didn't expect they could make improvements, and I began wondering whether this class was helping them to learn. However, their semester reports showed that their speaking and writing skills did improve and that they had gained confidence in learning English. Some students wrote the following comments:
>
> > Hiromi: *It was very difficult or almost impossible to have a 2-minute conversation even in October. I didn't know how to keep a conversation going. It's still difficult to ask new questions but I came to use conversation strategies more and more.* (Third portfolio, February 2003)
> >
> > Ichiro: *I couldn't speak English at all in April, but now I can use the expression 'How ya doin'?' to open a conversation, 'How 'bout you?' to ask the same question, and 'Nice talking with you!' to close a conversation. This is a big change for me.* (Third portfolio, February 2003)
> >
> > Kaori: *I didn't know any conversation strategies. But I now use the shadowing strategy and it is very helpful to keep a conversation going.* (Third portfolio, February 2003)
>
> For the speaking test in December, most students in the general class failed to have a 3-minute conversation. I gave a speaking test three times a year after I had covered a couple of topics. Students prepared for all topics but didn't know until the test started which topic they would have to talk about and who their partner would be. However, after writing their semester reports the students gained confidence. I was surprised that for the speaking test held in March, most students succeeded in having a 3-minute conversation.
>
> (Sato & Takahashi, 2008, pp. 216-217)

Action point

What kinds of documents exist in your classroom? Collect samples of those you use in one lesson. How could you use these documents as data for your AR? Brainstorm some ideas with your colleagues.

Are there documents you don't currently use, such as the student letter or the portfolios mentioned in the classroom voices above? Brainstorm some more ideas with your colleagues for using classroom documents creatively in AR.

3.3.5 Using/Incorporating technology into data collection

This is a big topic and I will only provide a very brief summary here. Of course, as we're all aware, rapid advances in technology now offer infinite possibilities for exchanging information and they are also a boon to action researchers. To get us started, here are just a few ideas from teachers in Malaysia about how they use technology to develop their reflections and insights on teaching and to collect information.

Classroom voices

The teachers were attending the second ***Teaching and Learning English in Asia (TLEiA)*** Conference, in Langkawi, Malaysia in June 2007. They shared these ideas about bringing technology into their teaching and research:

- Use video to record yourself when trying out different teaching strategies.
- Use a platform like WebCT for uploading materials, articles, photos which can then be discussed with colleagues/students.
- Use a mobile phone/digital camera for classroom photos/brief videos.
- Get students to send SMS text messages to each other to practise certain structures.
- Use PowerPoint to collate a classroom learning scrapbook (students can upload photos, texts and images that are significant to them).
- Use an MP3 player for recording classroom interaction or brief memos to yourself.

Hobson and Smolin (2001, pp. 83-103) offer other great ideas about using technology for action research. I'll highlight two of the main areas they cover:

1. *Expand your journal writing*: Use the computer to make entries, construct

tables, organise concepts (e.g., through the software program Inspiration), dialogue with other writers, create a web-based response journal (e.g, using Nicenet: http://www.nicenet.org), start a blog where you can post ideas and get responses.

2. *Conduct interviews and focus groups*: Use discussion groups, listservs and chat rooms to extend your research way beyond your own school, or even country. Discussion forums are electronic bulletin boards where you can interact with others and develop discussion threads on particular questions or topics. Try http://www.tesol.org/_tesol/index.asp (Teachers of English as a second language), go to Education and then click on Discussion for ones related to language teaching. You can find out what other teachers or researchers are saying about your topic, or what they are experiencing or finding that might relate to your own research. Listservs are operated through email and when you join a list you then get messages posted to your email account on different topics. This is an easy way of getting many responses and ideas about research questions or challenges you might want answered. For example, the American Educational Research Association offers one on action research (see http://coe.westga.edu/arsig/listserv2.htm). Chat rooms are another option. Unlike discussion groups and listservs, which are asynchronous, they are synchronous, that is you can chat to others who are present with you in the same chat room in 'real time'. If you can't find a discussion forum or chat room, you can create your own. Yahoo, for example, offers you this facility. Go to http://messenger.yahoo.com, click on Download and you can then register yourself to create a 'club' of members who can form a discussion room and share web links to discuss various aspects of your AR.

Hobson and Smolen (2001, p. 101) remind us that it remains to be seen how technology will affect opportunities to AR:

> How is what we learn shaped by conversations with people we never meet in person? How is that form of inquiry different from seeking out individuals in our schools and communities, conducting interviews, and forming focus groups to explore a research interest? Can a research project employ both face-to-face research methods and technology assisted methods with similar results or satisfaction?

None of the answers to these questions is very clear, but what is clear is that technology holds out many exciting possibilities for action researchers to enhance the ways they collect data and to be in touch with each other as they do so (see also Chapter 5).

3.4 Cross-checking and strengthening the information

One of the criticisms sometimes levelled at AR – and in fact at qualitative research more generally – is whether the data are just too subjective. Teachers and students new to research often wonder about this too, as these questions I have been asked show us:

Classroom voices

What's the point of doing piffling little research on my own classroom? What I find won't apply to any other classrooms, will it? (Australia)

Qualitative research sounds to me like something subjective and apt to be biased.

My question is: To what extent are the results credible? (Vietnam)

Of course, AR cannot claim to be able to generalise to other classrooms, as the first comment above asks. It is local research which we do in our own classrooms. Nevertheless, what we find might still have something to say to other teachers who are facing similar issues in their own teaching and our findings might give them new ideas. In other words our research may have *resonance* in other teaching contexts. The second question asks, quite reasonably, whether our results can be believed (*are they credible?*), and it is here that we need to find ways to strengthen the data, making sure we adopt an objective approach to the information we collect.

One key way to do this, which has been widely adopted in research requiring reflection and interpretation, is through *triangulation*. This term comes originally from the fields of 'navigation, astronomy and surveying', where different bearings and measurements are taken to make sure that a particular location is accurate (Bailey, 2006, p. 131). If we apply this to data collection it means that a combination of angles on the data will help give us more objectivity. This usually means collecting more than one type of data (it doesn't necessarily mean three types, although the term triangulation seems to suggest this). Then you can compare, contrast and cross-check to see whether what you are finding through one source is backed up by other evidence. In this way you can be more confident that your reflections and conclusions are supported by the data and not just by your own presuppositions or biases.

Classroom voices

Let's go back to Duong's research, which we have looked at several times in this chapter. She describes briefly how and why she ended up triangulating her data.

> My main research question was to see whether independent work or independent learning was practiced in my speaking-oral presentation classes and how it took place. I was largely researching my own practice ... (p. 36)
>
> The data were collected through document review, class observations and interviews. (p. 38)

Document review involved collecting, reading and taking notes about documents related to learner autonomy. She also looked at 'administrative documents, such as proposals, progress reports, agendas, announcements, minutes of meetings and other internal documents'. Class observations were conducted in two classes containing 99 students in all, by videotaping, taking observational notes, and keeping teaching logs. She also asked her students to keep journals of class events, and sometimes asked other teachers or students to comment on what had happened in class to compare with her own notes. Finally, she interviewed six students from two classes, three or four times each at the beginning, middle and end of the course.

She comments:

> I used these three main tools to collect the data, and then I classified and categorized it. I used multiple sources of data to identify patterns and avoid bias towards one set of data. (p. 39)

(Oanh, 2006, pp. 35-46)

Duong's data sources were extensive and you may find you don't need to collect data through such a wide range of methods. The number of sources will depend on your research focus, whether you are conducting the research for formal study, and the time and resources you have available to you. But you should try as much as possible to rely on more than one source of information.

Apart from different sources of data, sometimes called *methods triangulation*, you can also achieve triangulation in other ways. Denzin (1978, cited in Burns, 1999, p. 164) suggests four more types. Here I've illustrated how Duong's research included these different ways of triangulating:

- Time triangulation (data are collected at different points in time): Duong interviewed students at the beginning, middle and end of the course.

- Space triangulation (data are collected with different subgroups of people): Duong collected data in more than one class so that she could compare across two different groups.
- Researcher triangulation (data are collected by more than one researcher): Duong asked other teachers and students to collect data to compare with her own.
- Theory triangulation (data are analysed from more than one theoretical perspective): Duong consulted documents related to learner autonomy but also developed theoretical ideas from her own and others' observations and reflections.

Triangulation has a number of advantages. Not only does it provide a more balanced picture, it can also help to explain things that seem to contradict or not support each other. It also allows us to get rounded perspectives from all the people involved (students, other teachers, school administrators, parents) rather than relying on a limited set of informers (Altrichter *et al.*, 1993). But it can also appear daunting if you are not used to collecting so much data (as you'll see in Jerry Talandis Jr's comments at the beginning of Chapter 4), or if the people concerned are not used to being involved in research. It can even mean doing a radical reassessment of your own biases as new insights emerge from different sources. This experience can sit uncomfortably at first and seem a bit threatening. The best advice I can offer is to be aware of how triangulation can help to make your research stronger and richer, and to adapt the idea of triangulation to suit the time, energy and resources you have available. In Chapter 4, we will look at triangulation again, along with other ways of making your data analysis more robust and credible. For the moment, keep in mind that it is something important to consider as part of the process of collecting data for AR.

3.5 Summary point

I hope this chapter has given you a better idea of some of the tools that can be used to collect data. We've looked at a range of observational tools (answering the question: *What do I need to see?*) as well as non-obervational tools (*What do I need to know?*). We've also considered documents that can double as data collection tools. In the process of collecting data it's useful to decide how technology can be incorporated as well as how your data collection procedures can be strengthened through triangulation to increase the quality and rigour of the research.

Please bear in mind that the ideas I've presented are not exhaustive. By building on some of these methods, you may be able to think of any number of original and exciting ways to collect data that will answer your questions. The way these tools can be used and adapted is only limited by your own imagination, creativity and experimentation as an action researcher. Don't be discouraged, either, if some of your attempts at collecting data don't always go the way you intended or fail to give you the results you wanted or expected. These experiences have certainly happened to me and lots of other action researchers! Like teaching itself, research is a 'messy' process and the best way to learn more about AR and about collecting data is to keep trying things out. To illustrate this point, Jennifer Weathers, who worked as a foreign English teacher at a university in northeast China, offers a very honest account of the trials, tribulations and errors of finding good ways to get data.

Classroom voices

During this initial stage of my research, I tried many methods of collecting data. After the first lesson of the term, I began keeping a teaching journal to help me record and process my observations and reflections. I also planned to survey and interview the students in the class after each cycle to discover their reactions to the changes … During the 3rd week of the term, I began tape-recording each lesson … However after recording two classes, I discovered that the sound quality was too poor to identify the speakers or hear their comments clearly. The following week, I tried tape-recording several small-group discussions instead … Unfortunately, the sound quality was even worse … In addition I observed that many of the students seemed uncomfortable or distracted by the recorders … I decided to discontinue recording.

> In the third week I also invited a friend, Ying, to begin observing the class [using a seating chart and checklist] … After the class, Ying expressed difficulty in accurately recording each student's participation because she was sitting behind the students and because often several students answered simultaneously during whole class discussions … Throughout the rest of the term, Ying continued to observe the class. I did not ask her to take notes … but we often discussed our impressions of the lessons and the students' responses to them.

Because obtaining … recordings and observations was largely unsuccessful, I proceeded with … my own perceptions chronicled in my teaching journal [and] by consulting Ying and the students themselves.

(Weathers, 2006, p. 175)

Jennifer's account reminds us of some of the things action researchers learn along the way about collecting data. To round off the chapter, I'll summarise the main points below. After reading the summary, why not go back to the pre-reading questions at the beginning of the chapter and see whether you now have a better grasp of:

- identifying the main ways used to collect data for action research;
- combining classroom activities and data collection;
- selecting appropriate methods for your research questions;
- considering a range of observation methods (observing, noting, recording);
- considering a range of non-observation methods (surveying, interviewing, journaling);
- incorporating technology into data collection;
- strengthening your data collection through triangulation;
- understanding the 'messy' nature of research.

Appendix 3.1

Tim Marchand is an EFL teacher at Kansai Ohkura Junior High School in Japan. He teaches oral communication to five classes of 14- to 15-year-olds. To improve his students' interaction in class he taught 'meta-communication phrases' (expressions used to keep the conversation going, e.g., *I don't understand, what's ... in Japanese?*). After teaching them, he wanted the students to indicate their responses to the various phrases he had taught. He devised this questionnaire for one of the phrases.

'How do you spell —?'	strongly agree 非常にそう思う	agree そう思う	neither agree nor disagree どちらとも言えない	disagree そうは思わない	strongly disagree 決してそうは思わない
I'm confident saying this in English この文は英吾で話す自信がある					
I will use this phrase in the future この文はこれから使いるだろう.					
I often used this in class この文はクラスでよく使いました					
Instead of saying this, I usually said this in Japanese to the teacher この文は英吾でじゃなく、だいたい日本語で話しました					
Instead of saying this , I usually asked another student この文を使いらず、だいたい他の生徒に聞きました					
Instead of saying this, I usually kept silent この文を使いらず、たいたい黙っていた					

(Marchand, 2008)

References

Aldana, A. (2005). The process of writing a text by using cooperative learning. *Profile: Issues in Teachers' Professional Development*, 6, 47-57.

Al-Fahdi, H. M. (2006). English teachers' use of oral feedback. In S. Borg (Ed.), *Classroom research in English language teaching in Oman* (pp. 40-46). Sultanate of Oman: Ministry of Education.

Altrichter, H., Posch, P., & Somekh, B. (1993). *Teachers investigate their work: An introduction to the methods of action research*. Abingdon: Routledge.

Bailey, K. (2006). *Language teacher supervision*. New York: Cambridge University Press.

Banda, F. (2009). Challenges of teaching academic writing skills to students with limited exposure to English. In L. Makaleli (Ed.), *Language teacher research in Africa* (pp. 7-20). Alexandria, VA: TESOL.

Brawn, P. (2005). Creating teaching materials that support learning. In A. Burns, & H. de Silva Joyce (Eds.), *Teachers' voices 8: Explicitly supporting reading and writing in the classroom* (pp. 54-61). Sydney: National Centre for English Language Teaching and Research.

Burgess, R. G. (1984). *In the field: An introduction to field research*. London: Allen and Unwin.

Burns, A. (1999). *Collaborative action research for English language teachers*. Cambridge: Cambridge University Press.

Denzin, N. K. (Ed.). (1978). *Sociological methods: A source book*. Chicago: Aldine.

Dörnyei, Z. (2003). *Questionnaires in second language research: Construction, administration and processing*. Mahwah, NJ: Lawrence Erlbaum Associates.

Fanselow, J. (1987). *Breaking rules: Generating and exploring alternatives in language teaching*. White Plains, NY: Longman.

Hobson, D., & Smolin, L. (2001). Teacher researchers go online. In G. Burnaford, J. Fischer, & D. Hobson (Eds.), *Teachers doing research: The power of action through inquiry* (pp. 83-118). Mahwah, NJ: Lawrence Erlbaum Associates.

Krueger, R. A., & Casey, M. A. (2000). *Focus groups: A practical guide for applied research*. Thousand Oaks, CA: Sage.

Marchand, T. (2008). The effectiveness of explicit instruction of 'meta-communication' phrases at breaking the culture of silence in a Japanese classroom. Unpublished paper. Aston University, Birmingham, UK.

McKay, S. L. (2006). *Researching second language classrooms*. Mahwah, NJ: Lawrence Erlbaum Associates.

Mendoza López, E. M. (2005). Current state of the teaching of process writing in EFL classes: An observational study in the last two years in secondary school. *Profile: Issues in Teachers' Professional Development*, 6, 23-36.

Oanh, D. T. H. (2006). Learner autonomy in an Asian context: Independent learning and independent work at the university level. In T. S. C. Farrell (Ed.), *Language teacher research in Asia* (pp. 35-46). Alexandria, VA: TESOL.

Patton, M. Q. (2002). *Qualitative research and evaluation methods.* 3rd edition. Thousand Oaks, CA: Sage.

Progoff, I. (1975). *At a journal workshop.* New York: Houghton-Mifflin.

Richards, K. (2003). *Qualitative inquiry in TESOL.* London: Palgrave Macmillan.

Richards, J. C., & Farrell, T. S. C. (2006). *Professional development for language teachers: Strategies for teacher learning.* New York: Cambridge University Press.

Santana-Williamson, E. (2001). Early reflections: Journaling a way into teaching. In J. Edge (Ed.), *Action research* (pp. 33-44). Alexandria, VA: TESOL.

Sato, K., & Takahashi, K. (2008). Curriculum revitalization in a Japanese high school: Teacher-teacher and teacher-university collaboration. In D. Hayes, & J. Sharkey (Eds.), *Revitalizing a program for school-age learners through curricular innovation* (pp. 205-237). Alexandria, VA: TESOL.

Simpson, M., & Tuson, J. (1995). *Using observations in small-scale research: A beginner's guide.* Glasgow: Scottish Council for Research in Education.

Spada, N., & Fröhlich, M. (1995). *The Communicative Orientation of Language Teaching (COLT) observation scheme.* Sydney: National Centre for English Language Teaching and Research.

Stevenson, C. (1998). *Teaching ten to fourteen year olds.* 2nd edition. New York: Longman.

Troudi, S. (2007). Negotiating with multiple repeaters. In C. Coombe, & L. Barlow (Eds.), *Language teachers research in the Middle East* (pp. 161-172). Alexandria, VA: TESOL.

Weathers, J. (2006). How does course content affect students' willingness to communicate in the L2? In T. S. C. Farrell (Ed.), *Language teacher research in Asia* (pp. 171-184). Alexandria, VA: TESOL.

CHAPTER 4

Observe – Observing the Results of the Plan

Pre-reading questions

1. What are your current ideas about how to make sense of the data you've collected? Make a 'start list' of your thoughts and reflections.
2. What materials, equipment, or facilities do you think you will need for data analysis?
3. What skills and knowledge will you need? How can you develop them? Who can help you to develop them?

Keep these questions in mind as you read the chapter.

Now that we have looked at what's involved in collecting data, in this chapter we turn to ways of analysing and synthesising your data and making sense of the various types of information you've collected. Because I've presented the discussions in Chapters 3 and 4 consecutively that might give you the impression that first you collect the data and then, when they are all collected, you analyse them. But in AR nothing could be further from the truth. We've already noted that AR is a recursive spiral or cycle of action and reflection, and that means you start examining and analysing the data in a dynamic way right from the very beginning.

4.1 Preparing for data analysis

Classroom voices

Jerry Talandis Jr teaches at Toyama College of Foreign Languages in Japan. Jerry was studying by distance in a postgraduate course at a university in the UK. Part of his course involved completing an AR study. His focus was on how an electronic discussion list supports students completing a distance course and what kind of communication strategies they use. This is what he told me about his experiences of preparing for data analysis:

A key challenge I faced on this project was the sheer mountain of data I had collected. I had hundreds of discussion list posts, private emails, phone conversation transcripts, theory memos, and scads of site user statistics to crunch. Finding a common narrative thread was a big challenge. I remember printing everything out at one point, laying it all out on the floor of an entire room in my house. In the end I was grateful to have a good amount of quantitative data, and I appreciated the opportunity to blend it with the qualitative sources.

(Personal communication, 28 October 2008)

Please don't be daunted by the idea of having to analyse data when you begin doing AR. Although it's true that, like Jerry, many people new (and even not so new) to AR can find this part of the process challenging, it is made much more manageable if you analyse as you go along. In fact, reflecting on your data *in combination* with doing the action is essential in AR. Begin by reading through the first set of data you get as soon as you can and noting down any ideas and thoughts that come to mind. I agree with Burnaford (2001, p. 67) when she says, '[o]ngoing reflection is satisfying and makes the research worthwhile; looking at a mountain of information at the end of a month of collecting data can be a hopeless process'.

Bear in mind that by analysing data as you go you are also finding a way to distance yourself from the hurly-burly of the classroom and its immediate activities and to get some rather more objective ideas. Another useful thing to do is to keep returning to your research focus or question. You can then begin to get at the meaning of the data by asking yourself reflective questions like:

- Do these data answer my questions? If so, how?
- What are the main messages so far?
- What are the gaps in the messages I still need to fill?
- Am I still asking the right questions or are the data telling me that something else is more important?
- Do I need other kinds of data to help me really see what I am looking for?
- To answer my questions, are some pieces of data more important than others?

Analysing AR data is a continuing process of reducing information to find explanations and patterns. There are no 'quick-fix' rules for this type of analysis. Try to extract the key meanings and messages and centre your attention on what the data are telling you. In this way you will refine your understanding about what is going on. You can draw out new concepts, develop personal theories and find fresh possibilities for classroom practice that you can test out in further cycles. Some people refer to this analysis process as 'squashing' or, as Jerry also called it, 'crunching' the data. Calhoun (1994, cited in Burnaford, 2001, p. 68) refers to it as 'squeezing' the data to see what meanings we can find.

Although it's a really good idea to begin scrutinising and reflecting on your data as soon as you can, you will inevitably get to a stopping point where you are ready to look back over the whole data set. There are then some useful steps you can follow to get an overall framework for your analysis.

1. Assembling your data
   - Collect all the data you have as well as any ongoing reflections you have made about them.
   - Review your initial and/or your revised questions.
   - Start going though your data and look for broad patterns, ideas or trends that seem to answer your questions.
2. Coding the data
   - Based on the broad picture you have developed, start refining it by coding your data into more specific patterns or categories (coding is discussed in more detail in the next sections).
   - Identify which of your data sources you can code qualitatively (e.g., journal entries) and which you can code quantitatively (e.g., questionnaires).
3. Comparing the data
   - Once your coding is complete, compare the categories or patterns across your different sets of data (e.g., interviews compared with surveys) to see whether they say the same thing or whether there are contradictions that you can highlight.
   - Develop tables, bar/pie charts or sets of quotes to set the data out and display them in a concise form (see later sections of this chapter).
4. Building meanings and interpretations
   - Think deeply about what the data are saying by reflecting beyond the immediate surface details.
   - Look for more abstract 'big picture' concepts and not just step-by-step

descriptions of what you have found.
- Pose questions, identify connections, and develop explanations about what the research means at the broadest level of your understanding of it.
- Refine your own 'personal theories' (more about these in Chapter 5) about the meanings of this research.

5. Reporting the outcomes
   - Think about how you can present your research and what you have found to tell others (we'll look at this again in Chapter 5).
   - Consider how you will organise the whole 'story of your research' from beginning to end and not just the analysis and findings.

(Adapted from Burns, 1999, pp. 157-160)

Classroom voices

Analysing data is challenging but rewarding work. For many action researchers it's a mixture of using well-known methods and procedures, as well as your own informed decisions, intuition, and inspiration! Over the years that I've been talking about data analysis with colleagues and students, they've certainly used some very picturesque expressions to describe this experience:

> Analysing data is a bit like drinking a glass of champagne. You think all you can see is just a whole lot of liquid until the bubbles start rising to the top. (Carol, USA)
>
> My student described it as 'wallowing' in a data swamp. She said she was beginning to feel like a hippopotamus! (Jenny, Australia)
>
> It felt like I was in a thick fog, but then the mists started rising and things got clearer. (Susannna, Hong Kong)
>
> It was like seeing lots of stars covering the sky, but then some stars started shining really brightly. (Abel, Kenya)
>
> At first I felt like I was in a long dark tunnel. I thought I would get stuck in there! But after a lot of effort, and help from my supervisor, I could see light at the end of the tunnel. (Dewi, Indonesia)

In the rest of this chapter I'll offer you some basic practical techniques for analysing qualitative and quantitative data. Bear in mind, though, that these techniques are just to get you started. Depending on the level of AR you want to achieve and how deeply you want to understand data analysis, it would also be worth referring to other volumes that cover qualitative and AR data analysis in more detail (see those listed at the end of this book).

> **Reflection point**
>
> What are your current challenges in analysing your data? Make a list of your most important 'burning questions' and discuss them with a colleague or mentor.
>
> Alternatively, refer to some of the websites or books listed at the end of this volume to start finding some answers to these questions.

4.2 Analysing and synthesising qualitative data

Qualitative data are those that are analysed without using numbers. You are likely to get quite a lot of qualitative information from data such as journal/diary entries, interviews, classroom recordings of interactions among yourself and/or your students, and observation notes (see Chapter 3). The main tools for analysing qualitative data that we're going to examine in this section are: i) catagorising; and ii) analysing talk.

4.2.1 Categorising

Sorting objects and information into logical groupings is something that human beings do constantly in daily life. Essentially, this is what categorising data is all about. Altrichter, Posch and Somekh (1993, pp. 123-124) provide a very helpful description that illustrates what's involved:

> Imagine a room in which a large number of toys have been left lying around and it is your job to create order. You will probably begin by walking round and having a look at things. According to your interests and the characteristics of the toys, features will come to mind which help you to order them: for example, colour, size, shape, state of repair, the age group for which they are suitable, and so on. Then you will choose two or more features by which to begin to sort them. Something similar happens when a researcher wants to create order from a quantity of data.

We generally treat qualitative data in AR though a process of what is known as *inductive coding*. In other words, we scan the data carefully, usually several times over, to see what categories suggest themselves, or 'emerge', from the data. The research term for this is an *emic* approach, which is sometimes also called an 'insider' approach. It means that we look at data from the perspectives of people closely involved in the research context and analyse their opinions and views exactly as we find them. In other words, the data give us the categories. This is a different approach from *deductive coding* where the researcher develops categories based on the literature or on theoretical knowledge and then looks for instances in the data to match those pre-arranged categories.

Classroom voices

Gao Xuesong (Andy) conducted his research in China. He worked in a university and was concerned about 'Chinese students' language learning experiences with a focus on their teacher independence in the learning process' (p. 61). He wanted to understand more about his students' apparent dependence on the teacher and how they viewed the teacher's role in the learning process. He conducted interviews with 14 student volunteers from his class to find out their views. He describes how he then analysed these 'biographical/narrative' data by coding them into categories:

> During the process, I searched for all the students' references to teachers in the data. For instance:
>
> > He was a serious teacher in class. But after class, he could be your nice friend. In fact many students like such teachers. (Jing Jing, September 19, 2004)
>
> I highlighted the words *serious*, *nice* and *like*, because they suggest that an ideal teacher in this particular student's opinion should be nice and strict. I identified the initial coding categories by carefully reading through one interview transcript, and I refined the coding categories by applying the initial categories in interpreting the other interviews transcripts. The process of data analysis was also interactive, and further categories of analysis emerged from the data. First, a reference to nice or good teachers in the past helped define the attributes of a good teacher, reflecting what these students wanted teachers to do for them in the learning process. I then critically analyzed positive and negative images of teachers to identify particular patterns of students' expectations. Finally, students' reflexive comments on teacher-dependence, especially at their college, were interpreted to see whether they wanted to be independent from teachers in the learning process and why or why not.
>
> (Xuesong, 2006, pp. 61-65)

Andy's description shows how the first step in the process is to develop pretty broad categories – all the references in his data to *teachers*. Once you have a broad category like this you can look for all the things that might fit or relate to that category – Andy mentions: i) different aspects of *good teachers*; ii) *positive and negative images* of teachers. The next step in the process is to scan the data further to find other concepts that might relate to the ones already identified. This third step for Andy was to look at patterns of *student expectations* of their teachers. Having made all these connections, Andy notes that he linked the students' *reflexive comments on teacher-dependence* to the previous categories he had found.

Action point

If you already started an AR journal after reading Chapter 3, use it for this activity. If not, keep a journal about your teaching in a format of your choice for two to three days. Come back to the rest of this action point after you've written the journal entries.

Now try some initial coding. Read the entries in your journal that you made over two to three days. Identify all the references to your students.

What are the main words used about your students? Do they cluster into themes or categories? If so, what are they? What do they tell you about how you view your students?

Coding the data in this way basically means that you are looking for the main 'themes' or concepts that will help to throw light on your research questions, puzzles or dilemmas. It's a bit like listening for the most prominent refrains or beats that keep repeating themselves in a melody. Here are some possible steps for working out categories for coding your data.

1. Gather together all the data you want to look at – for example, your/your students' journal entries or the comments made in an interview.
2. Read the data over several times to get a good feel for what is there. As you read, use a highlighter or underline anything that seems to make an impression on you (interesting, surprising, unexpected, and so on).
3. Now take a section of the data and give a label to the main idea or theme that is being expressed (e.g., *the role of the teacher, learning strategy, feelings and emotions*, and so on) – this will provide you with an initial category. Look for other things in later sections of the data that could also go under that label (for example, are the same words mentioned over and over again?).

4. Keep doing this until you have developed a number of different labels for the ideas in the data that group together. You may find that some statements don't fit neatly into any of the categories. You can put these into a 'miscellaneous' category in the meantime. Go back over them later to see if they form categories of their own or relate back in some way to the ones you have already developed. By the time you have finished the first round of categorising you are likely to have a better idea of where some of the miscellaneous ones might fit.
5. Make a list of your different initial categories on a sheet of paper or on a computer.
6. Now look back over your broad categories and see whether you can group them more into sub-categories that all relate to the main category label. Keep doing this until you are satisfied that you have identified all the ideas that cluster together.
7. Make a note on your category list (see point 5) of where the sub-categories fit in.
8. Show your categories to a colleague and see whether they agree with the way you have grouped them. Discuss the ones where you have a difference of opinion and decide how best to categorise them. Asking someone else to look over your analysis can give you more confidence that you have come up with some reliable categories.

Classroom voices

Sue Garton, who is a teacher educator at the University of Aston in the UK, makes a very useful suggestion about the first part of the process I've outlined here. Sue used interviews rather than journal entries in her study and says:

> I actually analysed my data by doing it one complete interview at a time, rather than one category across the whole data set (as in points 2–3). That made it less daunting for me. It might be worth trying the two alternatives.

(personal communication, 4 February 2009)

If you go over your data several times you should begin to get a pretty good idea of what the main themes and categories are. Doing this kind of analysis involves a lot of chopping up of the text – often literally! – and deciding how things group together.

It's very common for action researchers to develop a personal style for doing the coding. Drever (1995, p. 65) says:

> Researchers tend to develop their personal toolkit for analysing semi-structured interview data. This may include coloured pencils, text-highlighters, scissors, or a craft knife, glue or sticky tape, large sheets of paper, and other devices for marking, separating and reassembling the text.

He also offers other good practical advice, like working on copies and not originals of your interview transcripts, and marking each of the transcripts you produced on various dates with a different colour down the left-hand side. Researchers often cut up their whole set of data into statements, utterances or chunks that can then be pieced together in categories. Using the colour coding technique means you can easily tell where they came from originally.

Reflection point

Have you had any experience of categorising qualitative data? Make notes about your experiences or discuss them with a colleague. Maybe use the following questions as a guide:

- What kinds of data did you collect?
- How did you organise them?
- How did you go about developing your categories?
- What tools or equipment did you use?
- What challenges did you find along the way?
- What things would you do differently next time?
- What did you learn about this experience?

If you have not done any categorising, find a colleague or teacher educator/workshop leader who has. Ask them to reflect on these questions with you.

To provide a very concrete example of how coding can be done, let's draw again on Andy's research from the classroom voices section above. If you were in a similar situation with lots of interview data to code, you might begin by getting a large sheet of paper and giving it a provisional heading. Andy's was: *Views of good teachers*. A provisional heading is a temporary label that you've identified by reading over your data set several times – you can, of course, refine the heading if necessary as you go along. You then place all the pieces of data you've cut up that relate to 'views of good teachers' on that sheet. The next step is to sift again through all the pieces of data you've placed under your first heading. Andy found that his data broke down into sub-categories – *Positive views* and *Negative views*. Now you can refine the first heading into two (or more) sub-headings. Instead of having one sheet of paper you can now start using two sheets.

Once the sub-heading step is completed you can go further and see whether there is a third level of coding. For example, it might be possible to categorise the positive and negative views of teachers in relation to: the *role* of the teacher, the *behaviour* of the teacher, or the *skills* of the teacher. You can split the data up now across as many sheets of paper as you need for the different sub-categories. In Figure 4.1 you can see how the different levels of coding might turn out (I have not filled out all the boxes here but you should be able to get the general idea).

One of the challenges of doing coding in this way is that you may find that some pieces of data fit into more than one category. One way to handle this is to copy them and for the moment place them in both categories. Alternatively, you can put them onto a sheet of paper with the title 'miscellaneous'. Later, when you are further along in your analysis and things are becoming clearer, review them again to see whether it is now more obvious where they fit in. It might also be that the miscellaneous data start to form new categories of their own.

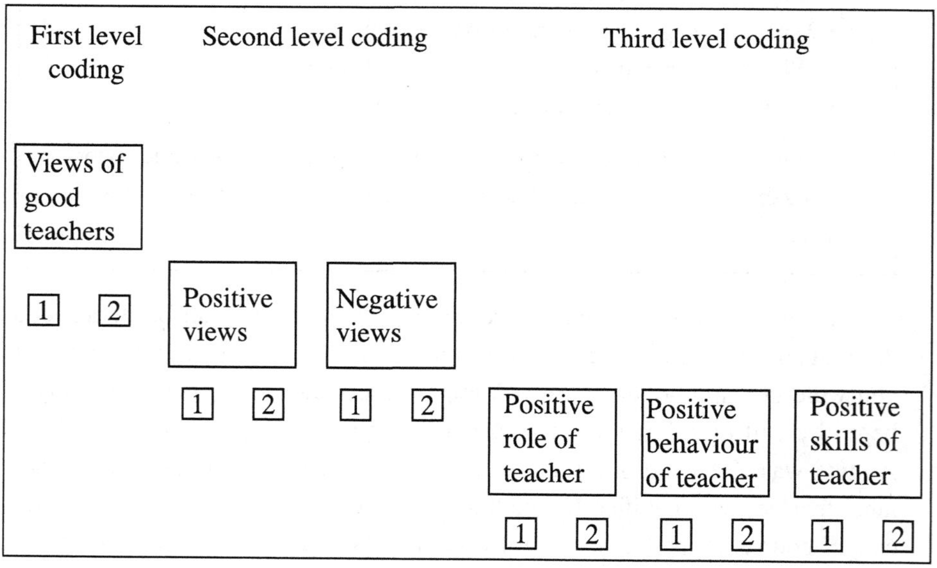

Figure 4.1 Levels of coding in qualitative analysis

Action point

Carmen Sanchez Chavez began her teaching in Mexico. These data are from an account she wrote on the topic of a 'significant event' in her development as a teacher. Read about Carmen's early experiences as a teacher and then try out the action point task at the end of this box.

> My first day of classes with the afternoon group was really disappointing: it was a group of about 18 students and most of them were teenagers (16–17 years old). They were taking their third level English course. Students at this level in our courses are supposed to have a basic level of English and hence be able to express themselves in English accordingly to the level. Nevertheless, they practically refused to talk, neither in English nor in Spanish. They just listened to me the time the class lasted and only spoke to say in Spanish that they did not like English at all and that they had enrolled for the English courses because it was their parents' desire but not theirs.
>
> During the first two weeks of classes I tried to make the class more interesting to them by keeping them busy working in pairs, trios or using games and contests in class. However, they were still very apathetic and reluctant to take part in the activities and I started to have some discipline problems. Thus, I could not avoid leaving my class every day with that feeling of frustration and disappointment, as my efforts to motivate them were useless.
>
> I talked with my peers about the problem, looking for some help. They asked me to tell them the students' name and the ones who knew the students said that was the way they were. They did not like participating in class and that it was very difficult to work with them. Most of the students were repeating the course.
>
> (Personal communication, 5 July 2005)

Analyse Carmen's data into categories and sub-categories. I have done one for you below as an example. I've also set out a second category where you can find quotes to match from the data above. See whether you can add any other broad categories and the sub-categories that go with them.

Broad category Feelings about classroom experiences **Sub-categories** • Disappointment • Frustration • Uselessness	 *My first day of classes with the afternoon group was really disappointing* *I could not avoid leaving my class every day with that feeling of frustration* *My efforts to motivate them were useless*
Broad category Expectations of students **Sub-categories** • Language abilities • Level of participation • Others?	

I've set out my version of the analysis in Appendix 4.1 at the end of this chapter.

4.2.2 Analysing talk

If you've decided to focus your research on classroom talk, your data will probably consist of recordings and transcripts you've made from all, or parts of, these recordings. The analysis of spoken interaction in the field of applied linguistics has become highly developed both theoretically and practically in recent years. If you are keen to learn more about the main approaches, it would be worth consulting specialist books. Richards (2003, ch. 4) is a good introduction to the main approaches of (critical) discourse analysis, conversation analysis, interactional sociolinguistics and ethnography of communication. His chapter will also point you towards the main authors for each area. In this section we will look only at some basic ways of analysing what classroom interaction data might be telling you in your AR project.

When analysing classroom talk it is worth referring back regularly both to the recordings and to the transcripts to deepen your analysis. Remember that the transcript can only ever be your written *interpretation* of the original interaction, so checking out what was actually said from time to time is very worthwhile. The basic, but most important, aspect of analysing classroom talk is that you are listening deeply to what you are hearing. Richards (2003, p. 185) suggests four steps in a basic analysis, and in the discussion below I will follow his model:

1. Providing a general characterisation
2. Identifying grossly apparent features
3. Focusing in on structural elements
4. Developing a description.

4.2.2.1 Providing a general characterisation

This step involves getting a general sense of the kind of interaction you are listening to and giving it a description. For example, compare these two extracts:

EXTRACT 1

1 Right, good morning everybody, we'll make a start
2 cos [because] you have three teachers this morning, then Pete, so four altogether
3 OK
4 so we need to start now
5 did you go to Cambridge at the weekend (ST) anybody else (ST) yeah (ST)
6 you went to Cambridge

(Taylor, 2006, p. 133)

(ST = student response)

EXTRACT 2

1 S1: No cauliflower (L1). Yeah cauliflower. Is this the cauliflower?
2 S2: cauliflower cauliflower
3 S1: er, first one cauliflower, second one
4 S3: car…what?
5 S4: carrot
6 S1: yeah, this one beans

(Burns, 1990, p. 49)

(L1 = first language)

Both extracts are from a language classroom setting. However, they differ in nature. The first could be labeled *the opening of a lesson by a teacher speaking to the whole class*. The second could be described as *students working in a group to complete an activity*. These two labels give the extracts a general categorisation and begin to provide a framework for looking at other 'gross' or obvious features like the number of speakers, who does most of the talking, and what kinds of things people say to each other.

4.2.2.2 Identifying grossly apparent features

Here we look more closely at the obvious features. We can see that in Extract 1, there is one main speaker – the teacher, who signals the opening of the lesson and begins to invite students to speak on the topic of the weekend. The student responses are not included but we can assume they are only minimal *yes/no* answers. In Extract 2, there are four students who take turns in speaking as they complete the activity. However, the nature of the turns varies. It is S1 who gets the most number of turns, asks the questions, moves the activity on to the next part, and also provides confirmation to the other students. We could also have noted that in these two extracts there are two 'dominant' speakers who may be the ones who control the interaction. However, Richards suggests that 'it is best to hold back on interpretations at this point if you can' (2003, p. 187) and just focus on the obvious. Looking more closely at the structural elements and what they tell us is part of the next step.

4.2.2.3 Focusing in on structural elements

This step is where we begin to examine the finer details of how the interactions are structured and describe the most noticeable features. Looking at Extract 1, we might produce this kind of analysis:

> From the data it can be seen that at this stage of the lesson the teacher controls all the interaction. She opens by greeting the students and stating that the class is about to begin (1.1), and then explaining that, rather unusually, the class will be taught by several teachers (1.2). The need to get started is emphasised again (1.4) possibly because of this fact. It is the teacher who decides on the opening activity and fields all the responses. Because the teacher asks a closed (*yes/no*) question, the responses from the students are minimal (1.5). The teacher's last turn (1.6) is a repetition of the question, but this time in the form of a statement.

If we turn to Extract 2, our analysis might go something like this:

> These data show that the interaction is between four students doing group work focusing on a task that involves identifying and naming vocabulary items (vegetables). However, there is one student, S1, who has more control over the interaction than the others. She takes three turns in which

she asks questions (1.1), corrects/ clarifies (1.1), confirms (1.3) the responses of the others, and initiates new turns (1.6). She can be said to take a role as the leader of the group and the way its interactions unfold. Each of the other students takes only one turn each – S2 rehearses a vocabulary item (l.2), S3 attempts to provide another item of vocabulary (l.4) and S4 assists S3 by providing the correct version (l.5).

4.2.2.4 Developing a description

Richards notes that once steps 1-3 are completed 'we are well on the way to a description' (2003, p. 187) which involves giving an objective picture of the interaction related to what we have seen in the data. Here are descriptions for Extract 1 and Extract 2:

> This is the opening stage of a lesson where the interaction is teacher controlled. Few turns are taken by the students at this stage. The interaction consists of a brief information-giving turn by the teacher followed by the start-up of the lesson. The teacher then introduces the first activity using a closed question. The few turns undertaken by the students are likely to be brief *yes/no* utterances or gestures in response to the question, as this kind of question does not encourage more elaborate replies. In the final turn, the teacher repeats the question in the form of a statement to which it appears she is asking students who have not yet replied to give further confirmation.

> This is an interaction among four students who are completing a vocabulary activity related to the naming of vocabulary items for vegetables. One student, S1, takes the dominant role in the interaction, as she produces more turns than any of the other students. In addition, her turns are more extended and complex in their structure. The other three students produce only one turn each, which consists mainly of naming vegetable vocabulary items. The exchange between two of these students, however, involves one, S4, assisting the other, S3, to name the item correctly. The interaction concludes with S1 again taking the lead by initiating a new vocabulary item in the final turn.

There will be many different aspects of a recording and transcript that you can focus on and, as Richards points out, it is not necessary to go through the whole text in this way. It's a question of becoming familiar with the recording and selecting the features that jump out as most important for your AR focus.

In fact, you may find that there are aspects of the interaction that you were completely unaware of when you began (as Isabella in Chapter 1 found) and these may well become your new focus of interest.

To illustrate how a teacher might investigate key aspects of his or her own classroom language, let us look further at the AR situation based on Extract 1. So far I have not given you the background to this interaction, so I will do this first.

Classroom voices

Linda Taylor works as a language teacher and teacher educator in England. She was interested in teacher talk in her classroom because one of her students – 'Colin', a new teacher–pleaded for 'rules' that he could apply to managing tasks that were not dependent on the teacher. Linda comments:

> I was embarrassed to admit that I had no rules to give. Until that time I had not thought of a language class in terms of applying a set of rules to be followed. I had thought of it rather as a purposeful interaction in which learning takes place. In order to help Colin, I had to shift my frame of reference, to observe and document my own and other teachers' relevant practices … I decided to carry out research in the context that Colin and I are typically involved with, that is, classes of adult students of English for general purposes.

Linda's research question was:

> *With specific reference to setting up teacher-independent tasks for language learning, in what ways do I and other teachers use language to manage learning, relate to individuals, and foster interaction in the language classroom?*

Linda made several recordings of her own upper- and lower-intermediate classes. She also recorded her students undertaking a practicum. She used a combination of discourse analysis ('why a particular speaker utters particular words at a particular point in the unfolding communication process') and conversation analysis ('how relationships are manifested through interaction') to investigate:

1. general issues of staging and interaction arising from the use of tasks;
2. issues specific to structural features of pretask, teacher-fronted stages;
3. issues specific to interactional features of pretask, teacher-fronted stages.

After recording, Linda transcribed the data, focusing mainly on the teacher's language. She highlighted each time a student uttered a word, phrase or sentence by inserting '(ST)' and used this as a 'crude measure of how much interaction went on between students and teacher at each lesson stage'. She continues:

> I next made charts for each lesson, showing lesson stages and associated interaction patterns. I also listed how transitions from each lesson stage to the next were signaled … From these charts, it was possible to identify teacher-fronted pretask extracts and to

contextualize them within the staging and interaction which occurred during the entire lessons … I then went back to the transcripts and refined my transcription conventions over several exposures to the audio recordings, during my detailed analysis.

Taylor (2006, pp. 125-132)

Here is the full version of Linda's transcript with her detailed analysis of the lesson she conducted with her lower-intermediate class:

1 Right, good morning everybody, we'll make a start
2 cos [because] you have three teachers this morning, then Pete, so four altogether
3 OK
4 so we need to start now
5 *did you go to Cambridge at the weekend* (ST) *anybody else* (ST) yeah (ST)
6 you went to Cambridge
(Latecomer enters)
7 morning
8 **OK first of all**
9 because it's Monday morning and we all feel a bit sleepy … tired
10 **I'd like you to come into the middle please … come into the middle here**
11 **everybody into here**
(Students move)
12 **OK, just go round and talk to each other, and what you're going to find out is**
13 **what do you like most and least about England**
14 OK
15 **so talk to as many people in the group as you can**
16 yeah
17 **just for three minutes**
18 yeah
19 **just to each other** (Task begins)

(Taylor, 2006, p. 133)

Linda refined her analysis by using a coding system. To show the setting up of the tasks she used bold type. She highlighted teacher questions in italics and underlined personal and social references to the class. All the students' turns are marked with (ST) but are not shown in their actual form as her focus was on teacher talk.

Classroom voices

By analysing her data and the data of the novice teachers, Linda gained a number of insights about managing tasks.

> I discovered that most of the language for setting up tasks was managerial (shown in bold [in the Extract]), but there were elements used by the teacher to encourage or simulate interaction (italicized [in the Extract]), and there were instances when the teachers referred to shared knowledge (underscored [in the Extract]).
>
> (pp. 131-132)
>
> I found that lessons in my data were staged in teacher-fronted and teacher-independent segments, with an attendant balance of teacher–student and student–student interaction patterns ... I have identified in my data three broad categories of functions for teacher-generated language in task-based language lessons as follows:
>
> 1. Teaching function – help students construct, extend, or activate knowledge and understanding of language.
> 2. Structuring function – Structure and manage procedures conducive to language learning.
> 3. Rapport-enhancing function – Create and maintain positive affect through rapport. (pp. 136-137)

(Taylor, 2006, pp. 125-132)

Linda's research is a great example of how a teacher can use interaction analysis and work collaboratively with others in an AR process to get deeper insights into what really happens as a lesson and its tasks unfold.

Action point

Have you already collected data like Linda's that focus on classroom interaction? If so, use your data for this task. If not, record a short segment (up to 15 minutes) in your classroom. You might want to examine how you are interacting with your students to set up a task. Or you could focus on your students' interactions with each other as they complete the task (as in Extract 2 above).

Use the tools for analysis outlined in this section to find out what is occurring in the interaction. If possible work with a partner. You can do this in two ways: i) do the analysis independently and then see whether your ideas coincide; ii) do the analysis together and assist each other.

Write up a short description like the one in step 4 above.

The kinds of analyses and descriptions I have outlined here are likely to find their way into the accounts that you write up about your research (see Chapter 5). One really important thing to note about analytical descriptions is that they synthesise and summarise what is occurring, while at the same time being firmly based on the data analysis rather than on our own assumptions or biases.

Now that we have looked at two of the major ways of analysing qualitative data, in the next section we will consider data that lend themselves to quantitative analysis.

4.3 Analysing and synthesising quantitative data

As the term suggests, quantitative data analysis means presenting your data in numerical form. Some people assume that AR is not about using numbers at all, but quantitative data can have a very important place in the way we discover things and present our findings. We can gain insights about the extents, measures, or 'weighings up' of the main issues that are important to our research focus. A quantitative analysis is used:

1. to gain a concise numerical picture of the issues;
2. to characterise or describe a set of numbers;
3. to show numbers succinctly in terms of averages, frequencies, percentages;
4. to show how numbers disperse or vary around a central point.

If you decided to use surveys or checklists in your research, then you will certainly end up quantifying the results, unless you used only open-ended questions (see Chapter 3).

4.3.1 Numerical scales

The first thing we need to know about quantitative analysis is that once we have coded the numbers, they are generally presented in three main ways, called numerical scales – *nominal, ordinal* (or *ranked*), and *interval* scales (by the way, there will be several sets of three in this section, so be prepared!):

- A nominal scale categorises numbers by the groups the data fall into. There is usually an 'obvious' response. For example, in a survey, you may ask participants to state their age, sex, nationality, main language spoken, highest qualification, or most advanced level of English studied. The numerical values of the coding are just arbitrary – assigning 1 for male and 2 for female does not have any 'real' numerical value.
- An ordinal scale ranks numbers. One obvious example very familiar

to classroom teachers is that we are often asked to order students in a list of rankings from best to lowest score in an exam – 1st, 2nd, 3rd and so on. An ordinal scale gives you a way of ordering data across a continuum of numbers.

- An interval scale is a variation on an ordinal scale. It ranks numbers but also describes the interval or distance between them. Usually measures are taken to ensure that the intervals are at equal intervals. For example, a survey item for a question, 'How often do you speak English outside class?', might offer options like (1) very often, (2) often, (3) quite often, (4) rarely, and (5) never.

It's very likely in a quantitative analysis that you will use one of these scales. You might present your data in a similar way to the classroom voices examples below.

Classroom voices

One of my students, Diane Malcolm, teaches at the Arabian Gulf University in Bahrain. Her students come from many different countries in the Middle East and are studying English as part of their medical degree. As they have large amounts of reading to do for their studies, Diane became interested in the reading strategies her students use and whether their strategies change as they advance over the four years of the degree.

Diane had some specific research questions in mind:

1. Are there differences in the reported use of academic reading strategies among Arabic-speaking medical students studying through the medium of English at different years of instruction?
2. Do students of low initial English language proficiency report using different reading strategies than students with high initial proficiency in English?

Here is her description of the participants in her study:

Study participants

The participants in this study were 108 Arabic-speaking medical students in their first year of study at a medical university in Bahrain and 52 in Year Four of their medical programme. The students came from a variety of countries in the Arab Gulf region, with the majority being from Bahrain, the Kingdom of Saudi Arabia (KSA), or Kuwait. A smaller number of students came from Oman, the United Arab Emirates (UAE) or other Arab countries. A breakdown of the nationalities of the students in the study, along with their genders, is presented in Table One.

To summarise information about her participants precisely she presented a table using nominal scales.

Demographic breakdown of study participants

	Year One			*Year Four*		
Country	***Male***	***Female***	***Total***	***Male***	***Female***	***Total***
UAE*	–	3	3	1	3	4
Bahrain	10	22	32	7	17	24
Kuwait	7	12	19	7	3	10
KSA**	18	30	48	4	4	8
Oman	1	5	6	2	2	4
Other Arab	–	–	–	2	–	2
Total	36	72	108	23	29	52

* United Arab Emirates ** Kingdom of Saudi Arabia

(Malcolm, 2009)

Classroom voices

Noriko Ishitobi was a member of a collaborative AR group working with Professor Kazuyoshi Sato at Nagoya University of Foreign Studies. Noriko was teaching four classes of third-year students at a Junior High School. There were 35 students in each class.

Noriko was concerned about the 'huge aptitude gap between students in classes' and also the fact that the students were 'not used to using English as a communication tool'. She put numerous strategies in place over three months to provide opportunities for the students to speak more in English and to develop their abilities in an atmosphere of cooperation. Her strategies included introducing new grammar points and encouraging the students to develop noticing, communicative and meaningful drills, pre- and post-reading communicative tasks, and extensive reading for enjoyment. Each student also had the opportunity to hold a one-minute conversation with the native-speaking Assistant Language Teacher (ALT).

As part of her AR, she decided to survey the students at the beginning and at the end of her research. She gave them a short questionnaire designed to show their confidence in speaking English. She set out the results as percentages showing interval scales in a table.

How much confidence do you have?

		5 *strong*	4 *rather strong*	3 *so-so*	2 *rather weak*	1 *weak*
To read	February	4	16	35	28	17
	April	18	42	27	9	3
To write	February	4	12	26	36	22
	April	11	28	32	20	9
To listen	February	2	15	33	32	18
	April	17	30	39	9	5
To speak	February	2	5	28	43	22
	April	7	28	34	20	11
						%

(Ishitobi, 2007, p. 97)

4.3.2 Descriptive statistics

Having thought about how data values can be presented, we also need to know something about ways of using statistics. In AR, we are much more likely to be using descriptive statistics than complex inferential measures, statistical packages or correlation procedures, so I am going to focus in this section only on the main basic descriptive tools we can use.

Descriptive statistics offer a neat and tidy way of summarising quantitative data, but can't be used for generalising results beyond our own context and research participants (Dörnyei, 2007). They are an excellent way of reporting on a particular group of learners, for example. So, descriptive statistics fit in well with the local and specific characteristics of AR (see Chapter 1). There are two main ways to use descriptive statistics. Here are the technical terms with brief descriptions of what each term means:

- Measures of *central tendency*: a single value is given to the set of quantitative data.The number shows where the set of data collects around a central point.
- Measures of *dispersion* (*or variability*): an indication is given of how numbers spread (or disperse) across the data set. When a measure of variability is used with an average score, we get a concise description of the distribution.

In case you have little or no familiarity with statistics, in the next sections I'll take you through basic ways of dealing with each of these measures.

Remember, though, that if you really want to go into detail you should consult books that deal in much more depth with statistical procedures (see those listed at the end of this book).

4.3.2.1 Measures of central tendency

Let's look first at central tendency. There are three ways of reducing numbers that fall into this category – the *mean, medium* and *mode*. They are all different kinds of averages which can be used to reduce the numerical values in a set of quantitative data and show them more concisely.

MEAN

In everyday life, and especially in the media, we are frequently presented with facts involving the mean – *the average rainfall for Sydney in November 2008 was 100 millimeters, average hourly earnings in Mexico rose by 9% in 1995* and so on. If I asked you to look at a set of numbers you had collected, add them up and then divide the total by the number of items, you would end up with the *mean*, or average. To show the number of scores in a set the symbol ***N*** is normally used. Now give this a try yourself.

Action point

You get a set of test scores out of 10 for the students in your class.

8, 4, 6, 2, 9, 1, 5, 7, 10, 3, 6, 8, 7, 5, 3, 9, 6, 4, 1, 2

$N = 20$

What is the mean score?

You ask the students in your tutorial group to indicate how many notebooks they will need next term so that you can order and distribute them. These are their responses.

1, 4, 2, 5, 2, 2, 4, 5, 1, 4

$N = 10$

What is the average number of books needed for this group?

Calculating the mean works really well for some kinds of scores. Getting the mean of 5.3 (I hope!) for the first exercise is fine for reporting the way your students' scores worked out on average across the whole class. But calculating the mean can have its limitations. First, getting decimal points can be a problem if numbers don't reflect real life. For example, if we wanted to calculate the average number of book prizes students could receive at the end of term, a mean of 1.85 would be completely unrealistic. How could a student be presented with a .85 book?

And what about the average number of notebooks from the action point above? The mean for this exercise is 3. But you'd immediately have a problem if you distributed this number to each student. Some would get more than they needed while others would go without. No-one would get the exact number they'd asked for as none of the numbers in this set comes to the value of 3. You'd end up spending a lot of unnecessary time fixing up what the students really needed. So, the most reliable way to use the mean is when the numbers cluster closely together and are relatively evenly distributed. You will also want to be sure there are no extremes, or *outliers*, at either end (the very highest and lowest scores in the first example may be outliers). If the results are likely to be misleading because of these problems, we can use other kinds of averages instead. We'll look at one of these, the *median*, next. But before we do, here's a classroom voice to illustrate how you could use the mean.

Classroom voices

Nawal Mohammed Al-Farsi is an English teacher in the Batinah South Region of Oman. He was interested in researching the types of questions teachers in his school, including himself, asked in class. He felt that 'greater awareness ... would be useful for my own professional development as well as for that of the colleagues who participated in the study.' (p. 27)

He audio-recorded and transcribed four classes (A, B, C, D) and analysed the types of questions asked and their functions in the lesson. He found four main types of questions:

- Closed display (a limited range of answers is possible and the teacher already knows the answer).
- Open display (a range of answers is possible and the teacher already knows the answer).
- Closed referential (a yes/no type answer is possible but the teacher does not already know the answer).
- Open referential (any type of answer is possible and the teacher does not already know the answer).

The most common question used by the teachers was closed display.

Teacher	*Closed display*	*Open display*	*Closed referential*	*Open referential*	*Total*
A	33	8	–	1	42
B	48	8	–	2	58
C	61	15	3	1	80
D	20	–	3	–	23
Total	162	31	6	4	203

He also calculated the length of the learners' responses, in words, to the different types of questions. He was then able to work out the mean length of response for each type across all four classes (the total number of words divided by the total number of each type of question, e.g., 342 divided by 162 to get 2.11 for closed display). He presented the results in a table:

Types of questions	*A*	*B*	*C*	*D*	*Total words*	*Average length of response*
Closed display	50	125	124	43	342	2.11
Open display	9	30	33	–	72	2.32
Closed referential	–	–	5	2	7	1.17
Open referential	–	7	2	–	9	2.25
Total	59	162	164	45	430	2.12

As Nawal points out, in terms of the total number of words, it is not surprising that the closed display questions elicited the greatest number of responses. However, by calculating the mean he was able to show that open display questions elicited the longest answers. Of course, the numbers also show that on average none of the learners' answers was actually very long. Across all the classes, the learners averaged a total of only 2.12 words.

Al-Farsi (2006, pp. 27-32)

MEDIAN

The median, as its name suggests, is what comes in as the middle point in a set of numbers arranged from the smallest to the largest. We use the median if we want to show the central point in a range of scores. We can then identify which scores are ranged above or below this central one – something we can't do if we just calculate the mean. For example, what if you had a set of test scores out of 100 for a group of 15 students? You could rank them in order from lowest to highest to find out the median value:

45, 53, 57, 62, 65, 69, 72, 75, 79, 81, 83, 87, 89, 91, 93
$N = 15$

It's pretty easy to work out that the median score in a set of 15 will be the eighth number, in this case 75. But what happens if you have an even set of numbers? Say you had to add another mark of 47, making this a set of scores for 16 students.

45, 47, 53, 57, 62, 65, 69, 72, 75, 79, 81, 83, 87, 89, 91, 93
$N = 16$

This would give you two equal sets of numbers, 72 and 75 being the ones in the middle. You would then need to find the point which is half-way between them. You can also do this by adding the two numbers in question together and dividing them by two. I hope that your calculation, like mine, was 73.5.

Action point

Calculate the median for these sets of numbers:

4, 6, 9, 11, 16, 17, 19, 20, 24

12, 17, 53, 47, 19, 40, 0

30, 30, 30, 50, 50, 50

0.6, 5.6, 3.9, 2.7, 8.4, 5.3, 4.2

See Appendix 4.2 for answers.

We usually calculate the median for smaller rather than larger sets of numbers (imagine trying to work out the median for 100 or more numbers!), so it can be a useful measure for a single class or group – it can tell you who is above and who is below the middle point. Also, if there are extreme values (the outliers I mentioned earlier) and these change, the mean won't be affected. So, if you suddenly find that the student who got 45 in the list above really should have got 40, your median won't change. Also if you get an unexpected amount of low ('the test was too hard') or high ('the task was too easy') scores, you can still get the median or central tendency. Even if you need to adjust the task to get more realistic scores at one end, the scores at the other end are likely to stay the same. Overall, the advantage of the median is that it gives you a typical value for the set of scores. But it can't be said to select a 'representative' participant for the group as it doesn't show the range (see the section on measures of dispersion) of actual scores.

MODE

The mode is the number you find most frequently in the set of scores – we can think of it as the most 'popular' or modish number in the set! Let's take the test score numbers for the students mentioned in the action point on page 142 again.

8, 4, 6, 2, 9, 1, 5, 7, 10, 3, 6, 8, 7, 5, 3, 9, 6, 4, 1, 2
$N = 20$

The most frequent score in this set is 6 (it occurs three times), so 6 is the mode value. But say we had one more score of 8, bringing 8 up to three times also, and the total N to 21. Then we would have two mode values for this set – 6 and 8 – and we could refer to *a bimodal* distribution. If, on the other hand, we took the first set of figures in the last action point:

4, 6, 9, 11, 16, 17, 19, 20, 24

we would not be able to point to a mode at all as the numbers appear with equal frequency – once each only.

The most useful thing about the mode is that it can tell us what is typical, usual or normal. It can also be useful if the distribution of number sets is unbalanced, or *skewed*, in some way. For example, if we had a set of test scores like this:

1, 1, 1, 1, 1, 1, 1, 1, 2, 2, 3, 3, 8, 8, 9, 9, 9, 9, 10, 10
$N = 20$

and we used the mean to show the central tendency, then we'd end up with a figure of 4.50. But this would disguise the fact that for over half the class (12 students) the more typical score was under 4, so the mean is rather on the high side. The mode, on the other hand, tells us that 1 was the most frequent score, which means we might want to know why so many students were getting low scores on this test. The median (2.5) is also closer to the typical score.

All these measures can give us a quick and tidy picture of roughly what the central or 'middle' state of play is for a set of numbers. When deciding which of these three measures – mean, median or mode – will show the best kind of average for your data set, Clegg (1990, p. 19) suggests asking this question: Does the figure selected give a fair indication of what the scores are like? She adds that descriptive statistics don't have to give extremely precise decimal places. But neither should they give the nod to the popular impression that figures are just 'lies, damned lies and statistics'. Our aim is to select the figures that do not misrepresent the patterns in the data.

4.3.2.2 Measures of dispersion

As the name suggests, these measures tell you how numbers are spread, scattered or dispersed across the data set. There are two ways of showing dispersion that you are likely to want to use in AR, the range and the standard deviation. Let's take each in turn.

RANGE

The range gives you the spread across all the numbers you have. To calculate the range you identify the largest and smallest numbers, then subtract. So, say you have a set of survey scores from your students where the lowest number is 50 and the highest is 80, your range will be 30. This tells you by how many points individuals are scattered from the centre. The problem with range is that it can give a false impression if you have one score that is an outlier, an extreme score. For example, what if one student in the class scored a perfect 100? You would then have a range of 50 (i.e., 100-50) – and yet most of your students' scores would actually be scattered across 30 points not 50. So the range gives you the clearest picture when all the scores are relatively closely bunched together as in this next example.

Classroom voices

Nilton Hitotuzi teaches English at a university in Brazil. One of his strong teaching phil- osophies was to adopt a learner-centred approach in his classroom. But he suspected that when he met with his EFL elementary (EG) and intermediate (IG) groups, 'I was talking more than I should' (p. 101). Consequently, he wanted to disprove his hypothesis that most of the talk in his classroom was teacher-centred.

> The initial hypothesis was that teacher talking time was in the range of 60 to 80 per cent and 40 to 60 per cent during the elementary and intermediate lessons respectively (Table 2). In my view, these figures are beyond the adequate level of teaching talking time at any level of L2 classrooms whose focus is on oral communication.

Using a micro cassette recorder, Nilton recorded 240 minutes of his interaction with students in the EG classroom and 165 minutes in the IG classroom. Then he calculated the percentage of teacher talking time (TTT) he did in each class. He found that the hypothesis set out in Table 2 was not supported by his data.

As Table 3 illustrates, in the EG classroom, the actual amount of TTT was in the range of 40 to 60 per cent, and 0 to 20 per cent in the IG classroom.

Table 2 Hypothetical amount of teacher talking time in the EG and IG EFL classroom

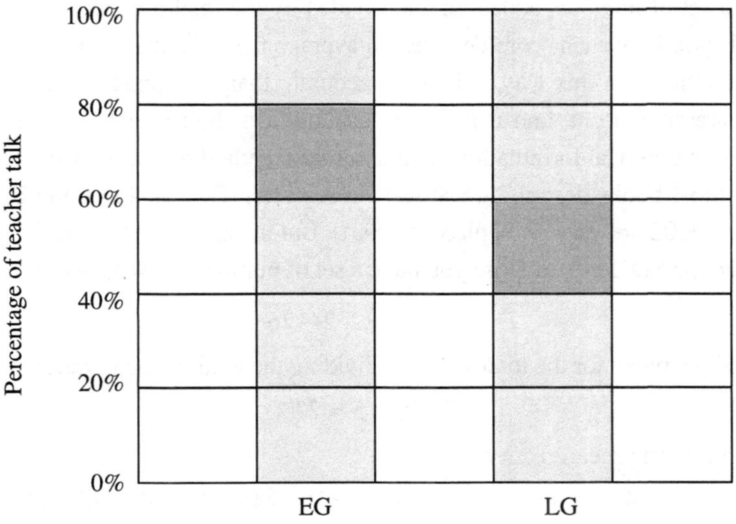

Table 3 Actual amount of TTT in the EG and IG EFL classroom

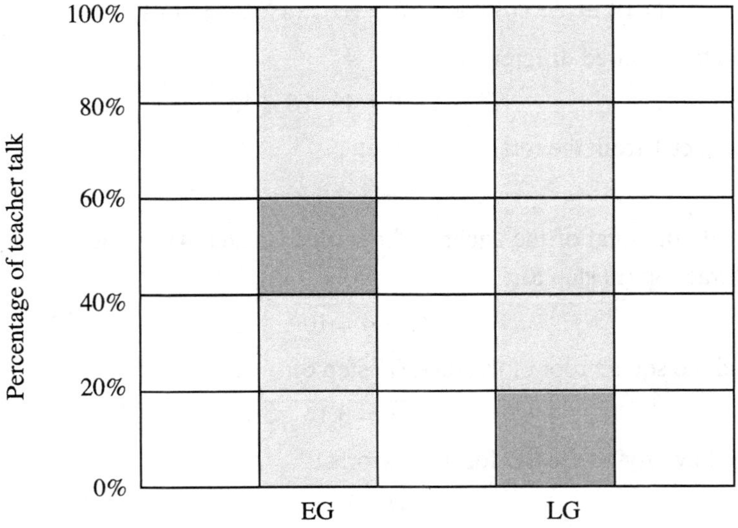

He concluded that 'despite the tentativeness of the investigation, the results somehow indicate a greater focus on the learners' (p. 105). He saw his AR as contributing to his development as a reflective teacher.

(Hitotuzi, 2005, pp. 97-106)

STANDARD DEVIATION

When we calculate the standard deviation (SD) we are getting an average of the distance of each score from the mean (remember, the mean means the average across a set of numbers added up and divided by the total number of items). The SD tells you how each score deviates on average from the mean. Because the SD averages things in this way, it is more accurate than the range in showing how scores are spread out, and if there are any outliers their effects are minimised. There is a numerical formula for calculating the standard deviation, which you will find in most books describing statistics in research (Brown, 1988 and Brown & Rodgers, 2002 are very good places to start). But in simpler terms, this is how you calculate the SD. Let's suppose you have a set of numbers ($N = 5$) like this:

$$18, 20, 22, 24, 26$$

1. Find the mean for the total score by dividing the total by the number of items:

$$110 \div 5 = 22$$

2. Subtract the mean from each score:

$$18 - 22 = -4 \quad 20 - 22 = -2 \quad 22 - 22 = 0 \quad 24 - 22 = +2 \quad 26 - 22 = +4$$

3. Square each of the differences:

$$(-4)^2 = 16 \quad (-2)^2 = 4 \quad (0)^2 = 0 \quad (+2)^2 = 4 \quad (+4)^2 = 16$$

4. Add the squared differences:

$$16 + 4 + 0 + 4 + 16 = 40$$

5. Subtract 1 from the total N in the set:

$$5 - 1 = 4$$

6. Divide the total of the squared difference (in step 4) by the total from the subtraction (in step 5):

$$40 \div 4 = 10$$

7. Find the square root of the total (in step 6):

$$\sqrt{10} = 3.16$$

8. You have found the SD for these scores!

$$SD = 3.16$$

(Adapted from Clegg, 1990, p. 155)

We've come to the end of the description of the main measures used in descriptive statistics. Here, I've given you only the briefest information. If you want to deepen your knowledge, use the excellent and user-friendly introductions I've referenced in this section to help you. For the time being, and just to make the discussion a little more concrete, let's look at how some of the measures we've covered – mean, median, mode and standard deviation– can be used in an actual AR project.

Classroom voices

Philip O'Gara works at a K-9 International School in Italy where he is the Head of Performing Arts. He was asked by the directors of the school to develop the drama programme. He decided to conduct some collaborative AR with three of his teaching colleagues. His aim was to see how drama could make an impact on the English language skills of students in the school, 80% of whom were native Italian speakers. Philip decided to adopt a quantitative approach, as there seemed to be little of this kind of data available in the literature he read.

He decided 'to explore the effects of drama techniques on understanding and use of verb tenses and compare them with the effects of the present traditional methods being employed at the school' (p. 159). Two Year 4 classes were involved in the research, with $N = 19$ in each class included in the evaluations. Philip explains:

> Two year 4 groups were given a blind pre-test of a simple worksheet to examine their understanding of and ability to use the past, present and future tense. The purpose of the research was then explained to both classes in an assembly, confirming that both groups would be taught using the treatment methodology but at different times.
>
> The research was carried out during two 45 minute classes per week over three weeks. The lessons were held on the same day for both groups and, where possible, at the same time. Students in the comparison group were taught using traditional teaching methods supported by exercises such as cloze procedure, conversion tables and paired reading in their classroom. The teacher of the intervention group facilitated exploration of the various tenses using a variety of drama exercises including role-play, hot seating, freeze faming and improvisation. At the end of the three week period, both groups were tested using the exact pre-test given pre-intervention to measure the development in understanding and application of the tenses.

Philip used a simple worksheet marked out of 10 for the tests. He analysed the data by calculating the mean, median, mode and standard deviation to compare the pre- and post- tests. He presented the results in a table.

Comparison of test results

	Intervention group	***Comparison group***		
	Pre-test	***Post-test***	***Pre-test***	***Post-test***
Mean	5.947	8.571	5.526	6.526
Median	6	9	4	7
Mode	6	10	4	4
Standard dev.	.870	1.228	.896	2.899

From these results we can see that the mean, median and mode all show greater improvement for the intervention group. Calculating the standard deviation provided the spread of the data from the mean and enabled Philip to do other tests to calculate the statistical significance of the results.

(Adapted from O'Gara, 2008, pp. 156-166)

When I asked Philip about the tests he did and his reasons for doing them he said:

> From these results, I did a test called a t test and used the results to calculate the p (probability) value, which gives us a significance value. The p value is a commonly used statistical measure of whether an intervention has brought about a 'true' effect, or whether the results could be down to chance alone.
>
> My results were statistically significant, therefore chance could be ruled out and the results produced by the intervention could be seen to be more reliable. The effect of learning language tenses through drama in this particular research proved more effective than learning through traditional methods.

(Personal communication, 9 March 2009)

In the examples I've used in this section, I've shown how numerical data are displayed in tables. They can, of course, also be displayed through figures, such as charts or diagrams (see Appendix 4.3 for some examples; see also Dörnyei, 2003, pp. 125-128).

4.4 Validity in action research: Making sure your conclusions are trustworthy

We have already touched on issues of validity in Chapter 3 when we discussed triangulation. Here we look at validity rather more broadly. An important question to keep asking throughout the whole of your AR process is: *How can I make sure that what I am finding results in reasonable judgements and conclusions?* This central question is crucial if we want to make sure that our research is solid and can stand up to evaluation by colleagues and peers. When I've worked with teacher colleagues, we've found it useful to go through a number of 'checkpoints'. This list may seem a bit heavy but we will be breaking it down and discussing it bit by bit in the next section.

1. Is the research focus the right one? Or am I really finding things that point to a different direction or focus?
2. Is the activity or strategy I am using to change the situation pedagogically sound? Is it of benefit to my students?
3. Do I need to go back and review my research questions? Do I need new questions?

4. Am I getting as rounded a picture as possible? Or am I relying on just one source of information that could be biasing what I find?
5. Am I being objective? Am I seeing things in the data as they really are, rather than how I want to see them?
6. Are there other people I can collaborate with or consult, who might shed new light on my data analysis?
7. Am I giving enough time to examining the data? Am I too hasty in drawing conclusions without seeing the deeper meanings of the data?
8. Am I coming to conclusions on the basis of too little evidence? Am I finding enough support in my data for the claims I am making?
9. Am I looking for things that don't square with what the rest of my data seem to say? Can I find explanations for this?
10. Am I claiming too much about the results of the changes I made? Am I suggesting that my conclusions apply beyond my classroom?

In AR, we are dealing with validity in ways that are close to those used in qualitative research. Essentially, what we keep asking is: *Are our findings and conclusions as trustworthy, credible and accurate as we can make them?* Going back to these 10 checkpoints from time to time as you do the research and analyse your data will help you improve the quality of your research. It will also help you present findings that are realistic and credible. Let's look at four important issues that synthesise the questions in this list further.

4.4.1 Keep the pedagogical focus of your research in mind

This is to do with not losing sight of the fact that the whole point of AR is to make things better for your students and yourself. This issue is in keeping with the democratic and social justice philosophies that underlie AR (see Chapter 1). The focus you find, the questions you ask, the methods you use to collect data, and the way you analyse your data should all work towards improving your educational situation. So, the teaching actions you adopt in the research should not disadvantage the students' interests. For example, experimenting all term with content or tasks that do not cover the topics students need for a competitive exam would not benefit them (or you for that matter!). In this situation you would be doing AR for your own interests and not for your students'. You can also increase the trustworthiness of your research by remembering the ethical principles we discussed in Chapter 2 and ensuring that your students know about your research, have given their permission, and are willing to cooperate in working with you.

Reflection point

Check out how you are doing in this area by asking yourself the first three questions from the list above.

1. Is the research focus the right one? Or am I really finding things that point to a different direction or focus?
2. Is the activity or strategy I am using to change the situation pedagogically sound? Is it of benefit to my students?
3. Do I need to go back and review my research questions? Do I need new questions?

4.4.2 Use more than one source of information

In Chapter 3, we looked at the idea of triangulation. If you remember, this is where using more than one source of information gives you different lenses for viewing the situation, and allows for more objectivity. Another very important way to strengthen your research is to take your data analysis to your participants for their comments. Then you can find out whether they see things the same way as you and reassure yourself that you're not just making assumptions. Asking your participants questions like: *Is this right? Have I explained this accurately?* is a very good way to get fresh insights on your analyses. Also, it's very valuable to run things past colleagues or mentors, especially if they are not 'emotionally involved' in your research, and get them to comment on whether your analysis seems accurate and your conclusions are reasonable. They may be able to highlight other interpretations, or point to important aspects you might have overlooked.

Reflection point

Now think about the next set of questions from the checklist. If possible find an opportunity to check them out with close colleagues. This gives you another perspective on the accuracy of what you are concluding.

4. Am I getting as rounded a picture as possible? Or am I relying on just one source of information that could be biasing what I find?
5. Am I being objective? Am I seeing things in the data as they really are, rather than how I want to see them?
6. Are there other people I can collaborate with or consult, who might shed new light on my data analysis?

4.4.3 Immerse yourself in the data

Action research data will inevitably be 'messy' – so take your time! Classrooms are complex and hectic places, so the meanings of the data are unlikely to emerge all at once. Also, because you are wearing both a researcher and a practitioner hat in AR, it takes practice to start seeing themes, patterns and categories coming out of your data, especially if they are not ones you expected to find. Thoughtfulness, openness and reflection are key approaches at this point, as are patience and organisation. The process can be helped by such things as discussing your findings with your colleagues, talking to your participants, re-reading your data several times, going back to the literature on your topic, reading other teachers' AR accounts, thinking about the characteristics of your particular research context, going back to the major issues in your research focus, and reviewing your questions. These are all ways to refine your analyses and make sure they are sound and trustworthy.

> **Reflection point**
>
> Think through these questions from the checklist. Again, it might be helpful to talk to a colleague, especially one who is also doing AR.
>
> 7. Am I giving enough time to examining the data? Am I too hasty in drawing conclusions without seeing the deeper meanings of the data?
> 8. Am I coming to conclusions on the basis of too little evidence? Am I finding enough support in my data for the claims I am making?

4.4.4 Maintain objectivity and perspective

Sometimes parts of the data just won't fit into the categories or calculations you have come up with. These *discrepant cases*, as they are sometimes called, can be frustrating but they might also be telling you something about the way you've done your analysis. Are there other explanations? Does the exception 'prove the rule'? Do they alert you to something you've overlooked? Does the 'discrepant case' suggest new directions for research? Do you need to refocus your questions? By going back over the data several times, and using some of the techniques I suggested at the end of the last point, you can gradually decide how to handle these aspects of your research.

Remember, too, that AR is localised in your classroom or school, so you must be cautious about making large claims or generalisations about your findings. This is a challenge related to qualitative research more generally. We need to be careful to show how the research fits with and relates to the context where it's conducted. It's also important to recognise the complexity of classrooms and that your research will probably focus on only a small-scale part of teaching or learning. So it will be difficult, if not impossible, to claim direct cause-and-effect relationships as we might in statistical or experimental research. But, by providing a 'rich description' of the context, examining and reflecting on the data honestly and openly, and setting out the specific details of the research story, you can be more confident that you are not exaggerating the 'truth value' of your research.

Reflection point

These are the final questions in the checklist. What are your experiences of them in your own research? Share your ideas with a mentor, colleague, or others in your AR group.

9. Am I looking for things that don't square with what the rest of my data seem to say? Can I find explanations for this?
10. Am I claiming too much about the results of the changes I made? Am I suggesting that my conclusions apply beyond my classroom?

4.4.5 Focus on 'practical theory'

By practical theory I am referring to the fact that at the heart of AR is the extent to which you can reflect on, (re)affirm, refine, or understand your own classroom practice more effectively as a result of your research. Many teachers who conduct AR are able to express what the process meant for them and how it enabled them to articulate their own 'theories for practice' (Burns, 1996) more explicitly. I don't have a separate set of questions for you to reflect on at this point. But this particular 'test' of the trustworthiness of your research is whether you can explain how your AR has deepened what you've learned about your own teaching contexts and practices. Perhaps the best way to illustrate what I mean is by providing a classroom voice.

Classroom voices

Bill Derham was teaching a low-intermediate class of adult immigrant students in Melbourne, Australia. He was working to a competency-based curriculum framework, where the assessment outcomes are expressed in terms of what a student can do at the end of a course (e.g., *Can ask for directions*). The framework was used nationally by his teaching organisation.

Bill describes his group as 'a slow class'. He wanted to assist them with vocabulary development, which he saw as an important aspect of their early learning experiences. The focus of his research was whether teaching vocabulary explicitly would help the students to cover the tasks outlined in the curriculum more effectively. He selected certain themes and topics that were repeated frequently and classified the vocabulary into general categories such as furniture, insects, animals, containers, building materials and so on. He then developed worksheets containing large numbers of words as a basis for teaching vocabulary intensively to his students.

He had various trials-and-errors in using the teaching strategies he was trying out. But, by the end of the 10-week course, he felt able to say that 'the earlier vocabulary lessons had established a foundation of understanding'. He was also able to expand on the 'practical theories' about vocabulary teaching that he had developed by doing AR.

> From Week 4 onwards, I almost abandoned intensive vocabulary teaching, because the class had found it such heavy going and they were in danger of falling behind in other essential aspects of the course. I think it would have been better to present similar material but with less content on a single worksheet. Fifty words may be more helpful to look at than 130. The worksheets that dealt with a narrower focus worked better. The fact that the students found some worksheets difficult may actually be an argument for persisting with this type of instruction, although in a scaled-down form with a class as slow as this. Since students had so little time in a 10-week course, some form of vocabulary enrichment would seem to be a helpful way to clarify and focus their thinking.
>
> Materials to teach vocabulary are most helpful and also necessary to prepare students for some of our competency assessments, such as making phone calls in a pay phone booth or using an ATM to withdraw money. Slower-paced students may find it difficult to learn large numbers of unfamiliar words, but it may be this very group who need explicit vocabulary teaching the most. The challenge is to simplify the lessons and materials for slower-paced classes so as to teach necessary vocabulary, but not to present too much at once.
>
> (Derham, 2001, p. 32)

4.5 Summary point

In this chapter, we've looked at some basic ways to analyse the data you have collected during your research cycle. We began by recognising that you might end up with quite a lot of data to analyse and that the task might seem daunting. However, in AR, data analysis does not have to wait until the end. By following a simple plan and starting your data analysis early you can use the insights and findings you are gaining to (re)shape the directions for your research. Like the AR cycle itself, data analysis is dynamic, cyclical and recursive.

We then looked at two key ways of analysing qualitative data – categorising and coding, and analysing classroom talk. Categorising and coding involved identifying emerging content, themes and patterns in spoken and written data and breaking them down into categories and sub-categories. Analysing talk involved looking for the types of patterns that structure the interaction in your teaching situation. For each of these approaches, we went through a series of practical steps for developing the analysis. We then turned to quantitative ways of analysing data and looked at two major sets of measurements in descriptive statistics – measurements of central tendency, and measurements of dispersion. The first involved calculating the mean, the median and the mode; the second involved calculating the range and the stand- ard deviation. Finally, this chapter discussed ways of strengthening the validity of AR. We noted, however, that in AR the term validity is less applicable than in experimental studies. We are more likely to be using techniques that demonstrate the trustworthiness of the study.

At this point you should be getting a clearer idea of how to undertake data analysis and where it fits into the AR cycle. Look again at your answers to the pre-reading questions for this chapter – or if you didn't record them, reflect on them or discuss them again with the same colleague. Go through the list below and decide whether you now feel more confident about each of the topics discussed in this chapter. If you need to do more reading, follow up some of the references in this chapter.

- The main purposes of data analysis in your action research cycle
- Steps in preparing your data for analysis
- Ways to categorise and code spoken and written qualitative data
- Ways to analyse and describe classroom talk
- The key features of measures of central tendency
- The key features of measures of dispersion
- Ways to analyse and present your data using descriptive statistics.

Appendix 4.1 Possible category analysis of Carmen's data

The amount of data in this extract is small, so most of the text is included. If you were looking at data from several participants on the same topic (a 'significant event' in their development as teachers), you would look for other quotes that would also fit into the same categories. Or you might find that more categories emerge.

Teachers' feelings about classroom experiences	
• Disappointment	*My first day of classes with the afternoon group was really disappointing*
• Frustration	*I could not avoid leaving my class every day with that feeling of frustration*
• Uselessness	*It was very difficult to work with them* *My efforts to motivate them were useless*
Teachers' expectations of students	
• Language level	*They were taking their third level English course* *Most students were repeating the course*
• Language abilities	*Students at this level in our course are supposed to have a basic level of English*
Students' attitudes	
• Attitude to English	*They did not like English at all*
• Attitude to the class	*They had only enrolled for the English courses because it was their parents' desire but not theirs* *They did not like participating in class* *The ones who knew the students said that was the way they were*
• Attitude to class activities	*They were still very apathetic and reluctant to take part in activities* *They just listened to me the time the class lasted*
Teacher's reactions	
• In class	*I tried to make the class more interesting by keeping them busy, working in pairs, trios or using games and contests in class*
• Outside class	*I talked with my peers about the problem looking for some help*

Appendix 4.2 Answers for median calculation (P. 146)

Calculate the median for these sets of numbers:

4, 6, 9, 11, 16, 17, 19, 20, 24 = 16
12, 17, 53, 47, 19, 40, 0 = 19
30, 30, 30, 50, 50, 50 = 40
0.6, 5.6, 3.9, 2.7, 8.4, 5.3, 4.2 = 4.2

Appendix 4.3 Examples of ways, other than tables, to display quantitative data

Example 1 Line char t figure

Kristina Hedberg is an ESOL teacher at Deer Park Elementary School, in Fairfax County, USA. In the following example (Figure 4.2), she set out three of her students' test results.

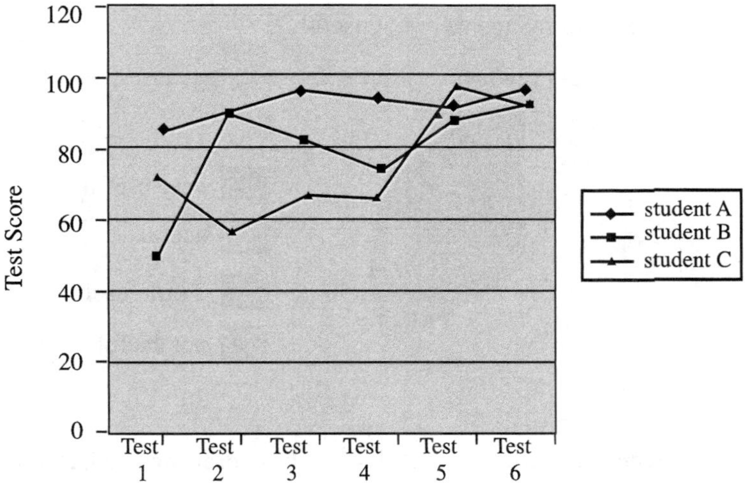

Figure 4.2 Chapter test results (Hedberg, 2002)

Example 2 Bar chart figure

In Appendix 3.1, we looked at a questionnaire by Tim Marchand, who teaches in Japan. The example in Figure 4.3, also from Tim, shows how he displayed his 14 to 15-year-old students' spontaneous use of the MCPs ('meta-communication phrases') he taught from June to October in his five oral communication classes (A-E).

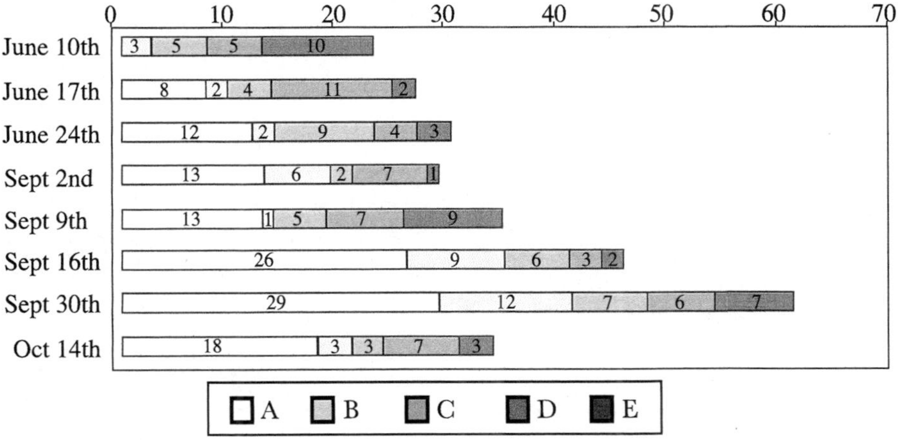

Figure 4.3 Total spontaneous MCPs by class (Marchand, 2008)

Example 3 Pie chart figure

Wang Lei teaches in Beijing and wanted to increase her junior Grade 1 students' motivation by providing brief drawing instruction. She believed that drawings would help the students understand the teaching materials better and foster their motivation to learn. At the end of her research, she asked the students how useful this technique was for them. She summarised the data she obtained from questionnaires in a pie chart (Figure 4.4). As you can see, no students responded that brief drawings were not useful.

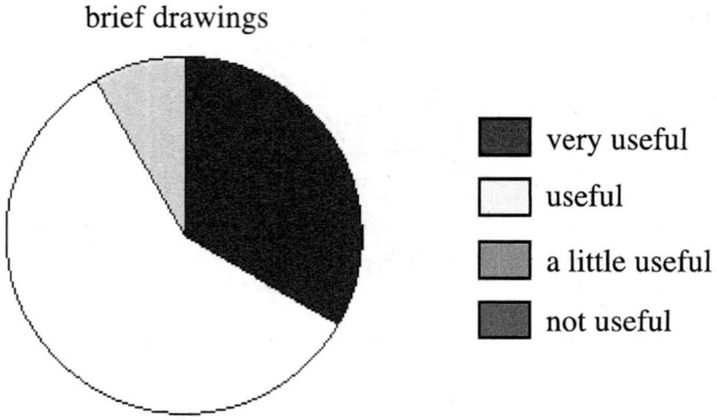

Figure 4.4 Students' views on the usefulness of brief drawings (Lei, 2001)

References

Al-Farsi, N. M. (2006). Teachers' questions in the basic education classroom. In S. Borg (Ed.), *Classroom research in English language teaching in Oman* (pp. 27-32). Sultanate of Oman: Ministry of Education.

Altrichter, H., Posch, P., & Somekh, B. (1993). *Teachers investigate their work: An introduction to the methods of action research.* Abingdon: Routledge.

Brown, J. D. (1988). *Understanding research in second language learning: A teacher's guide to statistics and research design.* New York: Cambridge University Press.

Brown, J. D., & Rodgers, T. S. (2002). *Doing second language research.* Oxford: Oxford University Press.

Burnaford, G. (2001). Teachers' work: Methods for researching teaching. In G. Burnaford, J. Fischer, & D. Hobson (Eds.), *Teachers doing research: The power of action through inquiry* (pp. 49-82). 2nd edition. Mahwah, NJ: Lawrence Erlbaum Associates.

Burns, A. (1990). Focus on language in the communicative classroom. In G. Brindley (Ed.), *The second language curriculum in action* (pp. 36-58). Sydney: National Centre for English Language Teaching and Research.

Burns, A. (1996). Starting all over again: From teaching adults to teaching beginners. In D. Freeman, & J. Richards (Eds.), *Teacher learning in language teaching* (pp. 154-177). Cambridge: Cambridge University Press.

Burns, A. (1999). *Collaborative action research for English language teachers.* Cambridge: Cambridge University Press.

Calhoun, E. (1994). *How to use action research in the self-renewing school.* Alexandria, VA: Association for Supervision and Curriculum Development.

Clegg, F. (1990). *Simple statistics: A course book for the social sciences.* Cambridge: Cambridge University Press.

Dörnyei, Z. (2003). *Questionnaires in second language research: Construction, administration and processing.* Mahwah, NJ: Lawrence Erlbaum Associates.

Dörnyei, Z. (2007). *Research methods in applied linguistics.* Oxford: Oxford University Press.

Derham, B. (2001). Vocabulary and a CSWE II class. In A. Burns, & H. de Silva Joyce (Eds.), *Teachers' voices 7: Teaching vocabulary* (pp. 25-32). Sydney: National Centre for English Language Teaching and Research.

Drever, E. (1995). *Using semi-structured interviews in small-scale research: A Teacher's Guide.* Edinburgh: Scottish Council for Research in Education.

Hedberg, K. (2002). Using SQ3R method with fourth grade ESOL students. Available at http://gse.gmu.edu/research/tr/articles/sq3r_method/sq3r/

Hitotuzi, N. (2005). Teacher talking time in the EFL classroom. *Profile: Issues in*

Teachers' Professional Development, 6, 97-106.

Ishitobi, N. (2007). Effective learning through communicative activities. In K. Sato, & N. Mutoh (Eds.), *NUFS Workshop 2007: Action research report* (pp. 96-107). Nagoya, Japan: Centre for EFL Teacher Development, Nagoya University of Foreign Studies.

Lei, W. (2001). Motivating students through brief drawings. Available at http://wyx.nbtvu.net.cn/ wyx/bk_jxsj_03q_10.doc

Malcolm, D. (2009). An investigation of English reading strategies, beliefs and practices of Arabic-speaking medical students at Arabian Gulf University, Bahrain. Unpublished PhD thesis, Macquarie University, Sydney.

Marchand, T. (2008). The effectiveness of explicit instruction of 'meta-communication' phrases at breaking the culture of silence in a Japanese classroom. Unpublished paper. Aston University, Birmingham, UK.

McKay, S. L. (2006). *Researching second language classrooms*. Mahwah, NJ: Lawrence Erlbaum Associates.

O'Gara, P. (2008). To be or have not been: Learning language tenses through drama. *Issues in Educational Research*, 18(2), 156-166. Available at http://www.iier.org.au/iier18/ogara.html

Richards, K. (2003). *Qualitative inquiry in TESOL*. London: Palgrave Macmillan.

Taylor, L. (2006). Aspect of teacher-generated language in the language classroom. In Borg, S. (Ed.), *Language teacher research in Europe* (pp. 125-138). Alexandria, VA: TESOL.

Xuesong, G. (2006). Understanding Chinese students' teacher dependence. In T. S. C. Farrell (Ed.), *Language teacher research in Asia* (pp. 61-74). Alexandria, VA: TESOL.

CHAPTER 5

Reflect – Reflecting and Planning for Further Action

Pre-reading questions

Think about these questions before you start this chapter. Make some notes or discuss them with a colleague or mentor.

- How does the reflection phase fit into the AR cycle?
- When is the 'right' time to end your AR?
- What are your views about teachers presenting their research to others?
- What are some of the reasons for sharing your research?
- What are some ways of presenting your research?
- What advice would you give to someone who wanted to continue doing AR?

Keep these questions in mind as you read this chapter.

In this chapter, we'll look at the final phase in the cycle of AR we've followed in this book – reflection. Eventually, you will reach a point where you want to bring the process to an end, draw out your overall conclusions and interpretations, and make statements about your research as a whole. This point involves thinking about the entire 'story' of the research and deciding where it will lead you next. In the first section in this chapter, we'll look at what it means to reflect on the process so far, and in the second section, at what the next steps for your research might be. I also want to stress the importance of letting other teachers know about your research. So, in the second half of the chapter, we'll look at ways to publicise what you've achieved.

Before we begin, I should point out that reflection in AR is much more dynamic than simply being the last phase in the cycle. Reflection involves creative insights, thoughts and understandings about what you have been doing and finding, and it happens right from the beginning. For action researchers, reflection flavours and moulds the whole AR experience.

5.1 Reflecting in the AR cycle

In this section, we'll look at different ways of reflecting on the processes we've undertaken and the knowledge we've gained from AR. But before we begin, I'd like to comment on the links between reflection and developing personal professional knowledge.

One of the most basic and essential aspects of our development as classroom professionals is to reflect on our experiences, whether these are experiences of teaching or AR. Deep reflection serves to build knowledge about curriculum development – in the widest meanings of that term. The possibilities for reflection and knowledge-building in AR are extensive, but they include exploring and expanding our understanding of how:

- the roles of teachers and learners interact;
- learners learn and how their diversity affects learning;
- to develop new modes of interaction with students;
- the curriculum works and the theories that underpin it;
- to develop and experiment with classroom tasks, texts and activities;
- to select and sequence units of work and the materials that go with them;
- to introduce and try out new classroom technologies;
- to assess students' progress and evaluate the course;
- to test out and apply current ideas and theories from the field of language teaching.

Building knowledge in AR is based on the deeper kind of reflection that comes from investigating your classroom systematically. So, reflection in an AR cycle often has a dramatic effect on how teachers build their personal knowledge about aspects of their teaching.

The idea of personal knowledge was put forward by Polanyi (1962). Others in the field of language teacher education have since built on this idea to talk about 'personal practical knowledge' (e.g., see Golombek, 2009). Polanyi believed that individuals bring their own personal knowledge into the experience of engaging in research, constructing knowledge, and creating meaning. As Polanyi said (p. viii), 'I have shown that into every act of knowing there enters a passionate contribution of the person knowing what is being known, and that this ... is no mere imperfection but a vital component of his knowledge' (cited in Fischer, 2001, p. 47). In other words, far from seeing the personal practical knowledge that is gained through research as irrelevant, Polanyi thought it was central. Practical knowledge allows us to create deeper meanings about teaching practices.

So, what kinds of reflection are important when we want to reach conclusions and develop interpretations in AR? And how do our reflections contribute to expanding and expressing our renewed personal knowledge? Let's look at four dimensions that are likely to emerge as you reflect on your AR. For each one I will suggest the kinds of questions you can ask yourself.

5.1.1 Reflecting on practice

Teaching involves classroom action on a continuing basis. In AR, ongoing practical action is the 'engine' that drives the research process along. Also, the actions, or practices that are part of your research are always subject to reflection, and reflection on action is what gives rise to further ideas for practice. So, practice and reflection-on-practice cannot be separated in the AR process.

Reflection point

Make notes on your responses to these reflection questions or discuss them with a mentor.

How did I select my practical actions to improve my classroom situation? Why did I select these particular actions?

How did the actions I selected work to improve the situation? For me as the teacher? For my students? For other people involved?

Were the actions effective? Did I need to change them?

5.1.2 Reflecting on the research process

All good teachers reflect on their daily teaching practices. In AR, however, the relationships between the teaching action and research are made close, systematic and ongoing. Your AR process is likely to have been a much more intense experience than regular day-to-day teaching. You will have selected certain issues that were problematic or challenging and given them special attention. You will have collected systematic information about these issues.

Essentially, you will have been involved in conducting a kind of 'practical experiment' to test out your ideas, hunches or 'hypotheses' about how to improve your classroom situation. Action and reflection are tied together as a central part of the research process if it is to keep going and achieve positive outcomes for you and your students.

Reflection point

Share your insights on the research process with colleagues, particularly those in your AR group.

How did I go about 'testing out' my practical actions?

How have I collected data to inform my practical actions?

How did I use the data to illuminate what was working in my classroom?

How have I used my data to change direction, if necessary?

How has my experience helped me to extend my knowledge of how to do research?

5.1.3 Reflecting on beliefs and values

Even if we are not consciously aware of them, our personal beliefs and values about teaching and learning affect everything we do in the classroom. The way we select particular language items or skills, the activities we use to teach them, and the different roles we take as the teacher are all based on what we believe about our learners and about teaching and learning. These are the 'practical theories' we also bring to our research. Action research aims to improve and change situations. And, our personal beliefs and values are central aspects of the process. Because AR allows for deeper engagement with a practical situation than routine teaching, we're also likely to end up examining, questioning, exploring, and expanding our 'personal practical knowledge'. This kind of knowledge doesn't just contribute to our own development as teachers. When we discuss our reflections with others and publicise our research, it adds to the development of the language teaching profession as a whole.

Reflection point

Explore these ideas in a personal journal or diary.

What are two of my strongest personal beliefs about teaching? What are two of my strongest personal beliefs about learning?

How did these beliefs affect the decisions I made as I did my research?

How has my research deepened my understanding of my personal beliefs and values about language teaching?

In what ways have my practical theories about teaching developed?

How has developing my practical theories helped to build my knowledge? About teaching? About research?

5.1.4 Reflecting on feelings and experiences

Action research doesn't only involve thinking about concrete actions and using techniques for collecting and analysing data. It also has an emotional and psychological aspect that brings personal feelings and experiences to the surface. Part of AR reflection includes dealing with the emotional reactions we have to the way our practices may be changing because of our research. In some cases, where our actions help to confirm our teaching practices, emotions will be positive. However, AR can also challenge our most dearly held teaching approaches or routines. Realising that our practices may need to change, or that we need to become more self-critical even, can be a confronting experience. At the same time, what happens in AR should not be treated as a 'test' of our success or failure as teachers. As Altrichter, Posch and Somekh (1993, p. 175) point out, AR means seeing and experiencing 'the art of the possible'. In other words, it means opening ourselves up honestly, and sometimes courageously, to the problems, dilemmas, possibilities and opportunities in our teaching contexts. It means trying to find the changes that make a difference, however small they seem to be.

Reflection point

Discuss your ideas with a close colleague. If you feel they are too personal, write notes in a diary.

What were your personal reactions to the changes that resulted from your practical actions? Were they positive or negative?

How did you deal with negative reactions? What impact did the positive reactions have?

Did the negative reactions trigger ideas that you had not thought about before? If so, how, and what did you do?

How did your personal feelings contribute to the way you did your AR?

What personal feelings and experiences arose from finishing your AR? Were they positive, negative or both?

5.2 Planning the next steps

I've already suggested that reflection is dynamic and happens throughout the AR cycle. If you've already done any AR you have probably experienced this aspect yourself. Nevertheless, at some point you will want to decide whether to continue or conclude the cycle of research. There are usually various pragmatic or practical reasons for deciding to end the research. For example:

- The issue you wanted to explore has been resolved to your satisfaction.
- You no longer have an external requirement (e.g., a course you are taking) to continue the research.
- The teaching situation you are in does not encourage research.
- For various reasons, you don't have time to do research right now.
- The group of colleagues you worked with can no longer meet.
- You have been asked to take on extra responsibilities in your school.
- You have become involved in another type of project or other forms of teacher development.
- Your action research mentor is no longer available.
- You have run out of energy for more research and want a break.

I have sometimes been asked by teachers I've worked with: *What's the ideal length of time to do action research?*, or *How many cycles should I do?* or *How long should I continue my research?* There are no ideal answers to these questions. We could say that AR is 'never-ending', but most teachers don't really want to spend the rest of their lives doing research! The number of cycles you complete depends on some of the factors listed above, as well as what your research itself suggests about whether you need to keep going. It will depend on whether you feel you have reached a satisfactory level of reflection and knowledge and you can see a logical stopping point, or whether you want or need to go further.

5.2.1 Continuing the action

From your point of view it may be that the first cycle of research has resulted in a mixture of both 'successes' and 'failures'. Or you have gradually realised that the issues or questions you started off with were not actually the main ones you needed to address. You may still have more questions than answers about the changes in your classroom. So, depending on where this first cycle has taken you, and the time and interest you have available, you may decide to keep going. Sometimes the second cycle will involve testing out the same issues with different participants to see whether your new teaching strategies continue to work well. Alternatively, you might go in a completely different direction because you realise you have not yet fully explored the issue you had in mind, or because the first cycle of research did not give you the outcome you were looking for. My colleague, Pam McPherson (see Chapter 3), provides a very good example of how AR cycles might continue but also change.

Classroom voices

Pam worked with students who were enrolled in adult ESL classes in Australia.

> My group was diverse in all the ways that make adult immigrant classes so interesting to teach. Ages ranged from 22 to 58 with equal numbers of males and females. They came from 15 different countries and spoke 17 different languages. Most had come to Australia because their country of origin was now unsafe for them ... My concern was with the wide variation in the levels of spoken and written English ... I was uncertain how to manage the class and I felt my planning was very 'hit and miss' ... I decided to read the literature on managing mixed-ability groups and to talk to teachers in [my centre] and in community organisations and primary school education about strategies they used ...
>
> As a result I decided to focus on developing materials and activities at different levels and to observe the response of the learners to these materials. I documented these observations [using a journal and drawing up diagrams of classroom interaction] and began to realise how much I tended to 'control' their learning by dispersing materials at 'appropriate' levels. When I allowed the students to take

> control, they worked with the [materials] in different ways which they found personally effective ...
>
> However, at this point I became concerned about another aspect of the class. I observed that the students would not cooperate to undertake joint activities. They were also starting to express exasperation, boredom, irritation and once, near hostility, as I brought to the classroom lessons and activities [about personal experiences] I thought were interesting and relevant, but which they were not prepared to participate in ... I decided on a strategy of individual consultation. I spoke to each student about what they were learning, how they were learning and how they could develop their skills. I documented their comments and followed with activities designed to enhance their requested learning areas. I also documented comments on their reactions to my classroom activities ...
>
> I began to see emerging patterns and to uncover the reasons for the rejected activities. Student comments and reactions indicated that discussions that revolved around cultural or social difference were not acceptable ... On a class excursion, I learned that the students were aware of deep ethnic, religious and political differences because of their experiences of the part of the world they had just left [former Yugoslavia] ... I suddenly realised how difficult it had been for them to maintain the veneer of courtesy and civility when I was introducing activities which demanded that they expose and discuss the differences they were attempting to ignore!
>
> (Summarised from McPherson, 1997)

Pam's first research cycle did not give her the improvements she'd hoped for in planning and managing her classroom activities better. In fact, her efforts seemed to be making things worse. Her students didn't want to cooperate when they did group work. Even more seriously, they were becoming hostile towards her and their classmates. As a result, Pam started a new cycle of research to try again to achieve a more positive outcome. This time she interviewed the students individually to try to understand how they wanted to learn, and what they felt about learning in her class. Over time, she realised that what she really needed to know about in this class was not how she could cater for the students' different levels of language ability, but how various social and cultural factors that were affecting their arrival as immigrants in Australia had an impact on their learning. In a later account, Pam highlights the emotional aspects that I mentioned earlier as part of the AR experience. As you read her account notice how many words she uses that are associated with her feelings.

Classroom voices

By the end of the course, I was pleased to have finally uncovered the reasons for communication difficulties in the class and impressed with the students' quick responses to the changed teaching approach. I felt relieved that they could finally let go of the early tensions and stresses, focus on their own learning, and achieve their learning goals. However, I was a little perturbed that in my investigations I had not taken good account of my students' thoughts and feelings ... I thought I understood the behaviours and events I observed in the classroom, but I was guilty of making assumptions about the causes instead of asking the students directly.

(McPherson, 2008, p. 129)

Before we move on, it would be useful to consider where you are likely to go next in your own AR process.

Action point

Where are you up to in your research cycle? Have you come to a logical end point?

If so, move on to the next section of this chapter. Select some of the strategies suggested there for finalising the cycle.

If not, start drawing up a list of issues from your first cycle that might need further action. Make a plan of:

a) the possible focus for the next cycle;
b) the actions you will put in place to try out new classroom strategies;
c) the methods you could use for collecting data on the actions.

When you are ready, consider the ideas in the next section for finishing off your research.

5.2.2 Concluding the action

As you reach the end of your AR cycle(s), more and more you will find yourself drawing together connections and building meanings about the whole process. This will be a period of reflecting back across the whole 'journey' or 'story' of the research. In order to bring out your interpretations of what the research means, you will probably be doing several of the following kinds of reflection:

- Reviewing and synthesising your whole set of data.
- Critically examining what the data tell you about the questions/issues you have explored.
- Relating your research to themes in the literature on your topic.
- Linking your discoveries to those of colleagues in your AR group.
- Using your colleagues' reactions to inform your interpretations.
- Examining your teaching assumptions, beliefs and values through a new lens.
- Expanding and elaborating your ideas about what your research means.
- Looking for the 'bigger picture' in your research.
- Considering ways to summarise and publicise your research.

One of the most useful support mechanisms you can have at this point in the cycle is a research partner, peer group or mentor. Your conclusions and interpretations will be greatly enriched by having others who can help you see what is valuable and meaningful about your work. The research process will almost certainly have been a 'messy' and complex experience – that is the nature of AR. So having an opportunity to dialogue with others can help recognise and crystallise the most important aspects. As Fischer (2001, p. 47) says:

> Research experiences are illuminated by the meanings we attach to them, and by the messages our colleagues find in them. Discussions with other teachers can help identify what stands out in our research, what we are trying to accomplish, and what further meanings we might discover in our inquiry. Importantly, such dialogue helps us put into words the complex experiences of our teaching that we are trying to understand.

Once you have had an opportunity to stand back a bit, and to reflect on and evaluate the research cycle as a whole, you will be in a good position to let others know about it. The next section suggests a variety of ways that you can spread the word to others by sharing the story of your research.

5.3 Sharing with others

Typically, language teachers have not been trained or encouraged to do research or to publicise it. However, over the last decade or so, ideas about second language teacher education and the skills and knowledge it should develop in teachers have changed a great deal (e.g., see Burns & Richards, 2009). Now language teachers are being encouraged more and more through certificate or masters programmes, as well as in-service workshops, to try out their own classroom inquiries and to share them with other teachers. In other words, you should not be shy about 'going public' about the AR you have completed, as more and more accounts of teacher research are appearing in the language teaching literature. Don't be put off either by the idea that the 'local' research you do in your school, country or region will be of no interest elsewhere. Language teachers the world over face similar challenges, as I hope the examples in this book show. As one colleague said to me, 'What's done in Mexico can resonate in the United Arab Emirates' (Sue Garton, personal communication, 4 February 1994).

The benefits of presenting your research to other teachers are clear. Teacher accounts allow good teaching and learning ideas to be shared around. Opening up what we do in the classroom inspires us to learn from each other and breaks down classroom isolation. Teachers usually enjoy learning about how other teachers have solved problems they may be experiencing too. They are often surprised, or relieved, to find out that they are not alone in dealing with various classroom issues. More generally, there is now a great deal of interest in the language teaching field in what real teachers do in real classrooms. And knowing more about how teachers actually operate in classrooms may be of value to second language acquisition research in general (see Zephir, 2000).

In this section, we'll look at several ways to publicise your research. But before we do, let's think about the possible audiences for teacher research – the range of people who might be interested in knowing more about the AR you have done.

Reflection point

Who are the possible audiences for your AR? Make a list of who might be interested in knowing about it.

Compare your list with the examples from the classroom voices below.

Classroom voices

The audience who attended the poster presentation and the seminar were high school teachers who taught English, teachers who taught non – English subjects who represented each public high school in Surakarta, committee members of

> the English Discussion Forum (Musyawarah Guru Mata Pelajaran – MGMP) and officials of the Ministry of Education from the district level. (Dewi, Indonesia)
>
> 15 teachers … completed the action research project organised by the Center for EFL Teacher Development at Nagoya University of Foreign Studies … After each monthly workshop, they made progress reports on their action research and shared their teaching materials. They made mid-term presentations in early August and final presentations in late March. (Kazuyoshi and Nancy, Japan)
>
> Nearly 1 month ago, 20th june marks the day that i'm officially graduated from my (1st) MA course and this is the envelope that flew all the way from singapore: [a photograph of the envelope follows at this point in the blog] … besides sharing the joy, here's my research for sharing … and here's the thesis in PDF format you may need to grab acrobat reader 8 or above to read the content. (Tan, http://edublog.net/mt4/2008/07/graduation-ma-thesis.html)
>
> At the end, the teachers who research[ed] could present their efforts to all the staff, so that they don't just 'get lost' in the printed form. (Carmen, Australia)
>
> It's really exciting to see that the seeds of our discussions have come to fruition, not only in the presentation we made at the conference in Mexico City but also in this article. (Carmen, Mike, Elisabeth, Patricia, Iraís and Teresa, Mexico)

As you can see from these comments, audiences can be people who are known to us or are in our immediate circle – members of our research group, teaching colleagues from within the school or region, school administrators or bureaucrats. Parents, students and members of the local community could also be involved. Or audiences can be unknown participants at a distance who attend a seminar or conference presentation, or read a written summary of our research.

5.3.1 Modes for sharing your research

One of the things to consider, of course, is which modes of presentation are most relevant for the different audiences you are trying to reach. In the next sections we look at various possibilities for presenting your research. Some of these ideas depart from the traditional presenter-to-audience approach and may be new to you – but I will leave it to you to decide which would work best for your own AR context.

5.3.1.1 Oral modes

In the immediate face-to-face situation, oral reports are a common way of presenting. These kinds of reports may be used as your research proceeds or as summaries for the whole research process. Not all of them involve facing a large audience. Occasionally, you might want to use an oral presentation just to develop your ideas further in a small group. The approaches I'll outline below begin with the more 'private' types of oral presentations and then move on to ones that involve an outside audience.

BRIEF UPDATES

If you are part of an AR group, you may be giving brief reports on your research to update your colleagues. These could be:

- progress reports outlining what you have done since the last meeting;
- interim reports summarising the research so far;
- 'show and tell' reports making concrete suggestions for classroom activities and sharing materials;
- case study reports demonstrating a particular case that serves as an example;
- 'future plan' reports running ideas for new directions past your colleagues;
- critical incident reports relating challenges you are facing and asking for solutions.

Brief updates could also be used in more general short presentations at staff meetings, teacher professional development seminars or workshops, or parent and teacher community meetings.

CONVERSATIONS

If you are not working with a group, it can be very useful to identify a 'critical friend' or mentor who can act as your sounding board. If you meet on a regular basis in a relaxed atmosphere, the conversation can become a continuing account of how your research develops from the early stages right through to the last set of reflections. Teachers who are new to research, or who are novice teachers, can find this particularly helpful. A variation on this approach is an interview where you ask the mentor to take you through a set of questions you have both agreed on in advance.

DISCUSSIONS

Sometimes there is not enough time in a group meeting to go into detail about an issue you desperately want to share. Discussions where you present a specific aspect of the research that you want to look at in more detail can be very useful. They could include ideas that you have had milling around at the back of your mind for some time or things that you are frustrated or unsure about. This kind of presentation can work well when you set aside an agreed period of time and one person acts as a discussion leader. The leader might raise the key issue and then ask for further input. This kind of presentation may include something you have read in the literature, or reflections from your research journal to stimulate the discussion further.

DEBATES

Another form of discussion is a debate where action researchers put forward different positions or findings about a topic and then debate them. For example, one teacher might find that giving students explicit instruction about how to ask questions in class improved classroom interaction. Another teacher might find that this kind of instruction made little or no difference to the way she interacted with her students. The various reasons for each position can be put forward and input can be invited from the audience in the form of questions, or comments on their own views or experiences.

RECONSTRUCTIONS

If you are working with a particularly creative and outgoing group, you may decide to perform your AR. You can do this as a kind of 'narrative' reconstruction (as is sometimes shown in television shows) illustrating different 'acts' or 'scenes' of how you came together, decided on your focus areas, put your plans and actions into place, collected your data, reflected on new information, and worked out solutions and outcomes. Although this is still an unusual approach to presentation, it may be a lot more engaging for particular types of audiences than the more traditional 'talking head' format.

WORKSHOPS

A workshop presentation gives you an opportunity to share your research interactively with other teachers who have not been involved. You can give a brief description of your issue or focus and then ask your audience what they would do in this situation. To get more discussion going, you can ask them to brainstorm in groups. You then share your own solutions with them and also ask for their ideas. You can finish the workshop by telling your audience what actually happened as the outcome of your research cycle. A variation on this approach is to give your audience samples from your data and to ask them to develop their own analyses and interpretations. You might find it useful to do this at a point where you want external feedback on the analysis of your data (see Chapter 4). Another variation on this idea is to involve some of your participants – students, colleagues, parents and so on – so that they can add their own perspectives on what happened in the research cycle.

VISITS

A rather unusual way to report on your research is to invite other teacher researchers into your classroom at some point during the research cycle, as you actually teach. They could be participants in your research group, or colleagues from neighbouring schools. This mode of 'slice of life' presenting can be especially useful if you are researching similar topics (e.g., how to motivate students, how to encourage greater oral participation in class, how to assess students' writing). Your 'audience' gets a first-hand view of your new teaching strategies and approaches by being a participant in your classroom. But you also get a chance to discuss what you are doing and get feedback after your lesson.

SEMINAR AND CONFERENCE PRESENTATIONS

The most typical way of presenting research to an external audience is through a formal seminar or conference presentation. Over the last two decades more and more regional and international TESOL conferences have encouraged teachers to present their AR. So I hope you will consider applying to do this when you have finished your research. There are several different ways to present at a seminar or conference. All of them include a time limitation, so you will need to think carefully about how much you can say in the slot allowed and how to cover the key points you want to get across.

- *Talk*: You give an overview of the research as a whole (usually 20-30 minutes, often including time for questions).
- *Panel presentations*: You are a member of a group of presenters who each gives a short account of their research (e.g., 10 minutes).
- *Colloquium*: You are a member of a group of presenters who each presents one aspect or idea (e.g., 5-10 minutes). Often there is also a 'discussant' who draws out the main themes from across all the presentations.
- *Poster presentation*: You construct a poster showing the cycle of your research in visual (e.g., diagrams, tables, drawings, cartoons) and/or written form (e.g., short descriptions, transcripts, quotes). You are allocated a place to show your poster (e.g., variable time but maybe 30-45 minutes) and discuss it with people who visit it.
- *Q&A (question and answer) presentation*: You are a member of an AR group 'interviewed' by a moderator or chairperson who asks members of the group to respond to questions (2-3 minutes) about their research.

Reflection point

Which of these oral presentation modes appeals to you most?

Which one appeals to you least?

Which would you find most useful? Why?

Which would you find the hardest to do? Why?

If possible discuss your ideas with a colleague or with others in your AR group.

Action point

With your group, or individually, select one mode of oral presentation that is not familiar to you but which you would like to try out.

Identify with colleagues the next opportunity you will have to present.

Make a plan for doing your presentation in the mode you have chosen.

After you have presented it, discuss with your colleagues how well you think it worked. Identify what you could do differently next time.

5.3.1.2 Visuals modes

Visuals are a great way of enhancing your oral presentations. PowerPoint slides accompanying oral presentations are now very common and can certainly help to structure your presentation and remind you of the points you want to make. Including photographs, drawings, illustrations, handwritten texts, diagrams, tables, video clips, clip art, sound, symbols, or animations makes the presentation lively and more appealing to the audience too.

The poster presentations mentioned above are becoming a strong feature of some language teaching conferences. If you are nervous about doing a face-to-face presentation, they can be a less threatening way of introducing your research to an audience.

Action point

Prepare a short PowerPoint presentation (no more than 15 minutes) on your research. Try to include visuals that show what happened in your classroom.

For example, can you bring in photographs, maps, samples of students' written work, diagrams or cartoons/clip art that illustrate aspects of your research?

Show your presentation to a group of interested colleagues in your AR group or school.

5.3.1.3 Written modes

You may find the idea of writing about your research rather daunting. Teachers are not usually given time off to write, and there are no obvious rewards in school systems for writing about your teaching. Writing demands time and effort, and it can be hard work (as I know myself) to structure your ideas and set them down on paper. This is especially true if you are not working comfortably in the language you prefer to communicate in. You might also doubt whether anyone will ever read what you have written or whether a small-scale AR study has anything worth saying that anyone else will be interested in. You might worry about what your colleagues' reactions to 'research' might be. Will they wonder why you bother? And it might just be such a long time since you've written anything like an essay or report (student days?) that you've simply forgotten how to do it. It may seem surprising, but many teachers don't generally get to write very much during their professional careers, so your writing skills might feel rather rusty.

Classroom voices

Some of the challenges for language teacher researchers are reflected in these comments.

> To think the content is one problem already; and to express it in English is another big problem. (Indonesia)
>
> I feel the results will be of limited value to a wider audience. (Australia)
>
> I found it difficult to find the right words so that my writing was very dry. (Japan)

Unfortunately, in the past, teachers' knowledge has not always been valued by educational experts. This means that the self-confidence of teachers in the language teaching and other educational fields to publish their work has not been high. Luckily this situation is beginning to change as more teachers, teacher educators and researchers are coming to see the value of understanding the experiences and knowledge of teachers and the realities of their everyday work.

So, despite all the common objections I just outlined, let me strongly encourage you to write about your research. There is much to be gained from putting down on paper an account of your experiences and articulating what your research contributes to insights about language teaching. The process of organising your thoughts, defining and outlining your topic, selecting and sequencing the events and experiences, setting out your data, and searching for the concepts and interpretations that explain what your research means is in itself a deep form of analysis. It allows you to reflect further on the learning processes from your AR. It also means that your work reaches a wider audience, adds to the research voices of teachers, and acts as an impetus for language teaching and learning research in general to connect with real classrooms. The next set of classroom voices from teachers in different countries affirms the rewards that the effort of AR writing can bring.

Classroom voices

When I read my report, it convinces me that I actually have conducted research. I could hardly wait to show the report to my friends. (Indonesia)

Writing about the steps of the research has been for me another moment of reflection, as it has made more solid the basis on which to build a new research cycle. At the same time it has made clear that in fact the object of change was not only the single aspect of my teaching practice I investigated, but the whole idea of teaching and learning ... (Italy)

The project which forced me to make a report and make a presentation encouraged me greatly. It led me to trace what I did in my research. (Indonesia)

During the research I have become more aware of the 'strength' that resides in writing. Writing has been for me an effective means for fixing ideas that were occurring to my mind and to make them clearer. Vague ideas would take the form of concepts with definite contours. (Italy)

Writing up – time for reflection, depth of perspective. (Australia)

Writing allowed my research to be shared by other teachers. (USA)

As you begin to gather your thoughts about writing, it's invaluable to identify who you are writing for. If you are writing for other teachers, you can think about what kinds of style professional teachers in a similar position to your own might appreciate. To get you started, try out the questions below.

Reflection point

Make brief notes on the following or discuss with a teaching colleague.

Who is my audience?

What do they already know about AR?

What kinds of reports do I like reading myself?

What kinds of texts have I enjoyed reading during my own research?

What were the good features about them?

What were not so good?

As in our discussion on oral modes, I'll start with more 'private' and informal types of writing, and then move on to ones that involve a more formal style.

CHAT ROOMS, BLOGS AND DISCUSSION LISTS

Using technology to communicate is now commonplace in daily life. It's a great way of being in contact with other action researchers, particularly if you don't have the opportunity to work with a collaborative AR group. It also has the advantage of putting you in touch with people all over the world who share your particular research interests and passions. This mode of reporting is a kind of half-way house between oral discussion and written reporting, but it can be an excellent way of developing your reflections, getting input, feedback and interpretations from other keen action researchers. Using Google or another search engine it's very easy to find sites where you can read about topics, view other people's responses and join in yourself. One site I found on the Web is Venus To's blog (see http://fivewisdom. blogspot.com/2008_02_01_archive.html) where Venus describes the project she is doing on new technologies in language teaching and then posts regular messages.

Classroom voices

Here's an exchange between Venus and her mentor, Christoph.

Christoph said:

> Hi there,
>
> Very good start on this project: it already looks very neat. Here are some things that you could consider:
>
> > Will you design tasks that encourage students to create (I'm not sure what exactly) based on the readings that they have engaged in?
> >
> > Will there be opportunities for the students to contribute to the site?
> >
> > What kind of comments are you expecting in the guestbook? Do you expect this to evolve like a discussion board?
>
> Christoph
>
> March 6, 2008 1:14 PM

Venus To said:

> By 'create', do you mean the students will write something after reading? online or offline?
>
> I expect the students to comment on the usefulness of the website and give some suggestions on further improvement.
>
> March 9, 2008 12:18 PM

Christoph said:

> Hi Venus,
>
> That is more or less what I meant by 'create'. It could also refer to creating video, audio, images with descriptions ... what do you think you and your students can manage? I think it would be nice to see if you could facilitate something online. What do you think?
>
> As well as the kind of comments that you are expecting in the guestbook (which would be helpful for further development) it might be useful to have some cmc [computer-mediated communication] tools that are explicitly oriented to student learning activities.
>
> Christoph
>
> March 10, 2008 2:05 PM

In this exchange Christoph gives Venus feedback on what she is proposing but also poses questions that encourage her to think about things that she might include as teaching actions. Christoph acts as a sounding board for her ideas at what seems to be the planning stage of the AR and also provides additional ideas for her to think about incorporating into her research.

BRIEF REPORTS

These kinds of reports can have a number of functions. Sometimes they are prepared as summaries of what has happened over the most recent period of the research. The update can then be copied and shared among a teacher research group. The group might decide to use a heading format something like this, and the comments could be no longer than a sentence or two:

Researcher:
Date of report:

1. Actions completed
2. Data collection techniques used
3. Data collected
4. Insights/Findings
5. Reflections/Observations
6. Questions/Challenges
7. Where next?

If the AR group meets regularly, this kind of ongoing summary can be very useful when it comes to writing up a longer account of your research. Other kinds of brief reports could be written as an update, perhaps to be placed on a staff noticeboard, or included as a short article for a school or professional association teacher newsletter. Another interesting way to update people quickly is to use a research 'portrait' or 'exhibit' which gives a quick overview of the whole process. This kind of brief report could be included as part of a poster presentation too. There are no fixed rules about the formats or headings you use for a brief report – so you can use your imagination about the way you want to design them.

Classroom voices

Here's an example of a brief report from a teacher who was part of an AR group in Japan. It summarises what the teacher did over the whole project.

March 2007
Takemi Morioka
Junior High School

1. Title: Increasing students' motivation by [using] interesting communicative activities.

2. Context

Grade: 1st grade in junior high school
Class size: 17 and 18 students each
Textbook: *New Horizon* (Tokyo Shoseki)
Level: Some students learn English outside junior high school (juku or English conversation class) but others began English at school.
Problem: Some students do not like homework and are poor at writing. Some students like to speak but others are too shy.

3. Goal

To increase students' motivation to learn English.

4. What I did

I gave the students some communicative activities.

(1) How many? (Unit 5)
Students write questions on the handout, ask each other, and write the results in English on the handout.

(2) Where/Whose?
Students listen to dialogues and draw pictures on the handout. Students write their names on the cards of a pen, a pencil, a book, etc. I collect them, give one card each to students. They ask, 'Whose ... is this?' and write the names on the handout.

(3) Telephone conversation (Speaking Plus 3).
Students ask their classmates and teacher to join them. If the answer is OK, they can get the signature or stamp.

5. Results

I gave communicative activities mostly in classes with the AET (Assistant English Teacher). Students enjoyed talking with him very much and especially loved games giving points. I sent out questionnaires at the end of the first term and at the end of the year.

6. What I learned

According to the results of the questionnaire, more students think English is more difficult than at the end of the first term. Especially writing sentences is the most difficult for them. To write English sentences they have to know the spellings of the word they want to use, and grammar and word order are also challenging. I spent a lot of lesson time on reading text aloud ... and speaking activities, and gave homework to practice spelling of words. I am glad if they helped students improve their English abilities. I felt that students were more interested in meaningful tasks than simple work. Presentations and speaking texts had students practice English harder. Combining assessment and activities in lessons is very effective.

7. Future issues

Half the students liked English, but the other half does not like English at the end of the year. I didn't ask why they don't like, but if I have a chance, I want to know the reasons. One of the reasons I guess is that English is difficult to them and they cannot understand or express themselves well. I need to make more devices to improve their weak points. And also I want to revise the activities used this year [to make them] more interesting and meaningful.

(Based on Morioka, 2007)

Action point

Look back over the suggestions in this section and the example above. Do the headings presented match how you would organise a brief report for your research?

Develop a set of headings that would suit you and discuss them with your research group or a colleague. When you have decided on a final list of headings, use them to write your own brief report.

ACTION RESEARCH ACCOUNTS

An AR account is a final write-up that gives a much fuller discussion of your research than a brief report. There are several good reasons for writing an account of this sort. Your group might decide to collate accounts of all the research you have done and publish it as a collection that other teachers can read. Publishing could mean producing it as an in-house volume or putting it up on a website for downloading. It may even be possible to approach a local publisher to see if they are interested in producing it. An example of a collection of teacher research accounts is the *Teachers' Voices Series 1-8* (Burns & Hood/Burns & de Silva Joyce, 1995–2005) which I published after working collaboratively on several projects with teachers in Australia.

Alternatively, as part of your own professional development you might want to contribute your research to a professional association journal or newsletter such as *The Language Teacher* (published by the Japan Association for Language Teaching, JALT – http://www.jalt-publications.org/tlt/) or *the TESOL-SPAIN Newsletter* (published by the TESOL-SPAIN Association – http://www.tesol-spain.org/newsletter/). Many local TESOL Associations are actively looking for AR reports from teachers as you can see below. If you are a member of a local organisation, you can look out for what opportunities they offer.

Classroom voices

The Word

Newsletter of Hawaii TESOL

Attention: ESL Professionals!

Here's a great professional development opportunity! Why not contribute a brief article to the Hawaii TESOL newsletter!? *Why would you want to do such a thing when you're already so busy, you ask? Here are a few reasons why (some self- serving; some not):*

> You get published (true, it's not a 'famous' refereed journal, but it still counts as a type of publication and if you're not published yet, this is a great way to get started).
>
> It's a great experience, and looks good on your CV.
>
> It's a great way to become involved in the local TESOL community and get noticed by some local employers, if you're planning to look for an ESL job in Hawaii.
>
> It's a fabulous way to share your knowledge, experience, teaching tips, etc. with other language educators.
>
> It's easy, painless and doesn't take much time. You can take a term paper, action research project, lesson plan, classroom activity, presentation you've given, or something else which you've already done or thought a lot about and simply turn it into a brief article (see examples below).

There are many possibilities for articles, but here are a few ideas: recommended internet sites (or a tech type column), book reviews, a grad student's perspective, field trips/learning outside the classroom, reports from members working overseas, content-based teaching ideas, using video and music in the classroom, online teaching, CALL, a 'gripes' column, DOE news/concerns, K-12 news, outer island news, applying theory into practice, interview with someone in the field, etc. This list is by no means exhaustive. Please feel free to send us any articles about these topics or others that you consider interesting to ESL educators in Hawaii.

(http://www.hawaiitesol.org/TheWord.html, downloaded 8 January 2009)

You'll need to decide how best to approach summarising your research so that your audience is engaged and gets good insights into the AR process, your findings and the insights you gained for improving professional practices. Currently, there are few 'set rules' for creating AR accounts, which means that action researchers are still in a position to experiment with different and creative ways. For example, Dadds and Hart (2001), who worked with special needs teachers, discuss innovative methods and styles of reporting – visualisation, conversation and fictional writing – that could also be of interest to language teachers. On the other hand, it's worth considering what Altrichter *et al.* (1993, p. 193) say, that:

> Part of teachers' antipathy to writing may spring from their perception that it is the traditional form of academic communication, but not the most meaningful method of disseminating knowledge within the profession. We agree with this to some extent, but believe that teacher researchers should master this form of communication until better alternatives are found.

In my experience, too, most teachers do like to have some recognised guidelines when they are setting out for the first time to produce a written account that is fuller than a brief report. So let's look at points you can use to set out your text. They will assist you to cover the main issues and share your account with a teacher audience or prepare it for publication.

1. Your name, where, and what you teach (background, experience, school, position).
2. Information about your school and class [location, setting, student population, class(es)].
3. Your issue, problem or questions (concerns, expectations, dilemmas, challenges and how they evolved, if applicable).
4. Reasons for the issue, problem or questions and their importance to you as a teacher (rationale, personal theories/beliefs about teaching).
5. Literature relevant to your research issues, if applicable (how it informed/motivated your research).
6. Teaching plans and actions for changing the situation (beginning of action research cycle, focus, expectations, reasons for selecting).
7. Tools/techniques used to collect data (why you chose them and how you used them to answer your questions).
8. First observations and reflections (happenings, successes/failures, insights from actions, examples from data).
9. Next directions, if applicable (further cycles, plans, actions, data collection, more samples from data).
10. Data presentation, organisation and analysis, as applicable to cycles (quotes, excerpts from transcripts, categories, samples, tables, graphs, figures).
11. Struggles, difficulties, dilemmas, questions coming from the research cycles.
12. Insights, findings, solutions, inspirations coming from the research cycles.

13. Reflections, interpretations on the findings.
14. Reflections, feelings, interpretations on the process.
15. Personal knowledge, learning and realisations developed from the action research experience.
16. Future directions (new questions, further steps, changes to practice, recommendations).
17. References, pictures, appendix.

This may seem a rather long list, but it is meant as a checklist of what could be covered (for another checklist, see Burns, 1999, pp. 184–185). Remember, the way you write up your account is not a 'set piece'. Your style and approach will vary according to the audience you are writing for, your own individual preferences, and also the context and nature of your research. In the end, it's up to you how you see the best way to tell the story of your research. At the end of this book in the Postcript, I've included examples of how two teachers have set out accounts of their AR, which might also be helpful.

Action point

Make brief notes on each of the points above most relevant to your research. This will help you to start preparing the ideas you will cover in your report.

If possible, run them past a colleague or mentor who is familiar with your research.

ASSIGNMENTS, DISSERTATIONS AND THESES

Of course, if you are enrolled in a formal course of study, you may have no option other than to write in a required style. Written assignments are standard in bachelor, certificate and masters courses. Action research has now become part of many such courses for language teachers around the world and you may be asked to prepare an AR proposal (see Chapter 2, Appendix 2.3 for one model) and/or to write a research report (see Postscript).

Classroom voices

This is how one teacher educator arranges the AR part of the course:

> My approach to teaching this seminar is that students attend 30 hours of lectures and discussions, they write a proposal for their own original research, they peer-review one another's proposals, they carry out the research (either singly or in teams), and they peer-review the drafts of one another's research reports, before giving formal oral presentations and submitting their final papers.

Especially if you are studying for a masters or beyond you may even write a whole dissertation or thesis for which you have chosen an AR approach. Outlining how to write a thesis is well beyond the scope of this discussion. But I can give you some brief advice on starting along a professional development pathway through formal study. These points are based on my experiences of teaching and supervising my own students (and I hope they will help you to get the grades you want!):

- Read the requirements of the assignment very carefully and make sure you have covered all the points you should include.
- Consult your tutor, lecturer, or supervisor if you have any uncertainties about the content and style (don't leave this until the last minute!).
- Read as widely as possible on your topic and try to go beyond just the set readings for your course.
- Try to find AR articles in books and journals and study the style in which they are written.
- Outline your arguments in a clear and logical sequence and provide theoretical support for your points and your claims.
- Display your data as fully as possible to support your claims.
- Develop a writing voice in an appropriate academic style.
- Signal the sequence of the research story to your reader. Draw attention at various points to where in the story you now are and what your readers can expect next.
- Use appropriate headings and sub-headings to structure the assignment – present your work well.
- Become familiar with styles for using headings and sub-headings and use them consistently.
- Become familiar with a well-known style for listing your references (APA, Harvard, Chicago are some of the ones commonly used).

- List all the references in the text that you have used.
- Number appendices, tables and figures clearly and in sequence if you have used them.
- Spell-check and proof-read your assignment!

Reflection point

If you are enrolled in a course of study, consider how the points above reflect your experiences of completing written assignments. What would you add to this list?

Discuss your ideas with other students in your course and/or with your course tutor.

Once you have completed your dissertation or thesis you will be in a very good position to consider submitting an article to a national or international journal. Your formal studies will have given you an idea about the range of journals interested in AR that you could target. I've written in more detail about writing for journals in a previous publication (Burns, 1999), but here, just briefly, are some of the things you should consider:

- Target the journal carefully to identify whether its aims and audience are in line with your topic.
- Find out about the editorial policies by looking at the information provided in the journal or on the journal website.
- Get hold of previous copies of the journal and examine the types of articles included in the journal and their style and format.
- Obtain the style sheets or guidelines for contributors for the journal.
- Follow the requirements for contributions to the journal carefully (e.g., length/layout of paper, referencing style).
- Write the article in an accessible and clear way suitable for the readership of the journal.

(Adapted from Burns, 1999, p. 189)

Some professional associations and conferences, such as the annual TESOL Convention, offer sessions involving journal editors speaking about their journals. If you get the opportunity, it is well worth attending to find out more about the range of journals available in the language teaching field.

In this section I've outlined a variety of oral, visual, and written ways of sharing and publicising your research. Of course, these ideas are not exhaustive and, as I mentioned, ways of presenting and reporting AR are still under development. In my opinion, there are no limits to creative ways of presenting that might be appropriate for the different audiences you want to reach. I encourage you to be as imaginative as possible in the way you publicise your research.

5.4 On with the action!

We have almost come to the end of this book and our explorations into AR. However, the last thing I want to do is leave you with the impression that AR is something that leaves no impact on you when you finish it. Most teachers find that even when their research cycles end and they want a break, their levels of awareness, knowledge and engagement with the world of teaching have shifted in ways they didn't expect. These classroom voices come from personal messages sent to me by action researchers from around the world.

Classroom voices

Doing a research study in my own classroom provided me with the chance to examine the daily work I do with my students. The results from the study's quantitative analysis were reaffirming. They clearly showed that my lessons facilitate language acquisition. No-one else could have given me this information. It was about me, my students, and our work together. (Jami, Mount Prospect School, Basking Ridge, New Jersey USA)

Doing action research has completely changed the way I approach a critical part of what I teach. It has made the link between theory and action in my teaching much stronger and given me new insights and the confidence to pursue them. Every time I complete a new cycle there are new ideas to think about and explore, and discuss with other teachers. Without the discipline of the research I would have missed many of these insights. (Heather, Auckland University of Technology, New Zealand)

I'd say that AR has opened a new perceptual avenue for me personally and professionally. Action research has helped me refine my question-making process concerning my teaching and my students' learning. After having been engaged in AR practice for some time, I realised that my discomfort with issues I didn't know how to deal with in my classroom could actually be explored, understood and maybe solved. (Heliana, Universidade de Minas Gerais, Belo Horizonte, Brazil)

Being involved in action research works inside you like a vaccine. Once you have been vaccinated, you are for life. Once you've been through an action research cycle your look on pupils and teaching changes in a way that is irreversible. (Mariacarla, a teacher who worked with Graziella Pozzo in Italy)

> To me the most impressive aspect of research was that it combined two roles into one: I, the teacher, who knows the real classroom atmosphere, became also the researcher, who can suggest things about teaching and learning. (Cem, a teacher who worked with Derin Atay in Turkey, Public Primary School, Umraniye, Istanbul)
>
> In carrying out research in their own classrooms, reflecting on the researched practice and underlying theory and sharing results with a wider audience, teachers often come to see the routines of preparing lessons, managing learning and marking students' work in a new light. (Antonia, National Institute of Education, on her experiences of working with many teachers in Singapore)
>
> During my first few years of teaching, I was painfully aware that I didn't have all the answers – and that was a tremendous source of anxiety. Was I really helping my students, or was I doing them more harm than good? After 14 years in the classroom, I am much more secure in the knowledge that I will never have all the answers, but that together with my students I can ask some intriguing questions. Action research is a way to examine those nagging doubts and come up with the answers that matter in our classrooms. I have found it to be the ideal way to instil the excitement and enthusiasm I had as a novice teacher into my practice as a more seasoned educator. Action research has helped me transform my questions from a source of anxiety into a source of curiosity. (Sharon, EARTH University, Guácimo de Limón, Costa Rica)

As these action researchers suggest, AR makes a striking contribution in numerous ways to the field of language teaching. Teachers deepen their professionalism when they plan, act, observe and reflect on their classroom actions. They develop awareness of the practical theories that drive them, either individually or with their colleagues. More and more, the voices of language teachers from around the world who have done AR are contributing to classroom practice, curriculum development, and knowledge about effective ways to teach English in different contexts. As a result, the quality of teaching and learning in our field should become ever more open to continuing change and improvement. As more teachers show they are willing to exhibit and share their knowledge about the successes and failures, questions and dilemmas in their classrooms, the language teaching field should become more inclined to open up its teaching practices to discussion and critique. This movement helps to broaden the knowledge base of language teaching (see Johnson, 2009) and contributes to our understanding of important issues in second language acquisition research. As I argued at the beginning of the book, AR is also a 'democratic' or 'participatory' movement for our field. It enables language teachers, who have usually been either the 'subjects' of research or excluded from research altogether, to enter an AR 'community of practice' and gain a stronger professional presence. Consequently, the gap between the work of educational theorists and the work of teachers becomes reduced. Rather than recommendations for practice being made at a distance from the classroom, teachers can become an integral part of testing out how feasible these recommendations really are in different contexts.

5.5 Summary point

In this chapter we have considered the role of reflection in the process of AR. We noted that reflection is fundamental to the way you start to change or improve situations in your classroom and develop your own knowledge and awareness about the meaning of your research. Deep and ongoing reflection contributes to developing 'personal practical knowledge' and finding the personal theories that lie beneath teaching. We then considered how continuing cycles of AR might become part of your research process, as well as when it might be appropriate to bring the research cycles to an end.

I argued that a very important aspect of the cycle is sharing with other teachers what you have discovered about the issues you identified in your classroom. We then looked at different ways that your AR can be presented – orally, visually and through writing. All these modes allow the reflections you've gained through AR to go even deeper. Not only do they summarise the research process, but they help you to identify and express to other teachers what has been important and meaningful about it.

We ended the chapter by noting that AR leaves its mark on us as professional educators. Teachers from different parts of the world, who have investigated and improved their classroom situations, reflected on what AR meant for them. Now that you have read this chapter, you should have increased your understanding about:

- why reflection is an essential part of AR;
- when and how reflection takes place in the AR cycle;
- how and why cycles of AR can go on developing;
- when to continue researching and when to bring the research to an end;
- the relationship between reflection and presenting your research to others;
- the reasons why teachers should publicise their AR;
- ways to present your research orally, visually and through writing;
- the impact of AR on teachers professionally and personally.

5.6 Final words

I wrote this book because of my many positive encounters with teachers all over the world who have told me they are interested in AR. Many of these teachers had never done research but were keen, committed, and enthusiastic professionals eager to make their classrooms the best places they could for their students. They were excited about the idea of AR and were looking for user-friendly guidelines to help them make a start.

As I leave you, my reader, who has accompanied me through these chapters, my sincere wish is that this book will inspire you to get started in AR. Of course, it is impossible for me to put myself in your exact teaching situation or to answer your questions directly. But I hope the classroom voices I've brought into this book – many of them known to me personally – will guide and encourage you as you try out the ideas yourself or with your colleagues. I'll leave you with ten things I've learned over the years about how to build success into the AR journey – and I wish you good luck!

1. Find colleagues interested in AR to work with.
2. Maintain a reflective and enquiring attitude to your teaching.
3. See classroom challenges and 'problems' as positive opportunities for change for you and your students.
4. Be confident in your ability to find good outcomes for classroom challenges.
5. Look for opportunities and take risks to change your teaching strategies.
6. Follow your interests and passions about teaching.
7. Keep reviewing and refining your personal practical knowledge.
8. Be a strong voice for teacher inquiry and professional development in your organisation.
9. Share your research with others.
10. Don't be discouraged – keep going!

References

Altrichter, H., Posch, P., & Somekh, B. (1993). *Teachers investigate their work: An introduction to the methods of action research.* Abingdon: Routledge.

Burns, A., & Hood, S./Burns, A., & de Silva Joyce, H. (Series Eds.). (1995-2005). *Teachers' voices series 1-8.* Sydney: National Centre for English Language Teaching and Research.

Burns, A. (1999). *Collaborative action research for English language teachers.* Cambridge: Cambridge University Press.

Burns, A., & Richards, J. C. (Eds.). (2009). *The Cambridge guide to second language teacher education*. New York: Cambridge University Press.

Dadds, M., & Hart. S. (Eds). (2001). *Doing practitioner research differently*. London: Routledge.

Fischer, J. C. (2001). Action research rationale and planning: Developing a framework for teacher inquiry. In G. Burnaford, J. Fischer, & D. Hobson (Eds.), *Teachers doing research: The power of action through inquiry* (pp. 29-48). 2nd edition. Mahwah, NJ: Lawrence Erlbaum Associates.

Golombek, P. (2009). Personal practical knowledge in L2 teacher education. In A. Burns, & J. C. Richards (Eds.), *The Cambridge guide to second language teacher education* (pp. 157-164). New York: Cambridge University Press.

Johnson, K. E. (2009). Trends in second language teacher education. In A. Burns, & J. C. Richards (Eds.), *The Cambridge guide to second language teacher education* (pp. 20-29). New York: Cambridge University Press.

McPherson, P.(1997). Action research: Exploring learner diversity. *Prospect: A Journal of Australian TESOL*, 12(1), 50-62.

McPherson, P. (2008). Exploring student responses in an immigrant language program. In A. Burns, & J. Burton (Eds.), *Language teacher research in Australia and New Zealand* (pp. 117-132). Alexandria, VA: TESOL.

Morioka, T. (2007). Action research report. In K. Sato, & N. Mutoh (Eds.), *NUFS workshop 2007: Action research report* (pp. 108-110). Nagoya, Japan: Centre for EFL Teacher Development, Nagoya University of Foreign Studies.

Polanyi, M. (1962). *Personal knowledge*. Chicago: University of Chicago Press.

Sato, K., & Mutoh, N. (2007). *NUFS Workshop 2007: Action research report*. Nagoya, Japan: Centre for EFL Teacher Development, Nagoya University of Foreign Studies.

Zephir, F. (2000). Focus on form and meaning: Perspectives of developing teachers and action-based research. *Foreign Language Annals*, 33(1), 19-30.

Postscript: Action Research in Action

Throughout this book I've offered ideas and excerpts from the action research of teachers around the world. As I've worked with teachers interested in AR, many of them have asked for concrete examples of how to write up accounts of their research. This postscript to the discussions in this book presents examples to illustrate how two teacher action researchers working with very different students in very different teaching contexts went about summarising their work. The examples are not meant to be idealised models but illustrations of two ways to create a short AR account. So they should be read in the spirit of possibilities and not 'recipes' for the approaches you could take.

The first author, Salima Khamis Al-Sinani, works in Oman and was undertaking AR as part of completing a BA (TESOL) programme through the University of Leeds in the UK. The programme was supported through the Ministry of Education in Oman and offered practising teachers the opportunity to upgrade their qualifications to degree level. Salima was teaching a Basic Education Grade 4 class of 30 children who were mostly 10 years old in the Muscat Region. She chose to investigate self-assessment in her classroom, an area which is of great interest to many teachers.

The second author, Ari Van Eysden, works in the Australian Adult Migrant English Program (AMEP) which offers English language tuition nationally to adult immigrants coming into the country. The programme focuses on helping students settle into and participate in their new English-speaking surroundings. Ari was one of the teachers I worked with in a national project which focused on how teachers could teach vocabulary effectively in order to help their students learn. In the project teachers worked collaboratively and shared their teaching strategies, research processes and reflections. When she conducted her action research, Ari was working in a small teaching centre in the north of Tasmania where her class was of very mixed levels and contained learners of different ages.

The third author, Cheng Xixu, works at the School of English for Special Purposes of Beijing Foreign Studies University. His paper is a report of a three-semester action research project implemented to improve the classroom interactions in the comprehensive reading course of a non-major English class.

As a follow-up to many of the ideas presented in this book, I hope you enjoy reading about their AR and the way they carried it out in their respective teaching situations.

Developing Learners' Self-assement Skills*

S.K. AL-Sinani

Introduction

The Basic Education curriculum for English in Oman provides learners with regular opportunities for self-assessment; my experience, though, is that learners often complete the self-assessments routinely and without much awareness of their purpose. In this study, therefore, I wanted to examine how my learners do self-assessment and what I might do to enable them to develop the ability to assess themselves more effectively.

Self-assessment in language learning

What is Self-Assessment?

Self-assessment (SA) is any assessment that requires learners to judge their own language abilities or performance against a set of criteria (Bourke, Poskitt & McAlpine, 1997; Brown, 1998). Its main purpose is to provide learners with the opportunity to develop an understanding of their own level of skill or knowledge by asking themselves 'How am I doing?' and then 'How can I do better?' (Sweeny, 1994).

Methods of Self-Assessment

Various methods of SA exist. One of these is a progress profile; this includes tools such as records of achievement and progress cards (Cram, 1995). Another popular method is the questionnaire; this can include statements of ability (using 'I can') for learners to judge themselves against or rating scales

* In S. Borg (Ed.), (2009), Investigating English language teaching and research in oman. Oman: Ministry of Education. Reprinted with permission.

on which they assess their knowledge or skill by marking a number. A third method is description and reflection, which involves SA through diaries and other forms of narrative self-reporting.

In *English For Me* (the coursebook used in the Basic Education curriculum in Oman), learners do SA at the end of each unit. In Grade 4, book 4B, there are five questions; the first two focus on vocabulary and spelling respectively, while questions 3, 4 and 5 focus on what learners can do, which activities they liked, found difficult and easy, and on their overall work on the unit (see the Appendix for an example). SA questions 3, 4 and 5 are the ones I focused on in this study.

Benefits and Problems in Self-Assessment

Benefits

Cram (1995) argues that through SA children achieve greater control over their learning – it helps them to monitor their own work, makes them aware of what they have done well and where they need to do more work. It enables them to define their own strategies for further action and to identify the sort of help they need to improve in any particular area. Furthermore, SA promotes autonomous learning (Dickinson, 1987) and encourages intrinsic motivation. For the teacher, Cram (1995) argues that SA alleviates the assessment burden.

Problems

Bourke, Poskitt & McAlpine (1997) point out that some learners find it difficult to praise themselves while others find it hard to critically evaluate their work. Another inevitable problem with SA is the language, as talking about learning will be a demanding task for younger learners (Curtz, 2005). There are also potential problems with the validity and reliability of SA; teachers' and learners' assessments may differ and learners may not apply the assessment criteria consistently. Finally, SA is seen to be more time-consuming; McAlpine (2000) in fact argues that sometimes the amount of time required to implement and sustain SA in the classroom is a major demand on teachers.

Making Self-Assessment Effective

Heilenman (1990) suggests that SA should involve simple activities that learners can already do. Learners also need help in learning how to assess themselves (Rolheiser & Ross, 2000; Curtz, 2005); for example, they need to see the teacher or other learners modelling the process and to have opportunities to talk about what it means to self-assess. Furthermore, as Muschamp (1996) suggests, SA needs to refer to learning objectives which have been made clear to the learners.

Ur (1996) also suggests that SA should make use of clear criteria and weighting systems which have been discussed with the learners and which they understand.

Method

Research Questions

Overall, my aim here was to develop my learners' ability to assess their own learning. To achieve this, I looked for answers to the following questions:

1. What are the problems that my Grade 4 learners have with SA?
2. What techniques can I adopt to address these problems?
3. How effective are these techniques in developing my learners' ability to assess their own learning?

Participants

Data for this study were collected in a Basic Education Grade 4 class. There were 30 children in the class (13 boys and 17 girls) and they were mostly 10 years old. This was their fourth year of learning English. In particular, I focused on six of these learners who represented a range of abilities in English.

Data Collection

This study followed an action research approach (Burns, 1999). I examined a problematic aspect of my own teaching, introduced changes, and evaluated the results of these changes. I worked through this process using one preliminary review stage and four main stages, in which I collected data through observation, interviews, and teacher and learner assessments. I describe each stage of the study below.

Reviewing Current Practice

In this preliminary phase I wanted to identify a focus for the study. I thus observed how I was conducting SA by examining its use in one lesson. I used the SA activities in the coursebook (see the Appendix) and followed the procedures recommended in the teacher's book – reading and explaining the statements for Question 3, helping learners to identify activities they liked, found difficult and easy for Question 4, and helping learners complete Question 5 to assess their overall work in the unit. My observation of this procedure highlighted one major problem: time. We had about 10 minutes at the end of the lesson to do the SA and it was clearly not enough. As a result, all the SA questions were completed in a rush.

After the lesson I interviewed the learners participating in this study as a group. One point that emerged here is that they had different understandings of the 'I don't know' option in SA Question 3 (which asks about whether they can do certain things). For example, learner F said that 'I don't know' was somewhere between 'yes' and 'no', learner A said it meant 'not sure', while learner E said it means 'not very yes and not very no'. This suggested that a focus for the first stage of changes in my use of SA would be to give the learners more specific SA scales to work with, in addition to allowing more time.

Stage 1: Changing Methods and Timing

I introduced four changes to SA. Firstly, I replaced 'yes, 'no' and 'I don't know' in the question where learners self-assess the extent to which they can do certain things with 'very well', 'quite well' and 'a little' (see Littlejohn & Hicks, 1996). Secondly, I ensured that every SA statement covered a specific skill, as some of the original statements in SA Question 3 covered two (e.g., reading and writing). Harris (1997) stresses that the more specific the questions, the easier they are for learners to answer and the greater reliability they are likely to have. Thirdly, in Question 4, where learners describe activities they liked, found difficult or easy, and say why, I supported the learners by supplying any vocabulary they needed to express their views. Finally, to address the time issue, I dedicated a whole 40-minute lesson to SA.

My observation of this SA lesson indicated that it went well. The learners had enough time to complete all the questions and to look back through the coursebook in doing so. However, when I analysed the learners' self-assessments and compared them with mine, I found that most of them had overestimated their learning (this applies to Questions 3 and 5 in SA tasks).

I interviewed each learner individually the next day. Some interesting points emerged. For example, learner E (a weak learner) said that she thought that I would send the SA sheets to her parents, and for this reason wanted to rate herself highly. Learner C said that because other learners could see what he was writing he was embarrassed to write down that he only understood a little. Learner D said he thought his self-assessments would be used in his final assessment for the year. These insights were useful in helping me understand why the learners overestimated their ability.

Stage 2: Modelling and Developing Awareness of Self-Assessment

In this stage of the study I focused on making learners more aware of the value of SA. I explained the purpose of SA to them and why it was important to express their actual views. I also used the modelling technique (see Rolheiser & Ross, 2000; Curtz, 2005) to demonstrate how SA can be conducted. I used myself as a thinker and modelled in front of the whole class how to self-assess; I modelled asking questions, asking why I am good at something, why I need to do more work on certain areas, and why certain activities were favourites, easy or difficult.

My observations of this lesson suggested that the learners understood my main points – they were able to repeat the key points back to me.

Stage 3: Sharing Objectives

In this stage, I used an idea suggested by Muschamp (1996) which involves sharing with the learners the objectives of our work. At the start of Unit 5, I introduced the topic of the unit, its main objectives, the outcomes I expected learners to achieve, and what kinds of activities they would be doing. Finally, I directed their attention to the particular aspects of the unit which would be the focus of the SA for that unit.

Stage 4: On-going SA

The final issue I examined in this study is whether I could (as Harris, 1997 suggests) integrate SA more fully into my lessons rather than dealing with it separately at the end of the unit. To experiment with this, I took the statements for Question 3 of the SA from Unit 6 (these statements ask the learners how well they can do certain activities completed in the unit); then, as we worked through the unit, before each activity referred to in the SA statements I asked the learners to predict how easy or difficult the activity was going to be. Then, after the activity, I asked them to complete the SA for it. This allowed me to integrate SA into the lesson, although Questions 4 and 5 of the SA had to be done at the end of the unit.

Findings

The description of the stages above has already highlighted certain findings to emerge from this study, particularly in relation to the problems learners experienced during SA and how these were addressed. Here, though, I want to focus specifically on the self-assessments completed by the learners during the study.

As noted above, I focused here on Questions 3, 4 and 5 in the SA tasks in the coursebook and I now discuss each of these in turn.

Question 3

I analysed learners' answers to Question 3 of the SA tasks for four units of the coursebook. I then compared the extent to which these assessments matched my own assessment of their work on the same units. Following Al-Jardani (2002), self-assessments were classified as overestimates, underestimates and matches. Underestimate means that a learner's assessment was lower than mine, over-estimate that it was higher and match that it was the same. Figure 1 summarises the findings of this analysis.

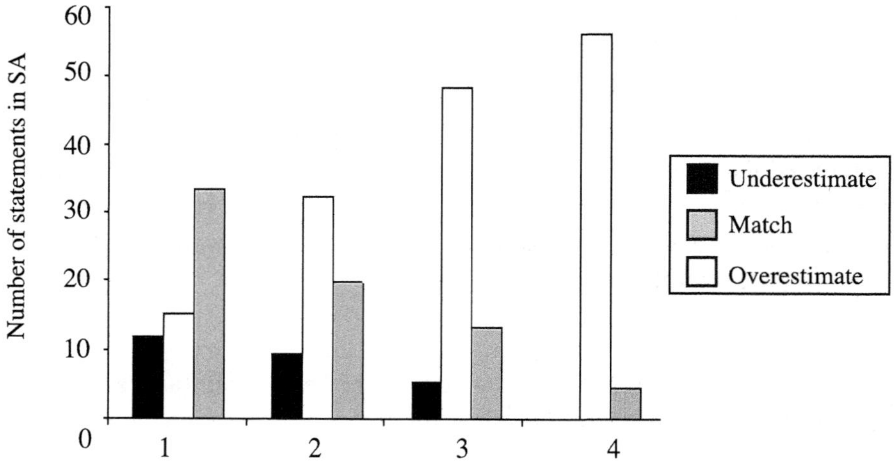

Figure 1 Comparison of learner and teacher assessment on Question 3 of SA tasks.

This figure shows that learners over-estimated their ability most frequently in Stage 1 of this study and that the number of overestimates decreased with each stage. By Stage 4 of the study less than 7% of the learners' self-assessments of their abilities were higher than my own and over 93% matched mine. This is evidence that during this study the learners became better at assessing themselves.

Question 4

Question 4 of the SA asked the learners to identify favourite, easy and difficult activities (and, ideally, to comment on these). To examine developments in learners' responses to this question I compared their answers in the preliminary stage of the study (before Stage 1) with those in Stage 4. I also drew here on the interviews I did after Stages 1 and 4.

At the start of the study, most answers the learners gave to this SA question were short, often just one word. Also, some learners named the same activities under the different questions – e.g., they named the same activity as both their favourite and as one which was difficult. This suggests that learners were not thinking carefully about their answers here. Even after I provided vocabulary they could use in commenting on the activities they mentioned, most learners were not able to explain why they liked an activity or found it difficult. This was true in the interviews too; when I asked learners why they said an activity was their favourite, the answer typically was 'because it is my favourite'.

At the end of Stage 4, in contrast, the learners were able to write longer, more complex and complete sentences. A wider range of activities were also mentioned in their answers. This was also reflected in the interviews I did after Stage 4. The learners were more confident in explaining why they liked activities or found them easy or difficult. For example, learner F said that doing a questionnaire about the environment was her favourite activity because she wanted to find out about her own views; she found out that she is green and likes to protect the environment and earth. These findings provide further evidence that the learners developed their ability to self-assess during this study.

Question 5

Question 5 in the SA tasks asked learners to provide an overall evaluation of their performance on the unit. I once again compared the learners' assessment for each stage of the study with my own. The results of this comparison are shown in Table 1, which shows, for each stage in the study, how often the self-assessments were higher (overestimate), lower (underestimate) or the same (match) as my own.

Table 1 Comparison of teacher and learner assessments of overall performance

Stages	*Underestimate*	*Match*	*Overestimate*
1	1	1	4
2	0	4	2
3	0	6	0
4	0	6	0

The trend here is quite clear; learners tended to overestimate their overall performance on the unit at the start of the study, but their assessments became more aligned with my own as the study progressed. In fact, in Stages 3 and 4, all six learners' self-assessments matched my own.

Discussion

At the start of the study I identified two issues which seemed to work against effective SA: limited time and rating scales which were open to interpretation. I addressed these in Stage 1 of this project by providing more time and making the criteria more specific; however, these changes, while desirable, did not produce very positive results as most learners overestimated their ability and performance.

Interviews suggested a number of reasons why learners self-assessed themselves positively: lack of understanding of the purposes of SA, lack of experience in assessing themselves, and fear of negative consequences (from parents, classmates, and the teacher) if they rated themselves too low. I would suggest that cultural factors were partly responsible for learners' fears, and a number of authors have noted that SA can be difficult in educational contexts (such as Oman) where learners and parents expect high assessment scores and may react negatively when this is not the case (Harris, 1997; Smith, 2000).

In Stage 2, the explicit discussion of SA I provided for my learners together with the modelling of the SA process seemed to have a positive effect on the learners' ability to self-assess as seen in the extent to which their assessments matched my own. The focus on sharing objectives I provided in Stage 3 also seemed beneficial, again as shown in the way learners' assessments matched my own.

In Stage 4 my focus was on integrating SA more fully into my lessons rather than doing it separately at the end. This technique (which I used for one of the SA tasks) seemed particularly effective as learners' assessments of their abilities matched mine in almost all cases.

Overall, then, the findings here suggest that my learners' ability to conduct SA did improve as we worked through the different stages of this study. The different factors described above and which I introduced at each stage of the study combined to promote this improvement. Additionally, it is possible that learners' on-going engagement in SA itself enhanced their motivation to learn English, developed their language, and hence was reflected in more effective SA.

Limitations

In interpreting these findings we must remember that I focused on six learners in one Grade 4 class and that studies with larger groups of learners are needed to further explore the wider effectiveness of the different strategies for improving SA which worked well here. In judging the reliability of learners' self-assessments I also relied solely on my own judgements; involving an additional outside assessor would have provided a further point of comparison.

Conclusion

This study suggests that key reasons why SA may not be effective are learners' lack of understanding of its purpose and the fact that many learners simply do not know how to assess themselves. SA can be improved, I believe, if teachers spend time in the classroom focusing on these issues. In addition, providing adequate time for SA and ensuring that the SA tasks themselves are clear can also improve the effectiveness of SA. Looking for ways of making SA part of the lesson, rather than a separate activity at the end of the unit, can also make SA more meaningful and purposeful for learners. Doing this study has allowed me to explore ways of using SA more effectively with my learners and I hope it provides other teachers with ideas they can use in improving the SA skills of their learners too.

Appendix: Self-assessment tasks in EFM grade 4

3 Norw I can

	Yes	No	I don't know
• talk about what things are made of	☐	☐	☐
• ask and answer questions about what things are made of	☐	☐	☐
• read about what things are made of	☐	☐	☐
• describe different types of homes	☐	☐	☐
• read about the types of homes people live in	☐	☐	☐
• write about my home	☐	☐	☐
• write about the types of homes people and animals live in	☐	☐	☐
• read about where people live	☐	☐	☐
• write about where people live	☐	☐	☐
• read a song about different types of houses	☐	☐	☐
• sing a song about different types of houses	☐	☐	☐
• read the story of The Three Rabbits and the Big Bad Wolf	☐	☐	☐

4

My favourite activity was______________________________

The most difficult activity was__________________________

The easiest activity was________________________________

5 My work in this unit was

excellent

very good

good

(*English for Me*, Grade 4B Skills Book, p. 43)

References

Al-Jardani, K. (2002). An on-going evaluation of the effectiveness of self-assessment in the new *English for Me* Grade 5 as a part of education reform in Oman. Unpublished BA TESOL Dissertation, University of Leeds, UK.

Bourke, R., Poskitt, J., & McAlpine, D. (1997). *Self-assessment in the New Zealand classroom* [Video]. Wellington, New Zealand: Ministry of Education.

Brown, J. D. (Ed.). (1998). *New ways of classroom assessment.* Alexandria, VA: TESOL.

Burns, A. (1999). *Collaborative action research for English language teachers.* Cambridge: Cambridge University Press.

Cram, B. (1995). Self-assessment from theory to practice: Developing a workshop guide for teachers. In G. Brindley (Ed.), *Language assessment in action.* Sydney, Australia: NCELTR.

Curtz, T. (2005). Teaching self-assessment. Retrieved 13 August 2005 from www.evergreen.edu/ washcenter/resources/acl/e1.html

Dickinson, L. (1987). *Self-instruction in language learning.* Cambridge: Cambridge University Press.

Harris, M. (1997). Self-assessment of language learning in formal settings. *ELT Journal*, 51, 12-20.

Heilenman, L. K. (1990). Self-assessment of second language ability: The role of response effects. *Language Testing*, 7, 174-201.

Littlejohn, A., & Hicks, D. (1996). *Cambridge English for schools: Starters student's book.* Cambridge: Cambridge University Press.

McAlpine, D. (2000). Gifted and talented students: Self-assessment. Retrieved 8 April 2005 from www.tki.org.nz/r/gifted/reading/assessment/self_e.php

Muschamp, Y. (1996). Pupil self-assessment. In A. Pollard (Ed.), (2002), *Readings for reflective teaching in the primary school.* London: Cassell.

Rolheiser, C., & Ross, J. (2000). Student self-evaluation: What do we know? *Orbit*, 30(4), 33-36.

Smith, K. (2000). Negotiating assessment with secondary-school pupils. In M. Breen, & A. Littlejohn (Eds), *Classroom decision-making: Negotiation and process syllabuses in practice.* Cambridge: Cambridge University Press.

Sweeny, B. (1994). Glossary of assessment terms: Self-assessment. Retrieved 9 April 2005 from www.teachermentors.com/RSOD%20Site/PerfAssmt/glossary.html#anchor96926

Ur, P. (1996). *A course in language teaching: Practice and Theory.* Cambridge: Cambridge University Press.

Watching to Learn or Learning to Watch*

A. Van Eysden

The setting

My action research was carried out in two very small AMES centres, based on the north-west coast of Tasmania and run by me as a single teacher. Participating in this research project gave me an opportunity to work collaboratively with AMES staff in the other two much larger centres in Tasmania, an opportunity that I valued very much as it gave me the feeling of being part of a team.

The two classes were held once per week, giving students only four hours per week to attend formal English classes. Almost all of the students were also involved in the Distance Learning Program. In Tasmania, we have only three terms per year, and this project took place in the third and final term of the year, which was ten weeks long. There had been no specific focus on vocabulary all year.

The two groups were disparate in nature, the students ranging from beginner to post-intermediate level learners CSWE I to CSWE III. Their ages ranged from 19 to 45 years.

* In A. Burns & H. de Silva Joyce (Eds.), (2001), *Teachers' voices* 7. Sydney: National Centre for English Language Teaching and Research. Reprinted with permission from the National Centre for English Language Teaching and Research, and in acknowledgement of research support from the Department of Immigration and Citizenship, Settlement Branch, AMEP Section, Australia. Full text is available at http://www.ameprc.edu.ac/docs/research_reports/teachers_voices/teachers_voices_7.pdf

Group A:

- six students
- males and females
- humanitarian and migrant entrants
- majority came from one language background
- different cultural, social and educational backgrounds
- none of the students had any prior English language learning experience.

Group B:

- four students
- only spouses of Australian men
- from different cultural backgrounds.

The decision to carry out the action research with students in both groups was based on the fact that they were only small groups and there existed a good bond between the students in each group. Both groups had been working together for most of the year and consequently knew each other and their teacher very well. Each class was quite different in terms of group dynamics. The students were informed about the project and from the beginning appeared keen to cooperate.

General aims of my research

As these learners spent relatively little time in the actual classroom, and all of them possessed a television, I wanted to find out if teaching them strategies to learn new words from television was a feasible method of helping them on a path towards autonomy. I was also keen for helping them to be able to use strategies to develop vocabulary in a range of other contexts – for example, when listening to the radio or while eavesdropping on casual conversations around them. I wanted to focus on the following issues in relation to vocabulary learning:

- television as a contextualised learning environment that provides imagery to facilitate comprehension
- comprehensive learning
- developing a systematic approach over an extended period of time.

A change in focus

Originally, my objectives were to enable the students to:

- listen for specific sounds
- transcribe the sounds into words by using the phonemic alphabet

- spell the words
- look up the meanings of the words in their bilingual dictionaries
- keep a list of new words in the back of their books.

However, it soon became apparent that the introduction of the phonemic alphabet served only to confuse the majority of students. This was due to a lack of time to teach the phonemic alphabet to students who were totally unfamiliar with it and probably my own lack of experience in using it as a teaching tool.

Consequently, I decided to allow the students to use whatever strategy they wanted to pick up new words while watching television. I encouraged them to write down what they heard in any way that was familiar to them. Then I asked them to share with the rest of the group how they went about *deciphering* their words. I hoped that they would be able to adopt new strategies for themselves, if appropriate. What followed was an enlightening and engaging exercise in which every student was able to participate.

Research method

I chose to do this research through teacher reflection. I set aside some time at the end of every teaching session to write down what had transpired in the class.

Pre-research activity

At the end of the second term I asked all the students to watch TV during their two-week holiday break. I asked them to come back to class with some new words they had learned from TV. I did not explain why. As expected, on our first day back, only two people in Group A had completed the task.

I administered a questionnaire about vocabulary development and helped the students with the questions, where necessary. I discussed the results of the questionnaire with the groups and explained how this was connected to a research project. This led to an immediate rise in interest in vocabulary acquisition and the action research project. At this stage nothing was mentioned about strategies for listening, as I wanted them to explain how they would go about listening for new words without any influence from me.

My next step was to determine if there was one TV program that the whole group would like to watch. After some animated discussion in both groups, Group A decided on *Water Rats* and Group B chose the *6 O'clock News*. It was decided that the students would use only the first segment of *Water Rats* (up to the first set of advertisements) and the first item of the news to listen for new words. The students were asked to come to the next class with at least one word they had learned from their TV viewing. The results of this initial viewing are outlined in the table [overleaf].

In Group A, we did not watch the program again in class. There seemed little point as all the words had been interpreted correctly, albeit with help from family members. The students were also not interested in watching it again.

In Group B, we did watch the news again and successfully deciphered the two words for Student 9. At this stage I introduced the phonemic alphabet to the group. I showed them a chart and where to find it in the dictionary. The purpose was to show Student 9 and the two weaker students how sounds could be translated into letters and then into words. Student 9 became confused and frustrated with this activity, but Student 8 became very interested and asked for more practice. Owing to lack of time, we were unable to continue with this activity during the class but we decided to watch another news item at home.

The next step

It was obvious at this point that few students had independent strategies for learning new words from watching television. In Group A, it also became difficult to decide on one program that everyone was prepared to watch. I decided that the students should learn one word from any program. They had to share the word and the strategy they used to learn it with the rest of the class. I stipulated that they were not to ask any other person for help. I asked the students to keep a very brief journal. They had to:

- record the TV programs they watched
- record the channel, the time and the day
- write down at least one new word from each program.

At the beginning of each lesson, I asked one or two students to tell the rest of the class their results. The students were told in advance when their turn would be and I started with the more confident ones. I also had a quick look at the journals of the other students so that they would be encouraged to participate on a weekly basis.

It was made clear that the point of the exercise was for them to become independent learners. From then on, the research began to resemble a steam train. It started off slowly and sluggishly but gradually gathered momentum until all students felt they could participate successfully. I think it is best described by giving details about each individual learner.

Group A: *Water Rats*					
	Level	**Sex**	**Age**	**Country**	**Strategy/Comments/New words**
S1	2/3	M	19	Bosnia	• didn't like it, therefore no new words
S2	2	F	40	Bosnia	• asked her daughter who had watched it with her for both the English word and its meaning • *collapse, oxygen*
S3	1	M	45	Bosnia	• too difficult for him to write anything while watching but he nevertheless enjoyed program
S4	1/2	F	23	Russia	• asked her husband whose English is excellent • *negotiate, violent, protest*
S5	1	M	23	Bosnia	• good program but no new words because it was all too difficult
S6	1	F	26	Bosnia	
Group B: ***6 O'clock News***					
S7	1	F	36	Indonesia	• asked husband who had watched it with her • *festival*
S8	1/2	F	26	Russia	• no words • she could not write them down because she could not spell them
S9	3 High oracy, low literacy	F	32	Cambodia	• she had scribbled down something that sounded like word but had no idea what the words were • words were only deciphered after watching segments again in class • *pre-purchased tickets, regular*
S10	3 Strong in oral and written skills	F	34	Fiji	• had written words down mostly spelled correctly • then checked the spelling and meaning in her dictionary • *interstate, contestants*

Group A

Student 1

Characteristics:

- son of S2.

Strategies:

- decided that if his mother (S2) could learn new words so could he
- biggest problem was having the patience to use a dictionary correctly, so almost a whole lesson followed on dictionary use
- total of his new words always remained less than his mother's – I believe this is due to the fact that basically his learning style was very different
- made it quite clear that he preferred to learn new words from mates as then he does not need to use a dictionary.

Student 2

Characteristics:

- wife of S3
- mother of S1
- spoke same language as S5 & S6
- student in this class for about one year
- arrived with no English
- from beginning displayed all the signs of a good learner.

Strategies:

- set the pace in this group
- soon convinced everyone in the class that it was possible to learn new words this way and that it could be done independently
- concluded that it was preferable to work independently as you did not need to bother anyone else that way and could do it when it suited you
- strategy was to listen carefully for a word, phonetically write down immediately what she heard, look at the context in which the word appeared in the program and broadly understand the context
- later tried to look up word in dictionary
- if couldn't find word, would look for another first letter that sounded the same
- discovered that usually, if she had the first three letters, she could guess rest of word by looking at all words in the dictionary starting with same letter and from reading all the meanings she was able to discover the word she wanted
- successfully did this with words such as *kolaps*, *diskastet*, *korapt*, *loja*, *wof*
- conceded not always possible but that did not matter because nobody is perfect and you cannot always be successful, e.g. had no success with

eksost (exhaust) and *polodjast (apologised)* – I helped her decipher these words by listening to her pronunciation and asking her for the context in which they appeared

- after she had finished her turn there was a lot of class discussion about letter/ sound connections as well as about unstressed syllables including suffixes and prefixes.

Student 3

Characteristics:

- husband of S2
- took up challenge of following wife's strategies but with less success
- much more insecure character and far less willing to take risks
- progressed from no words per TV program to 2 or 3
- became an avid fan of *Water Rats*.

Strategies:

- new words included *viktim, dispir, difend, keptred*
- words *disappear* and *captured* led to another class discussion on word stress and unstressed syllables and how to guess which letter could be represented by the unstressed sound
- conceded that it was better to work independently rather than to rely on his children
- decided that it was very difficult to learn new words if he was watching for pure enjoyment
- still preferred it if someone would simply tell him the word and its meaning.

Student 4

Characteristics:

- better reading and writing skills than all of the other students
- had some prior English in her native country
- listening and speaking skills were initially very poor
- whole activity became exciting as she discovered she could understand more and more words
- advantage was being able to spell the sounds more easily, e.g. *selebracion, perminent, hils, trust, desirabel, leeder, promicing*
- was learning up to a dozen new words per TV program.

Strategies:

- wanted to show off her ability to the other students by coming to the front of the class and writing all her words up on the board from memory

- at the same time explained some of the sound/spelling relationships she had rediscovered, e.g. the effect the letter *e* has on the end of a word and the sound of the letter *y* depending on its position in a word
- assured the other students that she was becoming less lazy and not asking her husband for the meaning any more but looking up the words in her dictionary instead.

Students 5 and 6 enrolled late and found it the most difficult. Both left before the end of the research project to go interstate. Student 6 was often absent.

Student 5

Characteristics:

- eventually decided to try learning new words from TV
- a risk taker but very impatient at the same time
- not very successful.

Strategies:

- in the end the only way to elicit any words from him was to do it as a class activity on the board from memory
- I recorded a local news story for the class from which all students had to listen for one new word and he heard *aspekt (expect)* and *fishel (official)* but could find neither in the dictionary without help – S2 explained how to find them.

Group B

The research took a slightly different turn with this group. Student 10, having had several years of English at school in her native country, Fiji, was the only one who had little trouble listening for new words. She also possessed all the traits of a good learner and was able to write down independently a long list of words from every TV program and find them in her dictionary – for example, *surveillance camera*, *ombudsman*, *moratorium*, *candidates*, *regulated*. She seemed to enjoy the exercise and acknowledged that her vocabulary had increased over the period of the research project.

Students 7, 8 and 9 continually came to class with no entries in their journals. Some said they could do it if they were allowed to ask their husbands for help, but they had collectively vowed not to do so. Student 9 often had a list of indecipherable scribbles in her book, the sounds of which she could not reproduce in class, so that I was unable to help her. Subsequently, I decided to record some programs for them and play them in class to see if we could come up with some successful strategies. I chose news items, as I had already ascertained that they all watched the news. We tried several, lasting from one minute to about ten minutes in length. The shorter the item, the more difficult they found it, mainly because it was too fast for them and they had no time to establish the context, let alone pick out individual words.

It was at this stage that Student 7 began to focus on the written words that often appear on the screen. She started writing them down as her new words and finding the meanings in her dictionary. Students 8 and 9 immediately liked this idea. I then asked them to listen for the same word again and, when they heard it, they were to call it out. I then stopped the videotape to listen to its sound. This did not always happen but several successful cases did occur – for example, with the words *murder*, *gambling*, *holdup*, *tourist attraction*, *seahorse*, *investigation*, *justice*, *offences*, *swimming pool fees*, *elections*, *motorists*, *road toll*, *annual*, *full bloom*. Once the words had been heard, we would look at the letter/sound relationships and examine the phonemic alphabet.

Student 9 continued to find this confusing, but Student 8 decided that this was an excellent strategy. Before long, she had mastered most of the sounds and from then on she became confident listening for new words and dared to write them down. Until then, she had consistently refused to write anything down, saying that she could not possibly do it.

I then asked the students to go home and do the same. This time they did come back with lists of new words. Student 9 turned her attention to SBS [Special Broadcasting Service, www.sbs.com.au] and wrote down whole sentences that she had been unable to understand, e.g., *He tapped his fingers to the thumping beat of the music* and *I gave a silent thanks*. Interestingly, she also came with words such as *occasionally*, which she had not recognised in their written form. They had remained meaningless to her, even after looking them up in the dictionary. However, as soon as she heard the spoken word she recognised it instantly. Student 10 left the class before the completion of the research project to take up full-time work and was soon replaced by a beginner learner from Thailand. This student was unable to participate successfully in the project at such short notice.

Conclusion

It was certainly possible for the students to learn new vocabulary from watching TV, regardless of their level of English language proficiency. However, most students needed a lot of initial support before they realised they could learn new vocabulary this way. Once the support was taken away, their ability weakened.

The ability to be successful appeared to be closely related to individual learning styles, and students seemed able to adopt new strategies only if they suited their learning styles.

Students from phonetic language backgrounds, such as the Balkan countries, appeared to be able to transcribe sounds more correctly than students from Asian language backgrounds.

The longer the program they watched, the more likely it was that they could pick up new words from it. Obviously, context played a large part in this, as learners had more time to understand the context of a longer program and they were also more likely to pick up a word that was repeated more than once.

Classroom discussions about vocabulary acquired, the difficulties encountered and the sharing of strategies led to an unusual bonding among the students, and lessons became entirely learner-centred.

Where the sound was too difficult to decipher, the research shifted to the written word that appeared on the TV screen, either with news items or as subtitles on SBS programs. This also became a valuable vocabulary acquisition tool.

A personal reflection

I enjoyed participating in this research project and found it to be an invaluable activity. I learned a tremendous amount about the learning styles and preferences of my students and understood much better what the difficulties were for them. However, I feel that my data collection leaves much to be desired. As most of the data was given orally in class discussions and I wrote my reflections mostly at the end of the day, much of the rich treasure that comprised the language used by my students to describe their efforts was lost. I should have recorded it and transcribed some of the more delightful evidence given by my students. Although I was made aware of this method of data collection at the very beginning of my research, it completely slipped my mind and ultimately I had to rely heavily on my own memory of events.

Written evidence, produced by the students themselves, would have been extremely beneficial (besides their word lists), but I overlooked that also. I do believe though that both of these methods of data collection have their disadvantages in that the spontaneity would have been lost had the students known they were being recorded or if they had been asked to write about it. One of the reasons why they were so frank in their discussions is the fact that we all know each other so well. I would like to thank my students for their unfailing cooperation throughout this research project.

打破大学英语课堂中的沉默
——提高课堂互动的行动研究*[1]

程熙旭[2]

提要：本文是针对情感因素影响大学英语阅读课课堂互动进行的持续三个学期的行动研究项目报告。针对大学英语课上时常出现互动不佳、学生沉默、课堂氛围不够好的情况，只加强对课堂互动重要性的认识，加强对教材的把握，采取积极的教学态度以及改进教学理念等还远远不够。情感也是影响课堂互动的重要因素之一。本研究发现，在采取了多项措施拉近学生与老师的心理距离、帮助学生建立互信合作的关系后，课堂上师生间、学生间的互动都得到了实质性的改观，课堂沉默显著减少。

关键词：大学英语教学；行动研究；课堂互动；师生关系

1．前言

在大学英语课堂上，尤其是在阅读课程（如精读）的课堂上，课堂沉默是一个比较普遍的现象。如谢元花（2006）与滕明兰（2009）等所说，在大学英语课堂上，常常是老师自顾自地在讲台上讲，课堂上的交际互动比较少，学生对老师所提出的问题、互动的要求反应冷淡，课堂气氛经常比较沉闷，场面有时非常尴尬。

在笔者的大学英语教学班级里就经常出现这种现象。笔者所教授的对象是某外语大学商学院一年级的学生，由两个自然小班合并而成，约48人。他们的入学成绩与该大学英语专业一年级新生相差无几。按照该大学的课程设置，商学院学生所学英语课程为双学位、双专业课程，即除了商

* 本文原载《中国外语教育》2011（1）。

1 感谢文秋芳、周燕、朱梅萍、任庆梅四位老师对本文的悉心指导，感谢杨华、修晨、张东英、叶如帆等老师给本文所提的宝贵意见。

2 北京外国语大学专用英语学院讲师。主要研究领域：翻译研究、英语教学。电子邮箱：chengxixu@bfsu.edu.cn

学方面的专业课程外，英语也按照英语专业的标准来进行教授。所用教材是由外语教学与研究出版社出版、杨立民主编的《现代大学英语》第一、二册。精读课程每周6课时。课堂互动不好、气氛沉闷，这使学生的学习兴致不高，教学效果也大打折扣。作为老师，笔者相当沮丧。

笔者是一位年轻教师，专业方向是翻译理论与实践，没有经过系统的教师培训。从事教学工作虽然已将近十年，但还不够自信，所以在教学中基本不敢跳出教材来教学，多数时候都是按部就班地按照词汇、课文、课后练习的顺序来教授课文，并没有认识到课堂互动的重要性。由于习惯于在课堂上以讲授语言知识点为主，很少设计课堂互动的活动，这在很大程度上影响了课堂上的互动。认识到可能是自己在对教材的把握、教学态度、教学理念等方面上的欠缺导致了课堂互动性比较差，笔者就试图从这些方面入手来改进自己的教学，可效果还是不理想。课堂上沉默现象还是时常出现，课堂上互动不起来。

2009年10月笔者成为教师—研究者互动发展团队的一员，参加了这个团队对课堂教学的讨论，了解和学习了行动研究方法。加上受罗淑兰（2002）、赖非等（2006）以及刘红梅（2008）等研究的启发，笔者使用了行动研究的方法对自己的阅读课进行了观察和反思，作出了改善课堂沉默、提高课堂互动性的努力。该研究从2009年10月到2011年1月持续了3个学期。本文是笔者对这一过程的报告。

2. 问题分析

2.1 最初的观察

在教授一年级阅读课一个学期的时间里，虽然加强了自己对教材的把握，改进了教学态度、教学理念、教学方法等，但笔者注意到在课堂上沉默现象还是比较严重。对笔者提出的问题学生主动回答比较少，即使在给学生充分的思考时间后，如果不点名让学生起来回答，学生还是经常沉默不答，最终结果往往是笔者提出问题，经过较长时间的沉默等待后由笔者自己尴尬地给出答案。课堂上除了基本的提问外，安排的一些相关活动，如小组讨论等，也都由于多数学生习惯于沉默而不能很好地开展。很多学生在对该课程的学期评估中也提到了课堂沉闷、课堂互动较少或者互动不成功的问题。

2.2 最初的反思

看到课堂上学生这么沉默、互动难以开展，笔者反思了自己和自己的教学，翻阅了研究课堂互动性或课堂沉默的相关文献。徐飞（2003）总结了影响师生课堂互动的五个因素：教师理念、学生理念和学习策略、课堂焦虑、师生关系以及教学技巧。贾晓琳（2008）提到课堂参与者、课堂任务和活动以及教材与班级大小等影响课堂互动的因素。

细想这些因素，其中有一个被笔者忽略了，那就是师生关系在课堂互动中的作用。项茂英（2003）认为不好的师生关系会减少或减弱课堂互动。谢元花（2006）与滕明兰（2009）则直接谈论了大学课堂沉默中来自教师方面的原因。谢元花（2006）认为教师要不断地调整自己的教学方式、方法，调整自己在课堂上的角色，努力创造一个有序的、宽松的、有趣的课堂环境，减少学生的紧张和焦虑情绪，使学生积极地参与课堂的各项活动。滕明兰（2009）观察到教师的性格特征、教学观念、教学方法和师生关系的亲疏对大学生课堂参与有较大的影响，认为良好的师生关系对于打破大学生课堂沉默，促进学生自主发展，全面提升教学质量有着重要的意义。国外很多研究者也研究了师生关系对课堂互动的影响。Walsh（2002）认为教师在课堂上使用的语言可以促进和优化或者弱化课堂互动。Poulou（2009）认为在互动积极的课堂上，师生在行为上常表现为相互尊重。Lewis & Hill（2009）认为和谐的师生关系对课堂互动有很大的帮助。反思笔者自己的教学，的确没有形成能够带来良好课堂互动的师生关系。作为年轻教师，笔者最想做的就是在学生中树立自己的权威。课堂上严肃的表情，课后刻意与学生保持一定距离，这些都让学生对自己敬而远之。在课堂上笔者几乎就是讲授知识，与学生没有多少交流，课后也没有留给学生多少时间和空间与自己沟通、交流。这样笔者与学生之间就形成了放任型的师生关系——语言知识成为连接师生关系的唯一纽带，认知与情感脱离；与学生之间很少沟通，有距离感（项茂英，2004）。笔者在教学中将认知与情感分离开来了，没有建立平等、互信的师生关系，增加了学生在学习上的焦虑和不安。笔者想如果笔者能够与学生建立平等和谐的关系，课堂沉默的现象应该会得到改善，课堂互动也应该会更好。

3. 行动干预的第一阶段

3.1 行动设计与实施

项茂英（2004）给出了四条改善师生关系的建议：（1）在教学活动中，教师应把学生看作客户和伙伴，认知与情感并重；（2）增加师生交往的时空，真正了解每一个学生；（3）真诚对待学生，尊重学生；（4）注意评价方式，保护学生的自尊心。根据这些建议，把如何实质改善笔者和学生的关系考虑进去后，笔者从以下几个方面作出了调整，对教学过程进行了设计和有意识的干预。

1）快速识记每位学生。笔者用两三周的时间记住了班上每一位学生的名字。记住学生的名字会拉近学生与笔者之间的距离，为真正了解学生打下基础，而且可以更好地针对每一位学生开展教学，作出适当的课堂评价。以前由于笔者叫不上很多学生的名字，课堂上让学生回答问题时只能这么提："第三组倒数第二桌的同学请回答一下这个问题"，对学生的反应也不能给予合适的反馈。识记学生后，每一位学生都觉得受到了老师的重视，对老师互动的要求会更积极地回应。

2）增加师生沟通的机会。创造和利用更多的时间、空间与学生沟通、交流，拉近与学生之间的心理距离。笔者在课间与学生聊天、谈心，谈他们最近的学习表现，交流学习体会，谈学习态度和学习方法/策略，增进了学生与笔者的亲近感。针对课堂口头报告，与学生谈论他们对课文的理解以及他们对课文内容所涉及主题的看法。笔者还抽出专门的时间来接待学生。为了方便学生联系，笔者把各种联系方式都给学生。此外，笔者对学生的课外生活给予更多关注，利用各种机会更多地了解学生，从更多渠道更好地了解学生的学习需求。

3）营造轻松的课堂氛围。笔者改变以往在课堂上不苟言笑的严肃态度，耐心、真诚、平等地对待每一位学生。在课堂上发现并引导学生表现自己的长处，及时给予表扬，不当众批评学生，而是把学生所犯错误提高到知识误区的高度来给全班同学讲解，解除学生在课堂上学习的焦虑与不安情绪。把学生对教师那种敬而远之的心态调整过来，去除他们心中对教师的敬畏感，营造出一个轻松愉快的课堂学习氛围。

4）努力做到认知和情感结合。在教学中笔者不再只重视认知，单纯传授语言知识，而是更多地注意情感因素对教学的影响。努力改变以往只按自己备课内容而不顾学生具体学习需求的上课模式。笔者采用了让学生写学习反思并匿名上交、问卷调查以及个别访谈等几种方式来了解学生对该课程的具体需求，了解他们学习的兴趣点和困难点，让学生明白教师不是想一味地教授课本知识，而是更想了解、倾听他们对英语学习的真实想法，不再片面强调学生是否掌握课本知识，而忽视能激发他们学习热情和创造潜能的师生情感交流。

3.2 **观察与发现**

令笔者感到高兴的是，课堂上沉默的现象有所改善，课堂互动也能开展起来，在小组讨论之类的活动中学生变得活跃了。这些改变主要体现在课堂话语量、参与度和课堂配合等几个方面。

1）课堂话语量增多。学生不再像以前那样不愿甚至躲避课堂互动活动，在课堂上发言时自信心更强，能更详细地阐述自己的观点。有些学习成绩好的同学，因为原本的语言功底好而更加愿意在同学面前表达自己的看法，而对自己语言能力不太自信的学生也能积极地回答笔者上课时的提问，与同学积极讨论课文主题。学生L1原先在课下跟笔者请假时说话都会结巴，甚至嘴角抽搐。在笔者找时间与他聊了几次之后，该生在课堂上能克服原本高度的紧张感，积极回答问题，甚至大胆与同学用英文进行辩论。

2）课堂参与度提高。通过采取收取和阅读学生的学习反思笔记、找学生访谈、问卷调查等一系列措施后，笔者更多地了解了学生的学习需求；与学生及时沟通后，笔者安排了更多的课堂活动，学生更愿意参加到课堂活动中来，大家的学习积极性大大提高，使笔者常常不得不适当延长课堂活动的时间。学生在两人活动、小组活动中更加投入，每次笔者让小组成员作总结发言时，他们都能得到同学的赞许或反驳。课堂上的口头报告也准备得更加充分，常常起到引人思考的作用，也更能吸引同学的注意力。角色扮演任务也都能完成得很好，给人留下深刻的印象。

3）教与学出现融洽的配合。学生与笔者在教学中配合融洽了。在与学生课下多次沟通、交流后，学生更加了解笔者在教学各环节中的目的和用心，笔者也更多地知道了学生在哪些环节可能会遇到困难和问题，这样在教学各环节中学生与笔者的配合就更好了。布置的课后任务有更多的学生完成得很好，课堂安排更加紧凑了，教学中因为没有学生接话而冷场的现象基本不见了。学生L2在作与课文话题相关的课堂口头报告前，对笔者就该问题的看法作了录像访问，让学生更多地了解到笔者对此话题的观点。学生Z在笔者提到要作调查后主动提出要帮助我设计问卷，并帮助笔者分析问卷结果。这些配合在干预措施实施前都不太可能出现。

虽然对教学进行干预后，课堂互动有所改观，可是笔者也发现有些学生在语言程度不够好的同学发言时表现出兴趣不高，甚至有时候会在课堂上发出嘘声。这对发言学生的积极性打击较大，以后发言也没有那么踊跃、主动了，总是要先大概写下来再说。还有些语言程度较好的学生在课堂上还是跟以前一样，不太认真，回答问题或者被叫起来发言时也没怎么准备。

3.3 反思

通过第一阶段的调整，笔者放下了教师的权威，努力增进师生情感，改变放任型的师生关系，建立了平等和谐的师生关系，课堂上的沉默现象得到了改观，学生不再像原先那么沉默，而是变得活跃了很多，课堂热闹了不少。从这些表现来看，老师与学生在课堂上的互动的确是有了改善、提高。可是部分学生对待某些发言同学的态度以及某些语言程度较好的学生课堂上表现还是不够积极，这说明课堂上某些参与者之间没有真正互动起来，实际的课堂互动效果还不是很好——学生与学生之间的互动不够理想。笔者之前未能意识到，学生与学生之间的互动和师生之间的互动共同构成课堂互动，任何一者的缺失或者不到位都会影响或减弱整个课堂互动的效果。笔者本来以为都是同龄人，学生彼此间更熟悉，产生互动应该比师生之间产生互动更为容易，事实证明并非如此。因此，需要进一步采取措施来提高学生与学生之间的互动。

4. 行动干预的第二阶段

4.1 行动设计与实施

由于观察到学生与学生之间的互动在课堂上还有所欠缺，在保留了针对前一个班建立平等和谐的师生关系的做法的同时，针对新的班级笔者又采取策略来建立互信合作的生生关系，并且在建立平等和谐的师生关系的同时利用教师这个身份去使师生关系积极地影响生生关系。一方面，帮助学生树立互信合作的观念。从第一次课起，笔者就反复强调学生不仅要向老师学习，也要向同学学习，学生与学生要互信合作，形成共同学习的集体，最好是能形成学习共同体，要求学生不仅在平常的生活中互相帮助，更要在学习上形成团队，提高学习效率。笔者抓住每一次机会给学生进行这方面的教育，让他们改变高中时期各自为政的学习观念。另一方面，帮助学生建立互信合作的机制。笔者请班级负责人带领他们根据自愿原则结成学习对子和学习小组，每次课堂活动基本上都是以集体的方式进行（例如，每讲一篇新课文之前都给学习小组或者是学习对子布置必须共同完成的任务），给每次活动记录成绩时都把集体协作这一项作为考察的标准之一，用机制让学生形成团队合作的学习习惯。这些围绕建立互信合作的生生关系的策略都是以平等和谐的师生关系为前提的，因此按照前一阶段的措施建立起平等和谐的师生关系是第二阶段行动的关键。

4.2 观察与发现

采取新的措施后，课堂上有了一些新的变化——学生与学生间能产生积极、正面的互动了。经过事先布置的课外学习小组讨论后，很多学生对文章理解得更好了，很多难句难词在课前就得到了解决。课堂上学生每次都会针对课文提出一些思考问题，有些问题是笔者作为老师都没有想到过的。比如，在 Christmas Day in the Morning 一课中，很多学生就提出作者为什么反复五六次提到星星，这在任何一本教学参考书中都没有提到过。问题都是学生自己提出来的，而且事先大家都在小组中进行了相关讨论，课前小组与小组间的讨论也经常发生。这使得课堂上学生们对笔者针对相关话题提出的问题兴趣更浓，课堂上的焦虑更少了。课堂上，不仅师生互动更好，学生与学生的互动也开展得很顺利。语言程度不够好的学生发言时再也没有同学发出嘘声了，大多数学生都会认真听其他同学发言并且积极作出回应。有一次轮到一位维吾尔族学生Y作口头报告，他认识到自己基础比较差，主动找笔者辅导他作口头报告。第二天，尽管他的口头报告没有同组其他几位同学那么好，但是大家给了他很多掌声和鼓励，并没有由于他做得不够好而不认真听或者取笑他。当笔者告诉他们这位同学进大学前才学了两年英语时，他们报之以更加热烈的掌声。事后，与他同组的一位同学M告诉笔者，笔者的辅导给了这位维吾尔族学生很大的鼓励，他很需要这样的鼓励。可见，平等和谐的师生关系积极地影响了生生关系，促进了课堂上各方面的互动。

不过，笔者也发现，在互动得到改善的课堂上还是存在个别学生上课懈怠、不认真听讲的现象。而且，尽管笔者多次强调并告知学生可以去完成什么样的学习任务，个别学生以及个别学习小组却没有认真完成笔者布置的针对课文提问的课前任务，只是抄袭别人的问题，学习小组里没有什么讨论，学习对子的活动也很少进行。

5. 对整个行动研究的反思

总体来看，采取措施建立平等和谐的师生关系和互信合作的生生关系后，课堂上出现了令人欣慰的变化。原先多数时候沉默的课堂变得热闹了许多，课堂互动也开展得更多、更好。行动研究中，笔者在认识到自己的错误观念对课堂互动带来的不良后果后采取适当的措施，在很大程度上提高了课堂互动性，也在一定程度上提高了教学效果。然而，也出现了一些新问题，如学生在更多地了解教师后，在课堂纪律上变得比原先随意起来，导致迟到现象时有发生。这应该是改善师生关系的措施不够严谨，导致教师和学生对课堂上师生关系的认识走向了另一个极端。还有个别学生不认真，不积极参与到课堂活动中去的问题。这些问题是改善师生关系、生生关系的措施和策略实施不够到位带来的，还是其他方面的因素导致的呢？这需要教师在教学中继续去发现、研究并努力解决。当然，行动研究本身的原则和基本方法告诉我们，作为研究主体的教学本身是一个在研究中不断改善和提高的过程，而不是一个一次性可终结的过程。就本次行动研究而言，建立平等和谐的师生关系与互信合作的生生关系也不是一次或三两次就能完成的，需要教师采取更多有效的办法，也需要更长的时间。

6. 结语

师生关系虽然不是影响课堂互动的全部因素，但是在很大程度上影响着课堂互动，继而影响教学效果。教师应该把理解和处理好师生关系作为自己教学上努力的一个方向。教师对师生关系认识错误的话，则不能与学生建立起平等和谐的关系，就不能取得好的教学效果，更谈不上教学相长了。教师，尤其是刚入职不久的年轻教师，面临如何在学生中树立威信的问题。在现代社会，传统大学英语教学中师道尊严的模式和做法不利于教师树立威信。教师应该拉近与学生的距离，了解学生的需求，建立平等和谐的师生关系。教师不仅应该在认知上、教学技术上，还要在教学情感上作出很大的努力，以有效地改善课堂教学，提高教学效果。同时，还需要认识到平等和谐的师生关系有助于建立互信合作的生生关系，进而对课堂互动中的学生与学生间的互动产生积极的影响，因此教师需要帮助学生建立起互信合作的关系，只有这样才会在真正意义上提高师生互动、生生互动，即整个课堂互动的实际效果。

参考文献

Lewis, M. & J. Hill. 2009. *Practical Techniques for Language Teaching* [M]. Beijing: Foreign Language Teaching and Research Press.

Poulou, M. S. 2009. Classroom interactions: Teachers' and students' perceptions [J]. *Research in Education 82*: 103-106.

Walsh, S. 2002. Construction or obstruction: Teacher talk and learner involvement in the EFL classroom [J]. *Language Teaching Research 6* (1): 3-23.

贾晓琳，2008，大学英语课堂互动问题研究[D]。硕士学位论文。长春：东北师范大学。

赖非、杨晶、韩芳，2006，大学英语精读课加强师生互动行动研究[J]，《山东教育学院学报》（3）：58−61。

刘红梅，2008，改善大学英语课堂互动性——行动研究报告[J]，《山东外语教学》（1）：75−79。

罗淑兰，2002，提高教师和学生在英语课堂上的互动性——一份行动研究报告[J]，《南昌航空工业学院学报》（1）：84−86。

滕明兰，2009，大学生课堂沉默的教师因素[J]，《黑龙江高教研究》（4）：146−148。

项茂英，2003，情感因素对大学英语教学的影响[J]，《外语与外语教学》（3）：23−26。

项茂英，2004，大学英语教学中的师生关系[J]，《外语界》（4）：37−42。

谢元花，2006，外语课堂学生沉默与教师的教学风格[J]，《广东外语外贸大学学报》（1）：30−32。

徐飞，2003，大学英语教学师生课堂互动的影响因素分析及对策研究[D]。硕士学位论文。重庆：重庆大学。

Further Reading and Resources

Here are some useful sources for expanding your knowledge about AR in English language teaching. I've tried to include some of the most recent publications and also some older 'classics'. I hope it's a useful starting point and not too overwhelming!

Chapter 1: What Is Action Research?

For general overviews of action research in English language teaching

Burns, A. (1999). *Collaborative action research for English language teachers.* Cambridge: Cambridge University Press.

Burns, A. (2009). Action research. In J. Heigham, & R. A. Croker (Eds.), *Qualitative research in applied linguistics: A practical introduction* (pp. 112-134). Basingstoke: Palgrave Macmillan.

Burns, A. (forthcoming). *Action research.* In B. Paltridge, & A. Phakiti (Eds.), *Continuum companion to research methods in applied linguistics.* London: Continuum.

Crookes, G. (1993). Action research for second language teachers: Going beyond teacher research. *Applied Linguistics*, 14(2), 130-144. Available at http://www2.hawaii.edu/%7Ecrookes/acres.html

Edge, J. (2001). Attitude and access: Building a new teaching/learning community in TESOL. In J. Edge (Ed.), *Action research.* Alexandria, VA: TESOL.

Freeman, D. (1998). *Doing teacher research.* New York: Heinle and Heinle.

Gebhard, J. G. (2005). Awareness of teaching through action research: Examples, benefits, limitations. *JALT Journal*, 27(1), 53-69.

Nunan, D. (1989). *Understanding language teaching: A guide for teacher-initiated action.* London: Prentice-Hall.

Wallace, M. (1998). *Action research for language teachers.* Cambridge: Cambridge

University Press.

Useful websites

The Internet is overflowing with sites providing readable introductions to AR – just try putting'action research' into Google! Here are two of my favourites which provide lots of resources:

http://www.scu.edu.au/schools/gcm/ar/arp/books.html

This is a very comprehensive list of books on action research, not necessarily related to language teaching. It is updated twice a year by Bob Dick at the Southern Cross University, Queensland, Australia.

http://carbon.cudenver.edu/~mryder/itc_data/act_res.html

This website is maintained by Martin Ryder, School of Education, University of Colorado at Denver. It is full of useful AR articles and information, including a link to a very comprehensive list of other AR websites: http://www.emtech.netactionresearch.htm

For extensive discussions of research approaches in English language teaching

Brown, J. D., & Rodgers, T. S. (2002). *Doing second language research.* Oxford: Oxford University Press.

Dörnyei, Z. (2007). *Research methods in applied linguistics.* Oxford: Oxford University Press.

Hatch, E., & Lazaraton, A. (1991). *The research manual: Design and statistics for applied linguistics.* Rowley, MA: Newbury House.

Hinkel, E. (Ed.). (2005). *Handbook of research in second language teaching and learning.* Mahwah, NJ: Lawrence Erlbaum Associates.

Holliday, A. (2002). *Doing and writing qualitative research.* London: Sage.

Johnson, D. M. (1992). *Approaches to research in second language learning.* White Plains, NY: Longman.

Mackey, A., & Gass, S. (Eds). (2005). *Second language research: Methodology and design.* Mahwah, NJ: Lawrence Erlbaum Associates.

McDonough, J., & McDonough, S. (1997). *Research methods for English language teachers.* London: Arnold.

McKay, S. L. (2006). *Researching second language classrooms* Mahwah, NJ: Lawrence Erlbaum Associates.

Nunan, D. (1992). *Research methods in language teaching.* New York: Cambridge University Press.

Perry, F. L. (2005). *Research in applied linguistics: Becoming a discerning consumer*. Mahwah, NJ: Lawrence Erlbaum Associates.

Porte, G. K. (2002). *Appraising research in second language learning*. Amsterdam: John Benjamins.

Richards, K. (2003). *Qualitative inquiry in TESOL*. Basingstoke: Palgrave.

Chapter 2: Plan – Planning the Action

Finding a focus for your research

Mann, S. (1999). Opening the insider's eye: Starting action research. *The Language Teacher*, 23(12), 11-13.

This is a very readable article with some good ideas on getting started.

Sagor, R. (2005). *The action research guidebook: A four-step process for educators and school teams*. Thousand Oaks, CA: Corwin Press.

See Chapter 2 for more good ideas on finding a focus.

Ethical issues

Flick, U. (2006). *An introduction to qualitative research*. 3rd edition. London: Sage.

Chapter 4 has a useful discussion and provides website addresses of organisations that present codes of ethics in the social sciences.

For a very extensive example of the ethical areas that need to be addressed at my university, go to: http://www.research.mq.edu.au/researchers/ethics/human_ethics. You may not need to supply nearly as much information as this for your action research! But it gives you an idea of the areas that have to be covered for university study in some locations and the kind of information required.

Chapter 3: Act – Putting the Plan into Action

Observations

Bailey, K., Curtis, A., & Nunan, D. (2001). *Pursuing professional development: The self as source*. Boston: Heinle and Heinle.

Chapters 7 on video and 9 on peer observation have useful practical advice.

Interviews

Richards, K. (2009). In R. Croker, & J. Heigham (Eds.), *Interviews: Qualitative research in applied linguistics* (pp. 182–199). Houndsmill, Basingstoke: Palgrave Macmillan.

Questionnaires and surveys

Dörnyei, Z. (2003). *Questionnaires in second language research: Construction, administration and processing*. Mahwah, NJ: Lawrence Erlbaum Associates.

An excellent guide and introduction to designing and administering questionnaires.

Diaries and blogs

Suzuki, R. (2004). Diaries as introspective research tools: From Ashton Warner to Blogs. *TESL-EJ*, 8(1). Available at http://www-writing.berkeley.edu/TESL-EJ/ej29/int.html

Chapter 4: Observe – Observing the Results of the Plan

I particularly recommend the following reader-friendly guides for data analysis:

Qualitative analysis

McKay, S. (2003). *Researching second language classrooms*. Mahwah, NJ: Lawrence Erlbaum Associates.

Richards, K. (2003). *Qualitative inquiry in TESOL*. Basingstoke: Palgrave.

Quantitative analysis

Brown, J. D. (1988). *Understanding research in second language learning: A teacher's guide to statistics and research design*. New York: Cambridge University Press.

Brown, J. D., & Rodgers, T. S. (2002). *Doing second language research*. Oxford: Oxford University Press.

Clegg, F. (1990). *Simple statistics: A course book for the social sciences*. Cambridge: Cambridge University Press.

Validity in AR

Newman, J. (1999). *Validity and action research: An online conversation*. Available at http:// www.scu.edu.au/schools/gcm/ar/arr/arow/newman.html

Provides an interesting online discussion on this thorny issue.

Schwalbach, E. M. (2003). *Value and validity in action research: A guidebook for reflective practitioners*. Lanham, MD: The Scarecrow Press, Inc.

Provides a short and user-friendly introduction to building quality action research and the role of validity.

Chapter 5: Reflect – Reflecting and Planning for Further Action

Accounts of AR conducted by language teachers

Burns, A., & Hood. S./Burns, A., & de Silva Joyce, H. (Series Eds.). (1995–2005).

Teachers' voices series 1-8. Sydney: National Centre for English Language Teaching and Research.

This is a series of eight books each with a different AR focus. Provides numerous examples of accounts written by Australian adult ESL teachers. To download books in this series go to http://www.ameprc.mq.edu.au/resources/professional_development_resources/professional_ development_resources?80032_result_page=6

Edge, J. (Ed.). (2001). *Action research.* Alexandria, VA: TESOL.

Provides interesting accounts of action research from teachers internationally.

Farrell, T. S. C. (Series Ed.). *Language teacher research in* ... Alexandria, VA: TESOL.

Each volume focuses on teacher research conducted in different regions of the world. There are six volumes with different editors: Asia (Farrell, 2005); Europe (Borg, 2006); the Americas (McGarrell, 2007); The Middle East (Coombe & Barlow, 2007); Australia and New Zealand (Burns & Burton, 2008); Africa (Makalela, 2009).

Hadley, G. (Ed.). (2006). *Action research in action.* RELC Portfolio Series 8, Singapore: SEAMEO Regional Language Centre RELC. Available at http://www.nuis.ac.jp/~hadley/publication/relcar/action-research.pdf

Action research by teachers in Singapore.

Tinker-Sachs, G. (2002). *Action research: Fostering and furthering effective practices in the teaching of English.* Hong Kong: City University of Hong Kong.

Provides reports on action research by teachers in Hong Kong secondary schools.

Warne, A., O'Brien, M., Syed, Z., & Zuriek, M. (Eds.). (2006). *Action research in English language teaching in the UAE.* Abu Dhabi: HCT Press.

PAC Journal

Many of the articles focus on AR conducted by teachers in Asia.

Profile Journal

Provides accounts of AR by teachers in Latin-America with a focus on Colombia.

Writing AR for formal study

Borg, S. (Ed.). (2006). *Classroom research in English language teaching in Oman.* Sultanate of Oman: Ministry of Education.

Borg, S. (Ed.). (2008). *Investigating English language teaching and learning in Oman.* Sultanate of Oman: Ministry of Education.

These two volumes arose from the action research conducted for a BA (TESOL) project offered by the University of Leeds and initiated by the Ministry in Oman for teachers to gain university level teaching degrees. The books contain short accounts written by teachers in this programme.

Warne, A., O'Brien, M., Syed, Z., & Zuriek, M. (Eds.). (2006). *Action research in*

English language teaching in the UAE. Abu Dhabi: HCT Press.

Gallagher, K., & Bashir-Ali, K. (Eds.). (2007). *New classroom voices: Action research and initial teacher education in the UAE.* Abu Dhabi: HCT Press.

Both these volumes highlight accounts by teachers of projects they undertook for Bachelor of Education degrees offered through the University of Melbourne.

Writing AR theses

Davis, J. (2004). Writing an action research thesis: One researcher's resolution of the problematic of form and process. In E. McWilliam, S. Danby, & J. Knight (Eds.), *Performing educational research: Theories methods and practice* (pp. 15-30). Flaxton, Queensland: Post Pressed.

Provides an interesting discussion of the challenges faced in writing up an AR extensive research study.

Index

action 4, 9, 17, 65-116; concluding the action 173-174; continuing in new cycle 171-172
action research 2, 12-17; cycle of 9-10, 170-174; definitions of 5-7; goals of 2, 5-6, 40; ideologies of 40-41; for teachers 1, 2, 5, 20-23, 193-194
action research accounts 187-190; examples 201-232
Aldana, A. 80-81
Al-Fahdi, H.M. 74, 79, 84
Al-Farsi, N. 144-145
Allwright, D. 21, 22-23
Al-Sinani, S.K. 199, 201-210
Altrichter, H. 84, 125, 169, 189
analytical observation 81-82
assignments 190-191
assumptions 19-20, 31, 32-33
audio-recording 83-84, 91, 95

Bailey, A. 48
Banda, F. 89-90
bar charts 161
Barkhuizen, G. 52-53
behaviour checklist 76-77
beliefs and values: examining 31-34; reflection on 168-169
books, consultation of 48-49
Boolean search 49
Bourke, R. 201, 202
Burgess, R.G. 88
Burnaford, G. 122
Burns, A. 6, 123-124, 187
Burton, J. 20

Calhoun, E. 123
Carr, W. 6
categorization of data 125-132, 159
chat rooms, presentation of research in 183-184
classroom activities 87, 107-110; observations during 70-86; use of to collect data 65-68
classroom documents, collecting data through 107-108
classroom interaction, analysis of 135, 137-139
Clegg, F. 147
closed items *see* yes/no items
closed questions 94
coding 126, 127-129; levels of 130
collaborative research 9-10, 53-55
colleagues 56; discussion with 153-154

Communicative Orientation for Language Teaching (COLT) 75
communities of practice 194
conference presentations 45, 179
confidentiality 43, 44-45
Cram, B. 201-202
credibility of research 112-114, 152-157
critical friend 54
cycle of research 9-10, 170-174

Dadds, M. 188
data 2, 67-68; improvements based on 2, 3, 5
data analysis 13, 121-125; of qualitative data125-139; of quantitative data 139-152, 161-162
data collection 13, 65, 67, 107-109; in diaries 105-107; in interviews 88-95; through observation 70-86; through questionnaires 95-105; triangulation 112-114, 154; use of technology 110-112
data recoding 56-57, 83-86
databases, search for resources in 49-50
debates, presentation of research in 178
Denny, H. 8
Derham, B. 156
describing 68, 80-87
descriptive statistics 142-151
Devine, J. 48
Dewey, J. 20
diaries 20; data collection in 105-106, 111; use to identify areas for research 24
disadvantage 44, 45, 153
discussion: forums 111; with others 20, 45, 173-174, 177
dispersion *see* measures of dispersion
dissertations 191-192
Dörnyei, Z. 95, 98, 100
Drever, E. 128-129

Ebbutt, D. 10
Edge, J. 7, 37
Education Resources Information Center (ERIC) 49-50
Elliott, J. 6
ELT Journal 49
ethics 40-47, 153-154; in interviewing 91
events checklist 76-77
experiences, reflection on 169
exploratory practice 23
exploratory teaching 21-23

feedback 178, 184; from mentors 184; from participants 45, 70; from teachers 74, 79; from visitors 179
feelings, reflection on 169
Fischer, J.C. 30, 174
FOCUS 75
focus for research 28; identification of 28-35; refining question 36-40
focus groups 91, 111
focusing circles 37

Griffee, D. 12
Griffiths, M. 20, 22
guided interviews 89
guided items in questionnaires 102

hardware 56
Hart, S. 188
Hedberg, K. 161

Heileman, L.K. 202
Hitotuzi, N. 148-149
Hobson, D. 111-112

informed consent 41, 42-44, 46; sample form 59
Internet 35, 55; to search for resources 50-51
interval scales 139-140
interviews 88-95; open 89-90; preparation for 92; questions in 93-94; semi-structured 89, 95; structured 88; use of technology 111-112
Ishitobi, N. 141-142
journal writing *see* diaries
journals 105-107, 110-111; searching for resources 49; submitting articles to 187, 192

Kemmis, S. 6, 9-10
knowledge: personal 16, 166; professional 166

The Language Teacher 187
language teaching, action research and 35-36, 193-194
Language Teaching 49
Lei, W. 162
Likert scales 97
line charts 161
listening 93-94
Liston, D.P. 18, 20
listservs 111
literature search 17, 47-53
logs 20, 80, 105-106

Malcolm, D. 140-141
Mann, S. 37-38, 55
maps 86-87
Marchand, T. 161
Marshall, C. 38
McAlpine, D. 201
McKay, S.L. 13, 43, 71, 91
McNiff, J. 10
McPherson, P. 171-172
McTaggart, R. 9-10
mean 143-145
measures of central tendency 142
measures of dispersion 148-152
medium 145-146
Mendoza Lopéz, E. 76-78
mentors 53, 55, 70; discussion with 173-175, 177
mind maps 38
mode 147-148
Morioka, T. 185-187
multiple choice items, in questionnaires 99-100
Muschamp, Y. 202, 205

narrative observation 82
nominal scales 139
non-observation 68, 69, 73, 88-109
numerical scales 99; analysis of 139-142
Nunan, D. 13

Oanh, D.T. 80, 83, 105, 113-114
objectivity 155-156
observation 4, 9, 68-69; checklists 76-79; modes of 70; notes 80; planning 71-74; recording 83-86
observation sheets 75-79

O'Gara, P. 151-152
open-ended interviews 89
open items, in questionnaires 101
open questions 94
openmindedness 20, 32, 155
ordinal scales 139
outliers 144, 146, 150
participants 53-54; information for about research 42, 44-45; informed consent 42-44, 45
permission for research 41-44, 45
perspective 155-156
photographs 86-87
pie charts 162
piloting 92, 105
planning 5, 9, 27-58
Polanyi, K. 16, 166
portfolios 108
poster presentations 45, 180, 185
PowerPoint 181
practical theory 156-157, 168
practice, reflection on 167
presentation of research 174-176; oral methods 176-180; visual methods 180; written records 181-183
privacy 43-44
Priyana, J. 54
problematic situations 2-5; identification of 6
professional development 8, 20, 35-36, 166, 187-188, 194; outline guide 60
professional knowledge, reflection and development of 166
progress reports 177
Prospect 49
publication of research 45-46, 187-190, 192
qualitative data, analysis of 125-139
quantitative data, analysis of 139-152, 161-162
QUEST analysis 52-53
questionnaires 95-96; closed-ended items 97-101; layout 103-105; open-ended items 101-103
range 148-149
rank order items 100
rating scales 97-98
recording of data 56-57, 83-86, 91, 95; use of video 44, 80, 83
reflection 2, 4, 9, 39, 165-195; -in-action/-on-action 17, 20, 22
reflective observation 80-81
reflective research 5
reflective teaching 18-23
repair 22
reports of research 185-187
research; difference of action research 12-17; ethics of 40-46, 153; outline guide 61; pedagogical focus of 153; teachers doing 7-8, 13, 22
research partners 53-55, 174
research questions 36-40
resources 47-51; evaluation of 51-52; preparation of materials 55-57; scaffolding reading 52-53
responsibility 20
retheorisation 22
review 22
Richards, K. 92-93, 132-135
Rossman, G.B. 38
Santana-Williamson, E. 104
Schön, D.A. 17

Schwalbach, E.M. 51-52
self-assessment, account of action research on 201-209
self-reflection 9
seminars 20; presentation of research in 179
shadow observation 83
sharing with others *see* presentation of research
Smolin, L. 111-112
software 56
Somekh, B. 6
standard deviation 150-152
starting point for research 28, 29
Stevenson, C. 83
structured items in questionnaires 102
structured observation 75
surveys *see* questionnaires

Takahashi, K. 109
talk, analysis of 132-139
Tann, S. 20, 22
Taylor, L. 136-138
teacher cognition 31
teacher dialogues 20, 53-54
teachers: beliefs and values 31-34, 168-169; doing research 7-8, 13, 22
The Teachers' Voices Series 187
technology: use of to collect data 110-112; use of to present research 183-185
television, role in learning, account of action research on 213-222
TESOL Association 187; publication of action research reports 187-188
theory 16-17
theses 190-191
transcribing data 85-86; analysis of 132
triangulation 112-114, 154
Troudi, S. 66-67

Ur, P. 202

Valeri, L. 43
validity of research 16, 31, 112-113, 152-157
Van Eysden, A. 199, 213-222
van Lier, L. 6
visits 179

Wallace, M. 13
Weathers, J. 115
wholeheartedness 20
workshops 178
writing up research 181-183; action research accounts 187-190; reports 185-187; use of technology 183-185

yes/no items 97
Yuesong, G. 126-127, 129

Zeichner, K.M. 18, 20